D1212039

A Moment in History:
The First Ten Years
of the Peace Corps

by Brent Ashabranner

A MOMENT IN HISTORY
A FIRST COURSE IN COLLEGE ENGLISH

In Collaboration With Russell Davis
POINT FOUR ASSIGNMENT
STRANGERS IN AFRICA
THE CHOCTAW CODE
WEST AFRICA: LAND IN THE SUN
CHIEF JOSEPH
THE LION'S WHISKERS
TEN THOUSAND DESERT SWORDS

A Moment in History:
The First Ten Years
of the Peace Corps

BRENT ASHABRANNER

DOUBLEDAY & COMPANY, INC.

GARDEN CITY, NEW YORK

1971

309.2
A819m

141819

MOUNT UNION COLLEGE
LIBRARY

First Edition

Library of Congress Catalog Card Number 74–139002
Copyright © 1971 by Brent Ashabranner
All Rights Reserved
Printed in the United States of America

For Martha
Who shared the Peace Corps years with me

367/71 - pub - $4.93

Table of Contents

We live at a very special moment in history. . . . Latin America, Africa, the Middle East, and Asia are caught up in the adventures of asserting their independence and modernizing their old ways of life. These new nations need aid in loans and technical assistance just as we in the northern half of the world drew successively on one another's capital and know-how as we moved into industrialization and regular growth.

President John F. Kennedy
Special Message to the Congress
on Foreign Aid, March 22, 1961

A Moment in History:
The First Ten Years
of the Peace Corps

My Peace Corps

My years with the Peace Corps spanned all of two presidential administrations and the early months of a third. I saw it grow from an idea in a campaign speech to an organization with more than fifteen thousand volunteers working in sixty countries around the world. Over thirty-five thousand volunteers and staff served in it during those eight and a half years, and I knew many hundreds of them personally.

Most of those I knew were strong-minded, strong-willed, high-spirited men and women, suspicious of anything that looked even remotely like a restraining bureaucracy and intent upon carrying out their service —or as later ones put it, doing their thing—as individuals, not as faceless pawns in a big Peace Corps machine. This insistence on individualism was almost universal among the young volunteers but was also present to a marked degree in the staff, most of whom were eager New Frontiersmen.

The result of all this individualism was an organization that initially, at least, built its administrative structures casually and often observed them with ill grace. There are those, in fact, who have suggested that "organization" is an inaccurate label for the early Peace Corps and that it more nearly resembled the mixture of a social movement and a revival meeting.

As the Peace Corps increased in size it did improve its administration because it had to in order to survive, but the Peace Corps even today is not remotely close to being a bureaucratic monolith. Former director Jack Vaughn often talked about the "sixty Peace Corps," referring to the great differences in the sixty country programs, and others have suggested that there are as many Peace Corps as there are Peace Corps volunteers.

Both of these ideas have a good deal of validity. It is true that volunteers go overseas in groups to teach, work with farmers, or serve in many other capacities. But the essential fact is that every Peace Corps experience is intensely personal. The individual shapes his own experience and sets his own standards for success or failure as in no other undertaking of which I am aware. This applies particularly to volunteers but to a considerable measure to overseas staff members also.

Yet there is a curious paradox involving all these individualists and their unique personal experiences, and it is this: Almost everyone who serves for any length of time in the Peace Corps builds up an intense concern for it. He develops an emotional attachment to the Peace Corps, or at least to the Peace Corps idea, that I cannot conceive of anyone ever developing for the Commerce Department, the Bureau of Standards, or the Agency for International Development.

I do not mean to suggest that choruses of former volunteers sing the praises of the Peace Corps organization and its management. Broadsides of criticism are more common. But they are concerned. They want the Peace Corps to be better than it is, more effective than it is. They write letters to the director; they visit Washington head-quarters at their own expense to give their views or express their concern; they organize former Peace Corps groups on campuses and in cities; they are great letters-to-the-editor writers on Peace Corps matters. They care about the Peace Corps as the Peace Corps.[1]

The answer to this paradox I believe lies not in the noble goals of service, friendship, and understanding upon which the Peace Corps is built, though they are probably an element in the explanation. The true answer is to be found in the tremendous emotional investment that everyone long in the Peace Corps—and particularly the volunteer—builds up in his personal experiences. These experiences consist of two years or more of the closest association with people—often the most desperately poor and wretchedly underprivileged people of the earth—under conditions that are frustrating, delicate, and strange. Under these circumstances, the concerns, the loyalties, the affections that develop have a powerful emotional base.

I believe I can illustrate my point better with a single letter than with a long recital of anecdotes. In 1968, Robert Neuhaus, a volunteer teacher in Malawi, left his village a few days before he was expected to leave in order to avoid the sad farewells. Just before his plane

[1] Sometimes the concern has a bitter love-hate flavor. Some members of the Committee of Returned Volunteers, an organization born out of America's Vietnam trauma, feel that the Peace Corps is being used as a tool of American imperialism and that it should be transferred from U.S. government sponsorship or killed.

departed, however, a messenger arrived at the airport and handed him a letter and a basket of thirty eggs. The letter was from two Malawi boys he had taught, and here is what it said:

Tactfully Mr. Newhouse,

I write this letter to you if you are very well I here with joy. Sorry to you sir, as I have heard that you will go on 4th December, but what I thought was that you would go on 9th of December.

I have only the simplest reward to you which are the eggs. Now the ration of the eggs will be like this: you yourself with 12 eggs, your father with 7 eggs and that is his salutation, 6 eggs for your mother and 5 eggs for your sister. These eggs from the numbers 7, 6, 5 are for thanking to your parents and have the best salutation with longer life and better living.

I hoped not to give you only 30 eggs but I wanted if I could give more than that perhaps 60 would be given but when I heard from Harry Kadzinje that you will be leaving on 4th of December, now then I have given you this 30 as our thankfulness.

Subjects here have gone on well. I was in number 2. And Levi in number 7. I don't know if whether we shall learn next year because of the school fees matter. I don't feel well without meeting you.

Give me your address and Remese's address. I had a hen but no money for the train fare.

Your lonely boys,
Richard and Levi

If Bob Neuhaus thought he could leave Malawi without a wrenching emotional experience, he knew differently when he stepped onto the airplane.

The experiences of a Peace Corps staff person are of course quite different from those of volunteers. He spends his time working with government officials in developing new programs and in trying, with sharply varying degrees of success, to help volunteers in their work. Between these two kinds of work, the staff man probably builds an emotional investment in the Peace Corps that, while different, is equal to that of the volunteer. My point is that, volunteer or staff, the Peace Corps becomes very much "his" through an accumulation of strongly felt, emotion-charged experiences and not through devotion to some abstract ideals of service.

My own personal Peace Corps contains such memories as that of a volunteer in Nigeria bitten by a green mamba and the tragic death in the Bay of Bengal of one of the loveliest women volunteers I ever knew. I remember my difficult decision to pull our volunteers out of the Punjab during the India-Pakistan conflict of 1965 and my even more difficult decision (as acting director of the Peace Corps during Jack Vaughn's absence from Washington) to remove our volunteers from Biafra. I vividly recall my tense, prolonged negotiations that determined, in the earliest days of the Peace Corps, whether we would be invited to have a program in Nigeria, where, in a sense, Shriver's reputation was on the line.

There are very different kinds of memories. I remember once at the end of a frustrating day of desk work in New Delhi picking up a letter from a schoolgirl in the south Indian city of Visakhapatnam, where we had a volunteer teacher assigned. The letter contained a poem entitled "Thank You, America, for Sending Margery Donk." The iambic pentameter was a bit shaky and the heroic efforts to find words that rhymed with "Donk" were only marginally successful, but there was no questioning the depth of feeling the girl had for her Peace Corps volunteer teacher.

Margery changed her name to Mrs. Richard Beeler when she married a volunteer who was teaching in a nearby town. They came to Delhi for the wedding, and I stood in for her father when the moment came to give Margery away. I'm not sure I can remember all of the Peace Corps brides I have given away, but they are a part of my emotional investment in the Peace Corps.

So is the day I appeared before the Senate Foreign Relations Committee for my confirmation hearing as deputy director of the Peace Corps. I was tightly strung for the hearings and crammed as full of Peace Corps facts and figures as an industrious staff had been able to cram me. There were only a few members present and after some routine questioning they all left except the chairman, Senator William Fulbright. He looked over my Curriculum vitae, saw that I had written some books, and commented on one called *The Lion's Whiskers,* which he thought was an eye-catching title. I told the chairman it was a book of folk stories of Ethiopia.

We had a discussion about education in Africa today and then the senator returned to *The Lion's Whiskers.* "That certainly is an interesting title," he said. "I wish you would tell me about the book."

So to my complete amazement I spent the last ten minutes of my confirmation hearing telling African folk tales to Chairman Fulbright, who seemed much more absorbed in these narratives than he had been in my profundities about the Peace Corps.

"My" Peace Corps was a very personal, individual one just like that of every other volunteer or staff member, but my interest in writing this book was not to record a personal memoir. Rather it was to chart the growth of the Peace Corps idea. Where stories of my personal experiences appear in the pages ahead, they are not there because they are my experiences but because they illustrate some point about the Peace Corps' development that I could make more clearly than with secondhand material. Fortunately, several memoirs by former Peace Corps volunteers are now in print,[2] and I have not tried to compete with them. I have tried to do what I think has not yet been done: tell the story of the Peace Corps' philosophical and political development.

[2] The two that I enjoyed most are *An African Season* by Leonard Levitt (Simon and Schuster: New York, 1967) and *Living Poor* by Moritz Thomsen (University of Washington Press: Seattle, 1969). Levitt's book is about teaching in East Africa and Thomsen's about community development in South America.

Part I

The First Decade of the Peace Corps

CHAPTER ONE

The Peace Corps Is Born:
1960–62

On the night of October 13, 1960, in New York, Senator John F. Kennedy engaged Richard Nixon, his rival for the Presidency of the United States, in the third of their nationally televised debates. Boarding their plane as quickly as possible after the debate, Kennedy and his campaign party flew to Michigan, where he was scheduled to speak briefly at the university at Ann Arbor. The drive from Willow Run Airport to the University of Michigan took about an hour, and it was nearing 2:00 A.M. when the motorcade arrived.

The night was clear and mild and, somewhat to the campaign party's surprise, a very large turnout of students, estimated at ten thousand, had waited up for the senator. Making his way to the Student Union Building with some difficulty and taking a position on the steps there, John Kennedy spoke his first words in public about the possibility of a Peace Corps. Speaking extemporaneously, Kennedy put his thoughts in the form of questions to the students. He asked how many of them would be willing to give up a part of their lives to work in Africa,

Asia, and Latin America for the United States and for freedom. He wanted to know how many of them who were
going to be doctors or engineers would be willing to work
in Ghana as technicians and commit not one or two years
but ten to traveling around the world in the foreign service. And then he said, ". . . on your willingness to contribute part of your life to this country, I think, will
depend the answer whether we as a free society can compete. I think we can, and I think Americans are willing
to contribute, but the effort must be far greater than we
have made in the past."

The idea of a Peace Corps did not originate with John
Kennedy, and he never suggested that it did. In an early
news release on the subject, he mentioned the pioneering
legislative work of Congressman Henry S. Reuss and
Senator Hubert Humphrey. As early as January 1960,
Reuss had proposed a bill in the House of Representatives
to study the possibility of establishing a Point Four Youth
Corps. Later that month Senator Richard L. Neuberger
proposed a similar bill in the Senate. In June 1960,
Humphrey proposed a bill for the creation of an agency
in which young Americans could serve in missions overseas; he actually used the name "Peace Corps" in propos-
ing the bill. And the idea of some kind of organization
to utilize the energy and idealism of American youth had
been discussed and written about long before these congressional proposals. In the years immediately following
World War II and the formation of the United Nations,
the idea of voluntary service to the world on a massive
scale was on the minds of many prominent Americans.

Just as the idea of a large-scale peace or service force

was not new in 1960, neither was the presence of Americans working in underdeveloped countries on a voluntary or low-pay basis. The International Voluntary Service, an organization funded by private contributions, began sending small numbers of young Americans to work in schools and hospitals in Southeast Asia and Egypt in the 1950s. And American missionaries, while not volunteers in any secular sense of the word, had for many years been working overseas, for low wages and often under conditions of hardship, teaching, building and running hospitals, and introducing better farming methods.

But despite this long background of ideas and example, people everywhere have always thought of the Peace Corps as John Kennedy's. It has been called his finest monument, and from the beginning it was known in many countries where volunteers served as the Kennedy Peace Corps. In the crucially important sense that he was the first man in American public life who believed in the idea and who had the skill, power, and desire to implement it, the Peace Corps does very much belong to John Kennedy.

Today a plaque at the University of Michigan commemorates the fact that it was there that Kennedy first publicly advanced the idea of a Peace Corps, and it is entirely possible that the American Peace Corps had its realistic beginning in those early morning hours on the steps of the Student Union Building. The idea had been floated by the Young Democrats on October 5 in a release entitled "Message of Senator John F. Kennedy to the Nation's New Voters," but it had said only that if elected Kennedy would "explore thoroughly" the possibility of

some kind of overseas Peace Corps service for the young
men and women of the nation.

No one knows why Kennedy decided to talk about the
Peace Corps idea that night at Michigan. Quite possibly it
came to mind because he had earlier asked Professor
Samuel P. Hayes of the University of Michigan to prepare
for him a paper on the possibilities of an international
youth service program. More likely it was the unexpected
sight of ten thousand young people waiting until long
past midnight to see him and hear what he had to say.
The response of the University of Michigan students was
enthusiastic, and within a few days a group had formed
an organization called Americans Committed to World
Responsibility. This group actively promoted the youth
service corps idea and sent a delegation to Kennedy to
discuss the idea further. Meanwhile interest spread to
other campuses, and Democratic campaign headquarters
received a heavy flow of mail supporting the concept. It
was clearly in the two weeks following his talk at Michigan that Kennedy realized he had connected solidly with
the young people of the country with the Peace Corps
idea.

On the night of November 2, in a major address at the
Cow Palace in San Francisco, Kennedy put on record his
intention to create a Peace Corps if he were elected
President. Speaking about the inadequacies of the American foreign service in its various manifestations, Kennedy
said:

"I therefore propose that our inadequate efforts in this
area be supplemented by a Peace Corps of talented young
men and women, willing and able to serve their country

as an alternative or a supplement to the peacetime selective service, well qualified through rigorous standards, well trained in the languages, skills, and customs they will need to know, and directed by the I.C.A. Point Four agencies. . . .

"This would be a volunteer corps, and would be sought not only among talented young men and women, but all Americans, of whatever age, who wished to serve the great Republic and serve the cause of freedom, men who have taught or engineers or doctors or nurses, who have reached the age of retirement, or who in the midst of their work wished to serve their country and freedom, should be given an opportunity and an agency in which their talents could serve our country around the globe."

The Peace Corps had now become a formal campaign pledge, and Kennedy forcefully underscored his belief in the idea in a speech in Chicago two days later and in his final television appearance before the election on November 7.

Richard Nixon, who during his second presidential campaign in 1968 was in general to speak approvingly of the Peace Corps and who was to retain it in his administration after his election, attacked the idea after Kennedy proposed it in 1960. He concentrated his attack on the dangers he thought it would hold for the selective service, and he expressed his belief that a Peace Corps would become a haven for draft dodgers. For good measure, he added his view that the idea was "superficial" and "conceived solely for campaign purposes."

Public interest in the Peace Corps idea continued to grow, particularly among college students. Pierre Salin-

ger, who was to become President Kennedy's press secretary, reported that after the Cow Palace speech over
thirty thousand letters supporting the Peace Corps idea
were received at the Democratic campaign headquarters,
far more than the total received on any other campaign
proposal or issue. Less than a week after the election over
one hundred students from many colleges met at Princeton to discuss what American youth could do in developing nations that would aid their development and serve
the cause of peace. In the few weeks between the election
and the end of the year, student groups on a number of
major campuses endorsed the Peace Corps concept and
signified the readiness of American college students to
serve.

The tremendous pressures of building the framework
of a new administration and searching for the key New
Frontiersmen to get it started meant that very little
thought could be given to the Peace Corps before
President-elect Kennedy's inauguration. But Kennedy
did ask Professor Max Millikan, Director of the Center
for International Studies at the Massachusetts Institute
of Technology, to prepare a paper with his ideas on a
youth service program. Kennedy also asked Chester
Bowles, well known for his imaginative and positive concepts of America's role in developing nations, to begin
thinking about the Peace Corps idea.

U.S. press reaction to the Peace Corps proposal was
predominantly favorable, though tempered with a good
deal of caution. C. L. Sulzberger in the New York *Times*
called the idea admirable but suggested that a volunteer
corps alone might not be "adequate to meet all the chal-

lenges before us." He raised the question of whether it might be desirable to pass legislation enabling the government to draft highly qualified civilians—on a short-term basis—to provide a technical capacity overseas that young volunteers might not have. A later *Times* editorial stressed the importance of competent and qualified volunteers: "It would be no compliment to any nation to send it young novitiates who have little to offer except personality and energy; we must not forget that in most of the underdeveloped areas labor is plentiful; skills are scarce." A Washington *Post* editorial endorsed the idea of a Peace Corps and suggested that it would serve as a valuable training ground from which to select career Foreign Service Officers.

Not all comment was favorable, of course. One writer called the Peace Corps another Henry Ford Peace Ship and remarked that he could only say of any underdeveloped country about to receive a shipment of idealistic young Americans, "Lord, save it from its friends." But such judgments were rare, at least in print. If there were severe critics of such a benign program as a Peace Corps, almost all kept their own counsel.

No further public announcement was made about the Peace Corps until January 9, 1961. On that day a routine release from the office of the President-elect proposed the establishing of an International Youth Service Agency. The story was extremely conservative. It suggested that the program should be considered strictly experimental and should be started on a small scale; probably no more than a few hundred young people would be placed in jobs overseas during the first year or two, and "there should be no pressure to achieve greater volume until there is sufficient experience and background study to give some confidence that expanded numbers can be wisely used."

Of great potential significance, the release suggested that the new youth agency should not develop and administer its own programs overseas but should provide necessary financial assistance to worthwhile programs developed by private non-profit organizations (such as universities, CARE, 4-H, etc.). The youth agency's role would be to develop information on manpower needs in underdeveloped countries, set standards for programs to be given assistance, stimulate the development of new programs where there was a demonstrable need, and sponsor research into and evaluation of overseas youth programs.

The release contained two final important points: (1) Service in the youth agency would not be a substitute for military service, and (2) The director of the agency would report to the director of the U.S. foreign aid program.

Much of the January 9 release was clearly based on the recommendations of Professor Millikan and on the earlier report of Professor Hayes. Both reports agreed that carefully selected, well-prepared young Americans could serve a useful purpose overseas. Both stressed that their jobs should be as "doers," not as advisers. Both urged a careful beginning with volunteers limited to a few hundred in pilot projects. Millikan in particular wanted to see the agency function by supporting programs of private non-profit organizations rather than by building its own programs.

The Peace Corps that emerged later in 1961 was to bear very limited resemblance to the kind of organization described in the President-elect's news release or in the recommendations of Professor Millikan.

Shriver and the Beginning

In later years, when his volunteer agency was basking in the warmth of both public and congressional approval, Sargent Shriver was fond of saying that President Kennedy had picked him to start the Peace Corps because no one thought it could succeed and it would be easier to fire a relative than a political friend. Shriver has speculated more seriously that perhaps the President chose him because some of Shriver's campaign duties had been to organize special groups to think through specific major issues such as civil rights, farm problems, and urban affairs. Thinking through the philosophy and operational considerations of a youth service corps for underdeveloped countries would not be a markedly dissimilar assignment in a general sense.

Whatever his reasons, the man the President selected to give him the definitive report on how to organize the Peace Corps, and then to organize it, was his brother-in-law, Robert Sargent Shriver, Jr. During the next five years, "Sarge" Shriver, through his qualities of decisive leadership and personal charm, was to make his name synonymous with the Peace Corps. He was also to launch a public career with such brilliance that he would be prominently mentioned as a candidate for the Vice-Presidency in both 1964 and 1968.

Shriver graduated *cum laude* from Yale in 1938 and received his law degree from the same school three years later, but he never became a practicing attorney. He was always interested in journalism and for a time was editor of the Yale *Daily News*. During World War II, Shriver entered the Navy as an apprentice seaman in the V-7 officers' training program and emerged from the war in 1945 as a lieutenant commander and a veteran of the submarine service.

In 1946 he took a writing job with *Newsweek*. That same year he met Eunice Kennedy at a cocktail party. There were a few dates and also a meeting with Eunice's father, Joseph Kennedy. When Joe Kennedy learned that Shriver was a journalist, he asked him to read some diaries that Joseph Kennedy, Jr., had kept during the Spanish Civil War and give an opinion on whether they might be publishable. Shriver read them and told the senior Kennedy that, in his judgment, they were not.

Joe Kennedy liked Shriver's style and his honesty and offered him a job as his personal representative in the Chicago Merchandise Mart. Shriver took the job, continued to court Eunice Kennedy, and married her in 1953. At the time John Kennedy announced his candidacy for the office of President, Shriver was assistant general manager of the Merchandise Mart with major responsibilities in promotion, advertising, and sales. He was active in Chicago public affairs and had been on the Chicago Board of Education for five years.

Like all other members of the Kennedy family, Shriver

pitched in full time on the campaign; in the weeks after the election he became the President-elect's chief talent scout in filling key administration jobs. Friends close to Shriver believe that it was he who put forward the names of Robert McNamara and Dean Rusk and argued for them most strongly.

Shriver maintains that, while he was glad to head the task force that built the Peace Corps plan, he did not want to run the agency. He asked the President to find someone else for the job, but Kennedy wanted Shriver. In his book, *Point of the Lance*, Shriver wrote:

> I resisted the assignment at first and proposed other people because I wished to protect the President from additional charges of nepotism and to enable the Peace Corps to start with the fewest possible disadvantages. It had already been dubbed "Kennedy's Kiddie Korps" by some. Mr. Nixon said the Corps would be a "haven for draft dodgers." Former President Eisenhower called it a "juvenile experiment." Others ridiculed it as a "children's crusade."
>
> President Kennedy wanted to make it tough and effective, and prove the skeptics wrong. A man of few words, he ignored my doubts, and just said, "Go ahead. You can do it."

In some ways Shriver's credentials for the job were not, in fact, blue chip. He did not have the experience with young people that a college president, dean of students, or professor would have had. He was not a development specialist and had no detailed knowledge of the developmental needs of emerging countries. His experience in the business world was primarily in promotion rather than management.

He was not without pertinent background, however. In the 1930s he had gone to Europe with other students in Experiment in International Living groups; later he had served as a leader for such groups. In the 1950s he traveled extensively in Asia, visiting such countries as Japan, Korea, Vietnam, Cambodia, and Thailand. After the Asia visits, he had worked on an idea for sending to developing countries three-man volunteer teams made up of young labor leaders, businessmen, and politicians. These teams would work with people at the grass roots level, "contributing to the growth of the economies, to the democratic organization of the societies, and to the peaceful outcome of the social revolutions under way." Nothing came of this idea, but the memory of it was in Shriver's mind as he began work on the Peace Corps.

The chief assets Shriver brought to the Peace Corps were a genius for persuading and leading men, decisiveness in decision-making, limitless but controlled energy, and an unwavering determination to make the Peace Corps work. A story in Peace Corps folklore has it that President Kennedy once told Shriver that he should find a word or phrase that would epitomize the Peace Corps for the public. Shriver is supposed to have replied, "How about *success?*" And in his five years at the helm, no one in public or—to the best of my knowledge—private ever heard him say that the Peace Corps was not making it big.

In one other respect—his close connection to the White House—Shriver was invaluable to the Peace Corps, especially in its infant stages. A handsome, glittering man, Shriver needed no one to help him build an image. Nevertheless, some of the matchless Kennedy charisma did rub off on him. Shriver scrupulously avoided trading on his relationship to the President when dealing with other government agencies, but they were still aware of its existence; and some members of his staff had less compunction about putting Shriver's name and the President's into the same sentence when something had hit a bureaucratic snag.

Shriver himself could invoke a gentle presidential pressure when someone he particularly wanted on his staff was reluctant to join. A senior university man that Shriver badly wanted in the Peace Corps once told me that he had about decided that he could not break away. One Sunday morning he received a call from Shriver in Hyannisport. "I'm with the President," Shriver said, "and he wants to know if you're going to take that job." The man took it.

In early February Shriver assembled a task force for in-depth consideration of creating a Peace Corps. No complete list was ever kept of the dozens of persons who flew in and out of Washington to make some contribution to the task force meetings, but the list would have included leading representatives from universities, business, government, foundations, unions, and private service organizations.

"The Towering Task"

At approximately 2:00 A.M. on the morning of February 6, Sargent Shriver was in his suite at Washington's

Mayflower Hotel reading through a stack of reports, memoranda, and suggestions about the Peace Corps. One of the papers was by Warren W. Wiggins, of whom Shriver had never heard. The paper was entitled "The Towering Task," and after Shriver read it he immediately sent Wiggins a telegram, at three o'clock in the morning, asking him to attend the first meeting of the task force that was to take place in a few hours.

Luckily Warren Wiggins lives in Hollin Hills, Virginia, a suburb of Washington. When he walked into the Mayflower conference room at ten o'clock that morning, he was astonished to find that copies of "The Towering Task" had been mimeographed and distributed to each member of the task force. Shriver opened the meeting by asking everyone to read the paper. When they were finished, he said that "The Towering Task" came closer to expressing his views about what the Peace Corps should be than anything he had yet read or heard. He suggested that their initial discussions be based on the paper.

From that moment, "The Towering Task" became the basic philosophical document of the Peace Corps-to-be. It is therefore necessary to examine it here in some detail in order to understand much of what happened in the years that followed.

The main theme of the paper was embodied in the title, which derived from a statement in President Kennedy's State of the Union message delivered on January 30: "Our role is essential and unavoidable in the construction of a sound and expanding economy for the entire non-communist world. . . . The problems in achieving this goal are towering and unprecedented—the response must be towering and unprecedented as well. . . ."

Wiggins began by acknowledging that almost all individuals and organizations that had advised the President about the possibility of a Peace Corps had counseled a cautious and slow beginning. They "suggest tentative pilot projects, involving small numbers of people and consequently a limited political, economic and psychological impact. This cautious approach is proposed by many because of the clear possibility of a fiasco . . . proceed cautiously . . . don't make mistakes . . . don't let this experiment get out of hand—in other words, find out the appropriate dimensions of the program by cautious exploration." Wiggins observed that most persons with this point of view were experienced in the matter of Americans working overseas.

Wiggins then reviewed the basic motives or justifications for the United States' having a Peace Corps:

—Program accomplishment abroad: Many persons felt it essential to add another tool or resource to those already available to help in social and economic development abroad. An agency that could move quickly and provide large numbers of persons for teaching, road building, malaria eradication, could prove invaluable.

—Training and recruiting ground for other activities: Peace Corps experience could provide an extremely valuable background for future members of the State Department, United Nations, government aid programs, foundations, business firms with foreign interests.

—Psychological impact abroad of American youth "pitching in" to work on the problems of developing nations: Some people believed that the better understanding of Americans that could result might be the most valuable outcome of the program.

—Impact on American society and American attitudes: Young Americans working in Africa, Asia, and Latin America would become much better oriented to the world scene and be better prepared to participate in world affairs and to influence other Americans through their experience.

—American youth want to serve abroad: Response from the college campuses made clear that large numbers of young Americans wanted to work abroad in developmental programs. This need, doubtless stemming from many individual motives, might be the most important national motive for creating the Peace Corps.

—Political motivation: Finally, there was a recognition that the proposed program had political support and was politically important both in the United States and abroad. "Religious, philanthropic and foundation-type institutions have already initiated their 'youth corps' programs with their own criteria in mind. What is now under consideration is the National Peace Corps that would be sponsored by the United States Government and developed by political bodies."

The paper then addressed the question of program magnitude. The basic thrust of the argument was that a small Peace Corps was more likely to fail than a large one because small Peace Corps groups in individual countries would not be significant enough to get the governmental and institutional support they would need.

. . . Sending one hundred students to a Latin American country won't be important enough to get presidential support from that country. Active support from a Minister of Agriculture, Health or Education would be surprising as a general rule. And if the country needed to give legislative or financial support it might not be forthcoming. However, one thousand or five thousand Americans, working on something important in a *single* country, would merit considerably more political, administrative and financial support. One hundred youths engaged in agricultural work of some sort in Brazil might pass by unnoticed, except for the problems involved, but five thousand American youths helping to build Brasilia might warrant the full attention and support of the President of Brazil himself.

The paper hammered away at the thought that a small program in a country might prove to be nothing more than an annoyance to the American ambassador and the foreign office and of no consequential help in a country's development program. "A small, cautious National Peace Corps," Wiggins asserted, "may be a diversionary path of inconsequential accomplishment . . . and major administrative and diplomatic trouble."

The paper pointed out that there were fifty or more countries in which Peace Corps volunteers might serve. If the Peace Corps started at the level of one or two thousand volunteers and grew even to five thousand by the end of President Kennedy's first term, that would be an average of only about one hundred volunteers per country—not enough to make an impact but plenty to cause a lot of headaches. Wiggins argued that a small Peace Corps would not respond adequately to any of the motives for creating such an agency: So few young people would have a chance to serve that it would only be a source of frustration; there would be no psychological impact abroad; there would not be enough feedback in the United States to make any difference; the Administration would receive little or no credit for bringing to life a weak, timid Peace Corps.

The paper then gave a concrete example, with an estimated budget, of a five-thousand man, one-country Peace Corps program. The country Wiggins chose was the Philippines, and the volunteer activity was English teaching in the public schools. English is not only the medium of instruction in the Philippine schools but also the official language of the government, trade, and commerce. English also has been a factor in building unity in a nation with seventy-five linguistic groups. Yet English is deteriorating alarmingly because of a shortage of qualified teachers, particularly native speakers of English. Americans could teach English with minimum preparation, Wiggins maintained, and demonstrated how five thousand Peace Corps volunteers could be phased into the Philippine schools over a three-year period.

Wiggins pointed out other countries such as Nigeria, India, Pakistan, and Mexico where large numbers of native speakers could be a real asset to English teaching programs. When other fields such as health and agriculture were included, the paper postulated that a Peace

Corps of perhaps one hundred thousand volunteers was feasible.

This remarkable paper concluded with a recommendation that the Executive Branch launch the Peace Corps in 1961 at a level sufficiently large to demonstrate that major programs could be undertaken. The paper further recommended that in order to make an immediate start the President should not wait for congressional approval or even a formal administrative structure to be built. Instead he should create the Peace Corps by executive order and make a major announcement that the new agency was in existence.

At the time Warren Wiggins wrote "The Towering Task" he was Deputy Director for Far East Operations in the International Cooperation Administration (later renamed the Agency for International Development or AID by President Kennedy). Wiggins was thirty-eight, holder of a master's degree in public administration from Harvard, and thoroughly knowledgeable about the federal bureaucracy and U.S. aid programs. He had started his government service in 1949 as a member of a Marshall Plan team in Norway. In 1952 he went to work for Averell Harriman in the Office of the President, where he coordinated U.S. economic programs in fourteen Western European countries. Later he worked as an economic adviser in the Philippines and as deputy director of the aid program in Bolivia.

Even without his provocative program ideas, a man of Wiggins' background and experience would have been very valuable in getting the Peace Corps off the ground. With them, he was unmatchable, and Shriver recognized this important fact immediately. From the morning Wiggins joined the Peace Corps task force at the Mayflower Hotel, he never went back to work for the International Cooperation Administration. Wiggins became Shriver's most important lieutenant, and it is impossible to overestimate his importance in terms of the form and philosophy that the Peace Corps took on.

Curiously, Wiggins would probably never have been in the Peace Corps if he could have found anyone in the new administration to listen to his ideas about how the foreign aid program should be reshaped. "I kept sending memos to people, but no one would read them," Wiggins once said. "No one in the New Frontier wanted to listen to insiders on the subject of aid. They figured new ideas had to come from outside."

But Wiggins very much wanted to be a part of the Kennedy administration and that is why he turned to the Peace Corps idea. "I figured no one knew anything about that," he said, "so my ideas stood a better chance of being looked at."

President Kennedy had asked Shriver for a report on the Peace Corps by March 1. When the general deliberations of the task force convened at the Mayflower were over, fewer than twenty days remained to sort out the thousands of ideas and opinions and produce a document that would give the President a clear picture of what the Peace Corps should be—its nature, purpose, and philosophy—and how it should operate.

An endless procession of idea men flowed in and out of Shriver's hotel suite during those February days, but a team of regulars began to take shape. Wiggins was there, and he brought over William Josephson, an imaginative and articulate young lawyer from ICA, to begin work on the legal problems of creating the Peace Corps. Harris Wofford, who had worked with Shriver in the campaign and would soon become a presidential special assistant for civil rights, served as liaison between the White House and the task force and put in his own special concerns about the relationship of the Peace Corps to higher education. William Haddad, a fiery young journalist, came down from New York on Robert Kennedy's recommendation and immediately involved himself in practically everything. A young man from Vice-President Lyndon Johnson's staff became excited about the Peace Corps idea and came over to work in those first weeks. His name was Bill D. Moyers. Richard Goodwin was there in the early days, and there were others.

The group worked around the clock in a fever of excitement. If any additional pressure were needed, the President called Shriver twice to find out how the report was developing. Basic questions had to be answered for the President on almost every phase of the idea: What would be the difference between the Peace Corps and the Point Four technical assistance program? Who would be eligible to serve? What exactly would volunteers do? Would the government operate the program or farm it out to other organizations? How would volunteers be selected? How would they be trained? How long would they serve? What should they be paid? Should the Peace Corps be a separate agency or a part of the foreign aid program? How and when should the Peace Corps be launched?

The questions seemed endless, and the answers were highly complex.

The final editing and typing of the report to the President was accomplished in the early morning hours of February 28 and delivered to him that day. The report, bearing the name of Sargent Shriver, recommended that the President establish a Peace Corps immediately. It suggested that this be done by executive order, under authority available to the President in the foreign aid act, and that separate congressional legislation and funds be sought later for the next fiscal year.

The report's rationale for recommending creation of the Peace Corps by executive order rather than through congressional legislation was speed. By organizing immediately, the report said, the most qualified people from the spring graduating classes could be utilized. Also college campuses would be available for summer training. The report was purposely vague about numbers but stated that, if the Peace Corps could be launched in a careful but determined way within the next few weeks, several hundred persons could be put into training during the summer for placement as volunteers in the fall. Within a year or two several thousand might be in service. The agency could then grow steadily as it proved itself and as the need for it was more fully demonstrated.

The report tried to answer in a general way all of the operational questions that might come to the President's mind. The Millikan, Hayes, and other reports were cited as evidence that Peace Corps volunteers could serve a useful purpose overseas. The report ended by asking if the Peace Corps would be worth the cost and the risks and provided this answer:

No matter how well conceived and efficiently run, there probably will be failures. These could be costly and have a serious effect both at home and abroad.

But as the popular response suggests, the potentiality of the Peace Corps is very great. It can contribute to the development of critical countries and regions. It can promote international cooperation and good will toward this country. It can also contribute to the education of America and to more intelligent American participation in the world.

With thousands of young Americans going to work in developing areas, millions of Americans will become more directly involved in the world than ever before.

With colleges and universities carrying a large part of the program, and with students looking toward Peace Corps service, there will be an impact on educational curriculum and student seriousness. The letters home, the talks later given by returning members of the Peace Corps, the influence on the lives of those who spend two or three years in hard work abroad—all this may combine to provide a substantial popular base for responsible American policies toward the world. And this is meeting the world's need, too, since what the world most needs from this country is better understanding of the world.

The Peace Corps thus can add a new dimension to America's world policy—one for which people here and abroad have long been waiting. As you said in your State of the Union message, "The problems are towering and unprecedented—and the response must be towering and unprecedented as well."

Executive Order 10924

The President astonished Shriver and his fledgling staff with his speed in acting on their report. On March 1, only one day after he had received the report, Kennedy sent to the Congress a special message on the Peace Corps which began, "I recommend to the Congress the establishment of a permanent Peace Corps—a pool of trained American men and women sent overseas by the U.S. Government or through private organizations and institutions to help foreign countries meet their urgent needs for skilled manpower.

"I have today signed an Executive Order establishing a Peace Corps on a temporary pilot basis."

The President's message, drawing heavily on the Shriver report, stated that the Peace Corps would be different from existing technical assistance programs in that volunteers would help provide the skilled manpower necessary to carry out development projects, "acting at a working level and serving at great personal sacrifice." The message stated that, while all qualified Americans would be welcome, the Peace Corps would undoubtedly be made up largely of young people just completing their formal education. The President assured Congress that his reason for establishing the Peace Corps on a temporary basis by executive order was to gain experience and information that would be helpful in planning a permanent organization. He stated that "a minimum of several hundred" volunteers could be selected, trained, and at work in pilot programs by the end of 1961. Adopting the vague language of the Shriver report, the President's message said: "It is hoped that within a few years several thousand Peace Corps members will be working in foreign lands."

The President's message on creating the Peace Corps received major press attention, and he challenged his new agency to "be in business by Monday morning." From that moment the Peace Corps became the one program in the Kennedy administration to which an unflagging spirit of urgency was attached. With its emphasis on youth, its idealistic aims, its combined aura of personal sacrifice and adventure, the Peace Corps was to become the trademark of the new administration and to symbolize the hope, energy, and idealism that people both in America and around the world felt in the young President. Kennedy's readiness to create the Peace Corps by executive order rather than take the safer but much slower route of waiting for congressional approval seems to indicate his understanding of the program's symbolic importance to his administration. Shriver and his early staff understood it also, as made abundantly clear by the almost frenetic pace at which they organized the agency and pushed the first programs overseas.

The Peace Corps' shingle was out the following Monday morning at the Miatico Building, a twelve-story structure with a fine view of the White House, reachable in a five-minute walk across LaFayette Park. The building belonged to the International Cooperation Administration, and the Peace Corps began by encroaching on the sixth floor where Wiggins had his office, as did one or two other ICA employees whom he had recruited for the Peace Corps staff. Shriver managed to get an office, but most of the others had to work in the halls, on the corners of other persons' desks, or on the floors of offices ICA had reluctantly vacated, taking all furniture with them.

Everything had to be done. An organizational structure for the new agency had to be worked out and the structure staffed. Personnel procedures had to be formulated; up to the time of the President's order creating the Peace Corps everyone working on its formation had been on loan from some other part of the government or, like Shriver (who continued to be a dollar-a-year man), had simply contributed his time. But before a structure could be created or many staff members brought on for planning and implementing programs, three decisions of the most fundamental importance had to be made:

How ambitious a start would the Peace Corps make?

Would it run its own programs or farm them out to universities and private organizations such as the Experiment in International Living?

Would the Peace Corps be a separate agency or part of the International Cooperation Administration or whatever new aid agency the President formed?

On answers to these questions hinged all future operational decisions and, indeed, the whole tone, style, and thrust of the Peace Corps.

A general program strategy for the start-up year was quickly agreed on. The President had said that "a minimum of several hundred" volunteers could be overseas by the end of 1961, and to Shriver and his staff that meant that they would be. Shriver decided that, because the first programs were supposed to be exploratory, they should cover a wide geographical area and be varied in the types of tasks undertaken. The staff hoped that program agreements could be worked out with two or three Latin American countries, the same number in Africa, and at least one or two in Asia. They also hoped that, for the sake of example and attracting wider attention to the Peace Corps, some of the first countries to receive volunteers would be politically important and leaders in their part of the world. Some naturals to be sounded out on their interest were Brazil, Colombia, Nigeria, India, and the Philippines. One of the first Washington tasks was to work up a background paper on the Peace Corps and send it to all U.S. ambassadors in developing countries so that they could talk more intelligently about the program with any interested country officials.

How large a Peace Corps to project when the first appropriation request was made to Congress was a question that would have to be thought about and worked on. All of Shriver's political and promotional instincts rejected the cautious, gradual build-up advocated by Millikan and many others. He bought Wiggins' concept of a big Peace Corps. The drama of starting big and the relevance that could come with being big were important for this very visible New Frontier program, and it could be argued —as Wiggins had—that bigness was essential to the success of the program. Still, no one knew what the African, Asian, and Latin American response would be; and "big" meant different things to different people, even on Shriver's own staff.

The question of whether the Peace Corps would primarily staff and administer its own programs overseas was intensely debated inside the Peace Corps and much talked about by private organizations outside. Millikan and the President's other early advisers had strongly urged that the Peace Corps have only a small central staff that would set standards for overseas programs and then award contracts to universities or other non-profit organizations to administer them; another approach recommended was for the Peace Corps to give financial support to private organizations which had already started worthwhile overseas programs.

Shriver's report to the President and the President's message to Congress asserted that Peace Corps volunteers would be made available to developing nations in four different ways:

—Through private voluntary agencies carrying on international assistance programs.

—Through assistance programs of international agencies such as UNESCO and the Food and Agriculture Organization of the United Nations.

—Through assistance programs of the United States Government.

—Through new programs which the Peace Corps itself would directly administer.

In many of Shriver's early speeches and press conferences and in his testimony before Congress, he empha-

sized that the private sector was going to be a full
partner in the Peace Corps and that in this way the Peace
Corps would not become another large government
bureau. The Peace Corps' official policy statement on the
issue was absolutely unequivocal:

> The policy of the Peace Corps is to give preference
> to the administration of projects by private agencies
> and universities. In cases in which a suitable and
> qualified university, voluntary agency or other in-
> stitution is interested, available, and acceptable to
> the host country, projects should be undertaken with
> such institutions.

There is no reason to believe that Shriver was not entirely sincere in his statements about wanting full private
sector participation in the Peace Corps adventure. The
fact is, however, that universities, private organizations,
international agencies, and other U.S. agencies were
never more than very junior partners in running Peace
Corps programs overseas or in receiving Peace Corps
volunteers for their own programs. By the end of 1966
they had been dropped from the partnership altogether.

The partnership ideal was the victim of the speed with
which the Peace Corps grew; equally important, the concept of contracting out a substantial part of the program
was not supported by most of the Washington staff. Warren Wiggins believed that in order to grow fast and big
and keep control of what was happening, the Peace
Corps would have to run its own show. It would take far
too long, he argued, to investigate all the possible ways
of sending volunteers overseas through private programs

and then evaluate the best and work out laborious contracts with the private agencies. Wiggins was by no means opposed to any private sector participation, but his main thought was to build a strong, centrally run Peace Corps that could do its own business.

Wiggins was put in a powerful position to urge this concept when Shriver appointed him Associate Director for Program Development. With the chief responsibility for determining what programs would be undertaken overseas, he was also in a strong position to recommend to Shriver how they should be run. Wiggins also succeeded in getting ICA men he respected and trusted appointed to a number of key positions. One of the most important of these was John Alexander, a brilliant, irrascible careerist in the foreign aid program. Alexander probably understood government bureaucracy and how to make it work efficiently better than anyone who ever served in the Peace Corps. He naturally supported Wiggins' idea of direct administration and, as director of Africa programs, was a formidable ally.

The probability is, however, that the concept of a strong central Peace Corps with its own programs and its own staff overseas would have prevailed even without Wiggins. This is true because of the nature of the men who made up the early Peace Corps staff in Washington. These men—the Moyers, Haddads, and Goodwins (and there were many such)—were imbued with the excitement of building something they believed to be new. They were fast-moving, ambitious, confident men who were sure they could do it—whatever "it" was—better than anyone else. Such men could not become passive directors of a Peace Corps holding company made up of university and private organization programs. They built the Peace Corps and they wanted to run it.

A few excellent men did support large-scale participation from the private sector. Two of these were Franklin Williams and Harris Wofford. Throughout his Peace Corps career Wofford worked tirelessly for a deeper, more meaningful role for universities than the routine training functions that the Peace Corps asked them to perform. A former law professor at Notre Dame and a man of exciting, wide-ranging ideas, Wofford visualized the Peace Corps and higher education in America merging into a kind of university in dispersion and producing a new kind of action-oriented graduate, both academically and worldly wise.

Wofford was a man of considerable influence. In those early days of the Administration, when campaign stories were still inhaled with lunch-time martinis at the Sans Souci or consumed with hors d'oeuvres at cocktail parties, the name of Harris Wofford was frequently heard. It was he, the story went, who had given John Kennedy the idea that had put the Negro vote safely in his column. In October, at the height of the campaign, Martin Luther King had been arrested and jailed in Atlanta, Georgia, for violating state anti-trespass laws. Wofford's idea was that Kennedy should call Mrs. King in Atlanta and express his sympathy for her and his support of the great Negro leader's cause. This Kennedy did on the night of October 27, 1960. The call, which took a strong measure of political courage, received wide publicity. Though no measurement of the call's impact was ever made, it was

generally believed to have solidified urban black support
behind Kennedy.

Whether Wofford's role in the incident was accurately
reported is not entirely clear; it is significant, however,
that President Kennedy made Wofford his special assistant for civil rights matters. Wofford's civil rights
credentials by no means rested on that campaign incident, however. He had made a study of non-violent
protest movements in India and had transferred his
understanding of this weapon of depressed people to the
United States. Burke Marshall, in a lecture later printed
in the *University of Virginia Law Review* (June 1965),
has said ". . . the first publicly articulated suggestion
known to me that the Gandhian techniques should be
applied by American Negroes was in a speech by Harris
Wofford, Jr., a white lawyer of great vision, at Hampton
Institute, in November of 1955, some weeks before the
Montgomery bus boycott, which is taken by many to
mark the beginning of the protest movement in this
country."

In addition to his special assistant's job, Wofford was
the White House liaison to the Peace Corps. A year later,
May 15, 1962, he joined the Peace Corps staff as director
of the program in Ethiopia and after that became Associate Director for Planning and Evaluation in Washington.

But all of Wofford's arguments and prestige were of
little effect in diverting the rapid formation of the Peace
Corps into a strong, centrally run bureau that was capable
of doing almost everything for itself. Shriver was genuinely interested in private sector participation and some

early contracts for administering overseas programs were signed with such institutions as Michigan State University, CARE, and the 4-H Foundation. As Shriver listened to the arguments, however, he consistently agreed with Wiggins, Moyers, Alexander, and others that the only sure way to launch the Peace Corps fast and big and maintain some quality control of the product was to do most of the job themselves.

In "The Towering Task" Wiggins had frankly conceded that political considerations had to play a part in the formation of the Peace Corps. It is impossible not to believe that Shriver was much more aware of this than any of his staff. The Peace Corps would not attract much attention or receive many headlines if its main purpose was to give money to institutions to run programs for it. Such an approach would have pleased many schools and private agencies and might have had some long-range benefits. But a Peace Corps that did its work in such a quiet, leisurely paced, and undramatic manner would never have become the symbol of the New Frontier. Shriver knew that.

While Warren Wiggins' ideas and administrative skill profoundly influenced the Peace Corps in its formative period, it would be wildly inaccurate to say that he dominated it. Sargent Shriver dominated the Peace Corps. He paid strict attention to detail, read all important papers, and approved all key staff. Most important, he made all policy decisions about Peace Corps structure, overseas programs, and volunteer terms of service.

Shriver's style of management was to encourage fierce competition and debate among his key staff and to make policy by being the arbiter of who had come out best in the competition or had been most persuasive in the debate. His staff meetings, where crucial operational decisions were often made, were sometimes bloody affairs. Any kind of question might be argued and translated into policy, questions ranging from whether volunteers should be sent to teach English in French-speaking African countries to whether staff should be allowed to have air-conditioners in their homes overseas. Shriver listened, sometimes added fuel to the debate, and rendered a verdict or expressed an opinion that soon had the weight of policy. There was always a winner and a loser in the staff clashes; many wounds were licked and tension was an everyday ingredient of Peace Corps life in Washington.

But morale was always high. Shriver was fair in his decisions, never playing favorites. A genuinely friendly man, he encouraged people to express their ideas and he listened to what they said. Above all, he was an exciting leader, and it was exciting to be a part of his team.

A Separate Peace Corps

One of the most crucial organizational questions facing the Peace Corps was whether it would be a branch of the Agency for International Development (the name given by the new administration to the old International Co-operation Administration) or whether it would be a separate agency, reporting to the Secretary of State but largely autonomous. As was perhaps natural for a career man in foreign aid, Wiggins, in "The Towering Task" had advocated that the Peace Corps be a part of ICA. There is some evidence that the President had assumed that the new program would be incorporated in the foreign aid structure. The President's news release of January 9 had in fact stated that the director of the Peace Corps would report to the director of the foreign aid program. Henry Labouisse, the retiring director of ICA, and David Bell, the director-designate of the new AID, strongly wanted the Peace Corps to be a part of AID.

Shriver passionately wanted the Peace Corps to be a separate agency. He was convinced that to capture the public imagination the Peace Corps had to have a life of its own. It could not afford to inherit the spotted past of the foreign aid program which had put such great emphasis on achieving short-term cold war political goals. Buried in the depths of AID's long-established and rigid bureaucracy, it would not be able to move with the speed and freedom necessary for an agency that was going to make its main appeal to youth. The Peace Corps was going to be made up of volunteers who would serve without pay under conditions of hardship; to be successful it was going to have to develop an esprit and distinctiveness that would be impossible as a division in AID. And, of great importance, the political value of the Peace Corps lay in its high visibility, which would be completely lost if it were submerged in AID.

Labouisse and Bell doubtless wanted the Peace Corps in AID not only because it made good sense administratively but also because it might be of some help to have something new in the foreign aid package when the annual appropriation struggles began with Congress. The President was apparently quite ambivalent on the matter and did not seem especially interested. Only Shriver and some of his staff, most notably Bill Moyers, felt that the very life of the Peace Corps depended on its autonomy.

The issue seemed to be decided on April 26. A meeting was called at the White House to settle the question; the President had been expected to chair the meeting but at the last minute could not attend and asked Ralph Dungan, one of his special assistants, to listen to the arguments and make the decision for him. The meeting came at a time when Shriver was overseas on his first visit to countries that might be interested in inviting the Peace Corps. His absence was perhaps fortuitous for, as the newly appointed head of the Peace Corps, and the President's brother-in-law, he would have been in an awkward position to argue that he did not want to serve under the director of the foreign aid program.

Warren Wiggins, who was acting director in Shriver's absence, was under no such handicap, however. If Wiggins was not converted entirely to Shriver's views on autonomy, he nevertheless represented his chief loyally and ably in the resolution of the issue. But at the White House meeting attended by Dungan, Bell, Labouisse, a representative of the Bureau of the Budget, and others, the demolishment of Shriver's hopes seemed complete. After listening to the arguments, Dungan decided that the Peace Corps should not be a separate agency, that the Peace Corps director should report to the AID director, that the AID director would have full and final authority on all Peace Corps decisions, and that the Peace Corps would not have its own legislation but that it would be a chapter in the foreign aid bill.

Wiggins' strategy after the meeting was, with Bill Josephson's help, to compose a long and masterful cable to Shriver outlining Dungan's decisions and then in a "comments" section expressing his concern that the White House meeting had concentrated almost exclusively on the administrative advantages of amalgamation and had not sufficiently concerned itself with the political importance of Peace Corps autonomy. He questioned whether the President had been made sufficiently aware of these political considerations.

As an experienced government official, Wiggins knew the psychological impact of a cable. He asked Bill Moyers to take a copy of the cable to Vice-President Lyndon Johnson and to discuss the problem with him further. The Vice-President read the cable and talked to Moyers about the political importance of a highly visible Peace Corps, which he understood very well. Johnson agreed to see the President.

On May 2 President Kennedy reversed all of Dungan's decisions. The Peace Corps would be a separate agency completely independent of AID. The Peace Corps director would report to the Secretary of State. The Peace Corps would have its own self-contained staff and its own legislative presentation to Congress.

Shriver's victory was complete and his gratitude to Lyndon Johnson extreme. In later years he called Johnson "a founding father of the Peace Corps." "The organizational charts would have looked better if we had become a box in a single foreign aid agency," Shriver wrote in *Point of the Lance*. "But the thrust of a new idea would have been lost. The new wine needed a new bottle."

With the basic decisions about a fast start, direct administration of programs, and agency autonomy made,
the Peace Corps staff, stepped up its already frenetic pace.
A basic organizational plan was drawn up calling for the
director and his deputy to oversee five major offices.
Despite his major contributions to the infant agency,
Warren Wiggins was not chosen as the first deputy director of the Peace Corps. Instead, the assignment went to
Dr. Paul Geren, a Harvard Ph.D. who had been a foreign
service officer in India and Syria and later executive vice-
president of Baylor University. Dean Rusk recalled Geren
to the foreign service and sent him to South Vietnam to
explore the economic situation there. Geren's combination of foreign service and academic credentials looked
valuable to Shriver, who asked him to become his deputy.

The five substantive divisions of the Peace Corps were
Public Affairs (which included volunteer recruiting and
informational services); Program Development and Operations; Peace Corps Volunteers (selection and training
responsibilities); Planning, Evaluation, and Research;
and Management. Though all of these divisions were
crucial to the functioning of the Peace Corps, Program
Development and Operations—run by Warren Wiggins—
was by far the most important; the other were essentially
service units for Wiggins' division, known as PDO. This
division, which included directors for Africa, Latin America, East Asia and the Pacific, and the Middle East and
South Asia, decided the activities of all volunteers everywhere in the world and was responsible for staffing all of
the countries' programs. It was the heart of the Peace

Corps, and the most coveted jobs were those of Wiggins' regional directors.

Many excellent men and women, attracted by the idealism and freshness of the Peace Corps idea, answered the urgent call for staff help. Douglas Kiker interrupted his career in journalism to become chief of Public Information. Dr. Joseph Kauffman, a specialist in student personnel matters, resigned as executive vice-president of the Jewish Theological Seminary to organize the Peace Corps' Division of Training. Charles Peters gave up a law practice and promising political career in West Virginia to become head of the Division of Evaluation.

Typical of the urgency of filling the jobs is the story told about Dr. Nicholas Hobbs, who organized the highly important Division of Selection, which would have to decide who would and who would not become Peace Corps volunteers. He received a call one day at George Peabody College for Teachers, where he was chairman of the Division of Human Development. Dr. John Darley, executive director of the American Psychological Association, who was scouting the selection job for Shriver, described the task and its importance to Hobbs.

"How much time do I have to decide?" Hobbs asked.

"Twenty minutes," Darley told him.

Twenty minutes later Nick Hobbs accepted the job. The selection procedures he developed in 1961 were used with little change for years.

Getting off to a fast start had not been Shriver's only motive in recommending that the Peace Corps be established by executive order. It was his judgment that the Administration in early 1961 was in no way ready to go before a skeptical Congress and talk nothing but theory. When the Peace Corps hearings were held before the Senate Foreign Relations Committee and the House Foreign Affairs Committee, Shriver wanted some concrete evidence of how Americans would respond to the Peace Corps idea, how foreign countries would react, and in general how the programming, selection, and training would take place.

As this information was being accummulated, Shriver set out on a marathon round of visits to the offices of senators and representatives. In this effort he received yeoman help from Bill Moyers, who understood the legislative temperament and traded on his own past service on the Hill. But Shriver himself proved to be a master at winning congressional confidence. On his visits to individual congressmen he explained the basic Peace Corps idea, he kept them abreast of what the young agency was doing, he answered their questions in detail, he supplied them with any information they wanted. By the time the hearing on the Peace Corps bill started, the basic groundwork of understanding had been thoroughly laid, and Shriver had won undisputed recognition as the most skillful congressional tactician on the New Frontier.

The Beginning Overseas

With a rudimentary structure and philosophy hammered out in Washington, Shriver and a few of his lieutenants set out in late April on a globe-girdling trip to tell the leaders of African and Asian countries about the new American Peace Corps and to get an idea of their recep-

tivity to the program. This was the first trip to those parts
of the world by a major official in the Kennedy administration, and Shriver's status as a member of the presidential family added an extra measure of excitement to
his visits.

But the word went out to American embassies, in what
was to become a standard instruction for Shriver trips,
that purely protocol dinners and receptions were out and
that Shriver wanted to spend his time in working sessions
with host country officials. An effort was made from the
very beginning to establish the concept of the Peace Corps
as something outside and apart from our traditional
foreign policy apparatus.

The second stop on the trip was Nigeria, less than a
year old as an independent country and, because of its
size, population, potential resources, and nucleus of experienced leaders and well-trained civil servants, considered a shining hope of emerging Africa. On April 25
in Lagos, the capital, Shriver met with Prime Minister
Sir Abubakar Tafawa Balewa, who warmly endorsed the
Peace Corps concept. Sir Abubakar expressed his belief
that Peace Corps volunteers could perform useful and important service in his country in both economic and social
development activities. He suggested that Shriver and his
team visit the regional governments for specific discussions of implementing the program.

Shriver also met with Dr. Nnamdi Azikiwe, Governor
General of Nigeria and powerful leader of the Ibo tribe,
and Azikiwe joined the prime minister in expressing his
support for the Peace Corps idea. The trip was off to a
good start.

Shriver then made flying trips to each of the three regional capitals—Ibadan, Enugu, Kaduna—and held meetings with all of the cabinet ministers and their permanent secretaries. He explained the basic concept of the Peace Corps as supplying volunteers who would work for and under the supervision of the ministry that requested them. In contrast to AID and United Nations technical assistance schemes, Peace Corps volunteers would not be advisers or expert consultants but rather "doers," persons who would do a job as teachers, surveyors, engineers, or in whatever fields jobs needed doing. They would work side by side with Nigerians. The idea of skilled workers as opposed to advisers was a popular one at the regional level where schools had to be staffed and roads built, and Shriver gave it major emphasis.

The ministers and permanent secretaries listened politely and invariably asked two questions: Would Peace Corps volunteers really be skilled and experienced? and what would the Peace Corps program cost their ministry?

The permanent secretaries particularly were concerned about the qualifications of the volunteers. As the chief administrative officer of a ministry, the permanent secretary directs all operations and deals with all personnel problems. Many of the "perm secs" were former British colonial civil servants who had been retained by the Nigerian government on a contract basis, and they were well aware that major questions were yet unanswered as to what kinds of persons would volunteer for Peace Corps service.

Shriver answered that the Peace Corps hoped to attract a wide range of skilled persons but that without a doubt large numbers of young men and women with fresh college degrees would apply. He emphasized, however, that the Peace Corps intended to exercise great care in selection and that any volunteer sent would be qualified to do the job for which he had been recruited. In addition to skills, experience, and knowledge they already possessed, volunteers would be given special training of any kind and duration necessary before being put on the job. The first step, Shriver explained, was to let the Peace Corps know what kind of help was needed; it would then do its best to meet those needs.

On finances Shriver stated that if necessary the Peace Corps would assume all costs in volunteer programs. He stated a number of times, however, that the Peace Corps would be "grateful" for any contributions toward cost sharing that the governments could make.

Shriver's candor, enthusiasm, and natural charm created a favorable impression everywhere, and when he flew on to Pakistan it was with the definite feeling that the Peace Corps program in Nigeria was "set." To be sure, Ministry of Foreign Affairs officials in Lagos had emphasized that, while discussions and planning could go forward, a formal decision on whether Nigeria would request a Peace Corps program would have to be made by the cabinet of federal government ministers. But a favorable cabinet decision was thought to be pro forma; and those Washington staff members who stayed on in Lagos for more talks sent messages back to headquarters saying that Shriver's visit had clearly established that a Peace Corps program for Nigeria had the full support of the federal and regional governments. Their early cabled predictions were that the program might number one thousand volunteers.

There was, indeed, a solid basis for such predictions. After the meetings with Shriver and follow-up meetings with his staff, the regional ministries quickly canvased their various departments and came up with an astonishing inventory of manpower needs. With a bureaucratic swiftness that would be considered dazzling in the most "developed" Western country, the Council of Ministers in the Western and Eastern regions by May 9 approved and transmitted to the federal government requests for more than twelve hundred volunteers. A somewhat later request from the Northern region added another two hundred to the total.

One cannot review those early lists of requests without sensing the desperate need of emerging countries for skilled manpower. Neither can one look at the requests without a feeling of considerable chagrin that in its early days the Peace Corps excited so many hopes it was unable to satisfy. A portion of the Eastern Region Ministry of Agriculture's list looked like this:

Job Title	Number	Job Description
Soil Conservationists	2	Prevention of erosion
Soil Surveyors	9	Soil surveys for farm settlement scheme
Irrigation Engineers	2	Farm settlement water control project
Farm Mechanization Officers	2	Farm mechanization scheme

Poultry Officer	1	To introduce broiler production
Farm Building Inspectors	6	To supervise farm settlement buildings
Rice Agronomists	2	To conduct agronomic trials with rice
Soil Analysts	2	Soil analysis
Boat Builders	2	Assistance in Opobo Boat Yard

This list continues in this vein at considerable length, and there was a similarly detailed list from the Ministry of Health for physicians, nurses, laboratory technicians, and many other kinds of health professionals.

From the Western Region came such requests as these:

Ministry of Lands

7 town planners
6 industrial site planning specialists
6 professional surveyors
12 sub-professional surveyors

Ministry of Works

3 electrical engineers (maintenance)
6 water engineers
6 structural engineers
3 architects
2 draftsmen
4 highway engineers
2 mechanical engineers
6 building technicians

Ministry of Industry

6 industrial engineers
4 business administration specialists
4 cost accountants
5 civil engineers
3 estimators (quantity surveyor)
3 rubber technologists

From each of the three regional ministries of education came requests for substantial numbers of teachers: teachers for secondary schools, technical schools, teacher-training schools, and a large request for junior instructors for the University of Nigeria at Nsukka. Orders for science, mathematics, and English teachers led the list; but practically every subject matter area was included: geography, history, shorthand, typing, technical drawing, metalwork, even French, German, and Latin.

Very little thoughtful analysis could have gone into this rain of requests, but it did indicate how easily government officials in a new or developing country could look over their staffing patterns and find major unfilled holes. And there is little doubt that the seeming absence of any price tag on Peace Corps volunteers whetted many bureaucratic appetites.

My own long association with the Peace Corps began with Shriver's visit to Nigeria. My family and I were living in Lagos, where I was education program officer for the Agency for International Development. I was asked to be AID's liaison to Shriver and his team, an opportunity I welcomed. John Alexander, an old friend from other days of overseas service, had written to me about the possibility of joining the Peace Corps staff if there was a program in Nigeria, and I was eager to learn more about the idea and the men behind it. I accompanied Shriver on his visits to the Western and Eastern regions, and in the process I became, for all time, a "Shriver man."

By May 10 the remaining members of the visiting Peace Corps team had either returned to Washington or had flown on to catch up with Shriver in Asia. Although I did not officially join the Peace Corps until August 9, I never worked another day for AID after the Shriver visit. It seemed to be just assumed that I would carry on the Peace Corps' business after the team left, and I did.

But Shriver was completely candid with me. He told me that he wanted me to set up the Nigeria program and run it as the acting Peace Corps representative until he could find an outstanding Negro educator to be the number one man; at that point I would become the deputy representative in Nigeria. Shriver felt very strongly that the most populous Negro nation should have a black Peace Corps representative who would have the stature, as he put it, "to almost be a second ambassador."

I understood Shriver's point of view and accepted on the terms he outlined. I told him, though, that if all went well, I would someday like to run a program without the "acting" in front of my title. Shriver said he understood, but he made no promise. I served as acting representative in Nigeria throughout the remainder of 1961 and into early 1962. The man Shriver finally chose as representative was Dr. Samuel Proctor, President of North Carolina Agricultural and Technical College.

Even before leaving Lagos the Peace Corps team was

showing some signs of nervousness that the federal cabinet had not yet passed a formal resolution inviting the Peace Corps to Nigeria. A decision had been made that the Ministry of Economic Development was to be responsible for all Peace Corps matters, and the team had a final meeting on May 9 with the able permanent secretary, M. E. G. Lewis, a Britisher. Charles Nelson, the team spokesman, told Lewis that program discussions at the regional level had gone very well and that he would now carry the more than twelve hundred requests for volunteers back to Washington. There the staff would analyze the requests and decide what portion of them it would be feasible to fill in 1961. Nelson promised to get this information to Mr. Lewis within a month or six weeks. Nelson then pointed out that of course nothing could be done beyond the planning stage until cabinet approval was forthcoming. If there was to be a Peace Corps program in Nigeria by the end of 1961, he said, the go-ahead signal would have to come soon. The recruiting and training of volunteers and detailed planning of their assignments would take several months.

Lewis said that he understood and that he hoped cabinet action would be taken by May 31. He said that he personally "firmly and heavily" favored the Peace Corps idea but that he wanted to alert the team to the probability that certain political questions or problems would arise when the cabinet considered the program. The question of what Nigeria's contribution to the program would be had not really been focused on, he pointed out. Also the question of size was certain to be raised, as would be the exact nature of the jobs volunteers would do, i.e., would they have staff or even line assignments within the federal or regional governments? Lewis said that he fully expected the opposition to ask how the government intended to ensure that volunteers are not "stealing state secrets and transmitting them to the United States Government."

It was on this sobering note that the Peace Corps' first visitors from Washington left Lagos.

In Washington a decision was quickly reached to concentrate on the request for teachers. Surprisingly little debate took place on this issue. The only way to get the Peace Corps launched with impressive numbers by the end of 1961 was to recruit from the May and June college graduating classes. Also, problems of selection, training, and over-all planning would be simplified by concentrating on one activity and essentially one slice of the population. Of course if older, experienced teachers applied for service they would certainly be welcome.

The argument prevailed that it would be very difficult and time consuming to recruit specialized agricultural skills, poultry experts, boat builders, experienced engineers, and other skilled types from the massive lists. Furthermore, it would be hard and expensive to set up a training program pointed at filling a jumble of different jobs. No one doubted that a small, hand-picked program of experienced specialists could be put together in time, but the dominant philosophy called for youth and numbers.

On one of my early trips to Washington a top Peace Corps official said to me, "If we can put a hundred thousand twenty-three-year-olds in those countries for two

years, keep them there doing something that isn't counter-
productive, and bring them back, the world may never be
the same again. I'm sure America won't be."

Such was the almost mystical Peace Corps belief that
young American volunteers working side by side with
Africans, Asians, and Latins would somehow bring about
fundamental changes to all.

Yet it would not be accurate to say that the Peace
Corps architects had unbounded confidence that volunteers could succeed at anything. Such men as Wiggins,
Alexander, and Josephson had real doubts about what
new college degree holders could do in these countries,
and their doubts were another major reason why teaching
projects dominated Peace Corps programming in Africa
and in many other parts of the world for several years.

Their reasoning ran that young volunteers' best chance
of success lay in having a highly structured assignment
such as classroom teaching with its well-defined responsibilities. They were not sanguine that volunteers would
be great teachers, but African and Asian secondary schools
wanted and needed college degree holders as teachers
and few were to be had. More important, Peace Corps
officials hoped and believed that volunteers would make
up in dedication, interest, and imagination what they
lacked in classroom teaching experience. Besides, they
would receive special pedigogical training.

When I communicated to the Nigerian federal government officials Washington's desire to concentrate initially
on supplying teachers, they were actually relieved and
quickly agreed that it was a good idea. It was clear that
they too believed schools would be the best and easiest

place to keep an eye on this untested new aid input. That
other departments were disappointed in their hopes of
getting this outside help was of lesser concern.

Almost at once I began to get anxious inquiries from
Washington asking when the federal cabinet was going
formally to approve a Peace Corps program for Nigeria.
They wanted something, anything, in writing that would
give them authorization to go forward with recruiting
and training plans. Spring semester endings were immi-
nent, and graduates were making their plans for the
future.

On May 30 I went to see Mr. Lewis at the Ministry of
Economic Development. He was very sympathetic, but
he emphasized that no one could give any kind of formal
or even informal concurrence in writing before the cabinet made its decision. Lewis told me that Jaja Wachuku,
the Minister of Economic Development, was holding the
Peace Corps paper and that it was Wachuku's prerogative
to place the paper before the cabinet for consideration.
He did not know why the minister was holding the paper.
He did state his knowledge of opposition to the Peace
Corps by at least two cabinet members.

The cabinet next met on the evening of June 6 but did
not consider the Peace Corps paper. I remember specu-
lating to Washington that Wachuku simply did not want
to appear too eager to accept Peace Corps help. It was
general knowledge that he was sensitive about Western
nations at that particular time and that he was unhappy
over a very unflattering picture of him that had appeared
in the London press and elsewhere. In any case, for whatever reasons, Jaja was sitting on the Peace Corps paper.

On June 9 Joseph N. Greene, Jr., deputy chief of the American Embassy and a good friend of the Peace Corps from the very beginning, went to see Wachuku and found him ready to talk. The minister observed that there were many misconceptions in the press and in the public mind about just what the Peace Corps was intended to be. He also noted that many American politicians and editorial writers seemed to think that it was a crazy or even dangerous idea. In any case, Wachuku said, it was naïve to assume that for a government to invite the Peace Corps into its country was not a political act. That was why he was giving it such thought.

He went on to say that if Peace Corps volunteers were invited to Nigeria, their quality would be much more important than their numbers. He made it very clear that he was not interested in "inexperienced youngsters just out of college." Another interesting point was his assertion that "Americans of African descent" should be included in any group of volunteers that might be sent to Nigeria. He expressed his unhappiness about an article by Harold R. Isaacs that had recently appeared in *The New Yorker.* The article dealt with the problems American Negroes were encountering in West Africa: problems of acceptance, understanding, and even discrimination. Wachuku wanted to make quite clear that they were welcome in Nigeria.

Greene's talk with the minister was enlightening but not at all reassuring to Washington because he did not indicate when he intended to take the matter up with the cabinet. The pressures on the Africa Division staff were becoming intense. Shriver wanted Harvard University to undertake the first training program for a Nigerian contingent of volunteers. The prestige of Harvard's name would be good for the Peace Corps both in the academic community of the United States and in those of West and East Africa, where educational elitism, based on traditional ties with Oxford and Cambridge, runs deep.

Harvard was interested but insisted they had to have an immediate go-ahead if they were to do the program; they did not want to be associated with a last-minute, slap-dash affair. Shriver could not understand the delay in Nigeria's requesting the Peace Corps to come in. He remembered the warmth with which he had been received and the cordial words of the prime minister and governor general, and he believed that his visit had got everything in place.

This was my first experience—but by no means my last —with the world of difference that exists between lofty agreements in principle by high-ranking government officials and implementation of programs through the political and bureaucratic mazes below.

Alexander and Wiggins assured Shriver that there was no real problem and that planning for a Nigerian program for the fall was going forward. Alexander in turn was frequently on the phone to me for assurance, which I did my best to give despite the obvious fact that nothing was happening.

On June 19 Jaja Wachuku left for a visit to the Congo, and Mr. Lewis told me that the minister had locked the Peace Corps cabinet paper away in his safe. In the following days I talked to both the prime minister's secretary and the permanent secretary of the Ministry of Foreign

Affairs, but both men professed to know nothing about the status of the Peace Corps program consideration.

That was the low point. Wachuku was in the Congo. Azikiwe was in London for six weeks, though he would probably not figure importantly in a decision about the Peace Corps. The prime minister was in his home country in the north and would not return until early July. Several other cabinet ministers were out of the country. At the very least it did not seem probable that the Peace Corps question would be acted on before the prime minister returned to Lagos.

Now it was summer in the United States. Colleges were out; people had to make decisions about their futures. Fortunately, agreements for Peace Corps programs were quickly reached with a few countries. The Latin American countries of Colombia and Chile, long accustomed to dealing with U.S. aid agencies, and the Caribbean island of St. Lucia responded favorably, as did the Philippines, another nation with a long and close association with the United States. There was rapid agreement with Tanzania, then known as Tanganyika and still a British colony, for a group of surveyors for road building. And, mildly surprising at least, Kwame Nkrumah gave his approval for fifty secondary school teachers for Ghana.

In Washington the Selection Division evaluated several thousand applications and results of special Peace Corps tests that had been given in late May and early June in five hundred different locations throughout the United States. An impressive total of 5,210 tests were administered on the two test days. Serious interest in Peace Corps service seemed to be running high.

The first firm invitations for Peace Corps service began to go out in June. In the case of Nigeria, however, prospective volunteers were talked to by phone and told that, while the Peace Corps was sure a training program would start sometime during the summer, formal invitations could not be issued for a while. Invitees-to-be were asked to preserve the Peace Corps option if they possibly could.

My own hopes for a program in Nigeria were kept alive during this period by one very significant fact. Talks with many education officials in the regional and federal ministries made it quite clear to me that they really wanted volunteers as classroom teachers. Their needs were great and real and they welcomed help from wherever they could get it. I received scores of requests for teachers from headmasters of private and government schools who wrote directly to the American Embassy when they heard about the possibility of Peace Corps teachers.

I had to this point resisted Washington's desires to send to Nigeria representatives from Harvard and the University of California at Los Angeles, with whom the Peace Corps was also discussing a training program for Nigeria. The two institutions wanted to make a firsthand survey in the country as a prelude to devising their training programs. I understood the necessity of this but thought their presence in Nigeria before the cabinet had approved the Peace Corps program might seem presumptuous and bruise the sensitivities of such officials as Wachuku.

Nevertheless, in late June I agreed to their coming as the only means possible to keep these two prestigious schools interested in doing training in this first key summer of the Peace Corps' life. I explained to everyone that their visits were purely conditional but necessary *if* volunteers were requested and if they were to be in Nigeria ready to begin the next school year, which would start in January.

Harvard sent John Usher Monro, dean of the undergraduate college, and UCLA sent Charles Young, at that time special assistant to the chancellor. Monro and Young traveled throughout the country visiting regional ministries of education and secondary schools. Both reported that they found deep and genuine desire for Peace Corps volunteer teachers.

These two men are again illustrative of the quality of persons attracted by the Peace Corps in its first year. John Monro was, a few years later, to give up his premier position in the educational world as dean of Harvard College to work in an obscure Negro college in the South. Chuck Young in 1968 became chancellor of UCLA, the youngest man to hold such a position in the California university system.

Jaja Wachuku returned from the Congo on June 27, but there was no immediate action on the Peace Corps paper. Word reached us that two or three other ministers had been made suspicious by Wachuku's inaction and that the whole Peace Corps question was now assuming political overtones which we badly wanted to avoid. But the ambassador, Joseph Greene, and I agreed that nothing more could be done. To push Wachuku further, to go over his head to the prime minister, or to try to get other ministers to intercede might make it seem as if we were trying to force a Peace Corps program on Nigeria. The result in a sensitive and proud young country might be rejection of the Peace Corps idea even though a majority was in favor of it.

And then on July 5 we were told by a friend in the Foreign Office that the cabinet had considered the Peace Corps paper and were in favor of a Peace Corps program, though there were certain reservations. We were not told what these reservations were, but we were told that the Foreign Office hoped to give us a response within two or three days.

On July 8 the permanent secretary of the Foreign Office confirmed that the cabinet had discussed the Peace Corps, and he said he would try to move the papers through the Ministry of Economic Development. He hoped that we would have an official response by the tenth. I relayed this good news to Washington, which then decided that invitations to prospective volunteers could now be confirmed and final negotiations for training could proceed.

On July 10 the permanent secretary called to express his regret that we could not expect an immediate response on the Peace Corps after all. He said that the cabinet was meeting again that morning to consider the program further. Though he did not say so precisely, we gathered that the further discussion was at Wachuku's insistence.

Despair reigned in Washington.

Two days later we learned from another reliable source that the cabinet had again approved the Peace Corps program in principle. They had, our friend said, decided not to use volunteers in government administrative jobs, and they had decided not to insist that some portion of the volunteers be Negroes. This was the first intimation we had had that Wachuku had taken his color concern to the cabinet.

Still there was official silence and it continued for over a week. Then on July 21 a Foreign Office official called to inform us that the Government of Nigeria was officially requesting a Peace Corps program. There were but two conditions: (1) Persons of all races and creeds would be welcome, (2) The first year the program would be considered on a pilot basis and would be limited to twenty-five percent of the numbers requested by the regions. This meant a figure in excess of three hundred, which we were not likely to reach in any case.

I cabled Washington that we were in business. Three days later, on July 24, forty-three trainees reported to Harvard to begin preparing to be Peace Corps volunteers in Nigeria. They had been literally standing by with their bags packed, and everything had been made ready to go into action at Harvard once the signal was given. It was a great piece of "provisional" planning.

The genesis of the Nigeria program illustrates two key facts of the Peace Corps' life. The first was Washington's driving determination to launch the Peace Corps with significant numbers of volunteers in important countries and to have them in place before the end of 1961. No one seriously questioned that a fast and dramatic start with all its loose ends and frantic midnight planning was worth the problems it would create. Everyone simply assumed that it was essential to have the Peace Corps in action in the field before the end of the President's first year in office.

There is no doubt that this speed contributed to the

troubles of the early programs and the volunteers who comprised them. Officials of receiving countries frequently did not understand who volunteers really were or what they were to do. Usually there was not time to see if the number of volunteers requested in any way matched the number of jobs—or in fact if real jobs existed. And in training, not even Harvard could put together in a few days a program that could do all of the things good Peace Corps preparation called for.

Perhaps a solid year of planning, of mutual education among Peace Corps staff, host country officials, and training institutions would have produced a smoother start. Still I am not sure. So much of what had to be learned could only be learned through trial and error. The heroes and the victims of this process were the volunteers.

A second fact illustrated by the Nigeria example is that the Peace Corps was not initially—and in fact, never— overwhelmed by unsolicited, wholly spontaneous requests for volunteers. The pattern was very much the same around the world. Someone in Washington would visit a country to explain what the Peace Corps was and what it might do; in some cases an ambassador or embassy official might raise the possibility of a Peace Corps program. If any interest was shown, someone from Washington or someone selected from the country, as I was, would continue the discussions until the program materialized or the idea was dropped. Of course, in some cases countries did make unsolicited inquiries or expressions of interest.

There is certainly nothing wrong with that pattern, and I hardly see how it could have been otherwise. It was necessary to get out information about what the Peace

Corps was, or at least what we thought it was. And never to my knowledge was any pressure put on a country to accept Peace Corps volunteers. Anyone who understands at all the psychology of newly independent or developing nations knows that any attempt at pressure would almost certainly result in indignant rejection.

Some persons have suggested that countries might have accepted the Peace Corps simply out of politeness or out of some sense of obligation since they were accepting U.S. financial aid. African, Asian, and Latin officials are certainly polite and considerate, but I have never known them to feel at all obligated to accept what they don't want. A not inconsiderable part of the skill they have developed is to accept from donor nations what they want or think is good for them and to decline politely all else.

As I think the Nigeria case makes clear, they were for the most part cautious about the Peace Corps. They weren't at all sure it would work; but they did have manpower needs and they were willing to try it.

The Peace Corps certainly had its manpower needs, too, in those early days. It was easier to staff the Washington positions than it was quickly to get the right men overseas on two-year tours of duty. The country program staffs were chronically shorthanded for years, and the cost was often high in sound program development and volunteer morale.

The first official Peace Corps staff member in Nigeria (I was still on AID's payroll) was William Hintz, a roofing contractor from Milwaukee who had been smitten by the Peace Corps idea. Bill served as acting deputy while

I was acting representative; and for several months the
two of us, plus a TDY (temporary duty) secretary from
Washington, made up the Peace Corps staff.

A bewildering range of actions and decisions confronted
us, as they did the implementers of all early Peace Corps
programs. In our case, the plan called for three groups of
volunteers, totaling something over one hundred, to arrive in Nigeria before the end of 1961: the Harvard and
UCLA groups plus another contingent to train at Michigan
State University. The Harvard and UCLA volunteers
would be scattered all over the country; the Michigan
State group would be concentrated at the University of
Nigeria in the Eastern Region as junior instructors.

The first priority seemed to be to establish specific
teaching assignments for the volunteers, but immediately
the problem of housing presented itself. There had been
much publicity in the U.S. about volunteers living in village mud huts, but mud huts are in no sense a part of the
life of secondary school teachers in Africa. Almost all
secondary schools are located in clean, well-kept compounds and surrounded by good to excellent staff houses.
A problem exists, however: Few schools have enough
housing for all of the staff they need. Furthermore, schools
are nearly always located at such a distance from any
town or village that commuting is a problem, even if any
kind of adequate house were available there.

The original team from Washington had been very em-
phatic in discussions with ministry officials that adequate
housing for volunteers was of highest importance. They
said that, to the extent necessary, the Peace Corps would
provide funds to add to existing houses, remodel unusable

ones, or even build new quarters as a last resort. There was even some talk of bringing in pre-fabs.

This talk of financial assistance with housing caused real excitement in the financially hard-pressed education ministries and private schools. But as I tried over several weeks to get from Washington some firm idea of how much money we might have to spend on housing, I discovered a strong sentiment developing there that housing should be a contribution of the host country. Feeling was particularly unified that the Peace Corps should not get into the business of building houses for volunteers.

While I was inclined to agree in principle that a contribution by the receiving country was a healthy sign of interest in the program, I did not relish the task of dampening all of the hopes and expectations that had been built up. But I did, and the obvious alternative was to choose schools for volunteer assignment only where housing was available. Of course, this sometimes meant that a school which needed a volunteer teacher most did not receive one. Everyone remarked on this unfortunate fact and then seemed to forget it.

Deciding on assignments for volunteers could be nightmarish. For reasons we could never fathom it took weeks to receive from the training sites the names and backgrounds of the trainees; invariably there were more English, history, and social studies teachers than the ministries had asked for and fewer science and mathematics. I also quickly discovered that members of the allocation committee tried to pick off for their region volunteers from "name" schools such as Harvard, Yale, Princeton, MIT, and the University of California. It even came to my attention that there existed in the Ministry of Education in Lagos a list of "unacceptable" American colleges. Fortunately, the list was never invoked in the case of a volunteer, but it reminded me again of the strong element of educational snobbishness that is a heritage of Africa's colonial past.

Once the tentative assignments had been made in the ministries, each school had to be visited to see if the need was genuine, the headmaster really interested in a volunteer teacher, and the house he was to occupy in fact a reality. I can't remember the number of times the house proved to be a foundation or a marked off plot plus a solemn and thoroughly well-intentioned assurance that everything would be in place by the time the volunteer arrived. I can't remember the number of times outraged volunteers wrote to me asking me how I expected them to live in a foundation.

Nigeria is twice the size of California plus something, and the roads are long and rough and dusty. Four of us, as the staff became shortly before the volunteers arrived, pounding through the country in Jeeps could do at best a very superficial job of checking schools. A site survey visit usually amounted to arriving in a cloudburst of dust, having a cup of tea with the headmaster, walking through the school, and looking at the volunteer's prospective house. Then it was on to the next location, a drive of from four hours to a whole day. Sometimes, of course, there was an overnight, and these were good for longer talks and a better feel for the realities of teaching in Nigeria. But even then the visits were superficial and made tolerable only by our ignorance of how little we knew about what we were trying to do and about what we were asking volunteers to do.

Washington correctly decided that each country should determine what the living allowance should be for its volunteers, and every country staff had to try to divine a figure that would permit the volunteer to maintain a healthy existence but that would not make him seem unduly affluent in comparison to his co-workers. This was, to be sure, an impossible task. From the moment a volunteer arrived at his site with camera, radio, quite likely tape recorder and phonograph, a full bag of new clothes, considerable supplies of toilet goods, and his own portable library, he was marked as a rich stranger from a rich land.

Still we worked at gearing the volunteer's income to his daily needs. We drew up lists of food costs, bus fares, servants' salaries, clothing costs (although there was a special clothing allowance); we guessed at needs for tooth paste, ink, postage, and the myriad other items that go into an American's life no matter where he is. I remember that we rather vaguely put in fifteen dollars a month under a general item called "recreation."

"Look," someone said to Bill Hintz and me, "if your volunteer drinks just one bottle of Star Beer with his friends at the end of the day, that will use up his fifteen dollars for recreation."

We raised that item.

We finally came up with a figure of $168 per month, which by only minor coincidence was the same salary that a beginning Nigerian secondary school teacher with a university degree would receive. The range for teachers in government schools went from $2,016 to $4,435 per year. Our theory was that, although our volunteer would have certain advantages such as a clothing allowance and a vacation allowance outside his basic $168 per month, a Nigerian teacher should be able to make a similar amount of money go further in his own country. This should make the volunteers come out about even with the lowest paid of their teaching colleagues.

As it turned out, the amount we decided on was considerably in excess of what volunteers needed to "subsist" in reasonable comfort. In later years subsistence allowances were reduced, not only in Nigeria but in a number of other countries, a painful process once the volunteer had become accustomed to a higher figure. The wise reps[1] were those who set the living allowance figure very low and raised it when the need was seen.

Washington and the field staff also decided in the formative days that the Peace Corps, both volunteers and staff, would not join embassy-AID commissaries, where many good material things of American life were available at duty free prices; nor would we patronize P-X's or use APO or diplomatic pouch for sending or receiving mail. We would not import duty free food or luxuries of

[1] The Peace Corps never really settled the question of what to call its top staff man in an overseas program. In the beginning the title used everywhere was "Peace Corps Representative." Later, most of the regions adopted the title of "Director" for those who ran country programs, but Latin America retained "Representative." But the shorthand term "rep" was universally used for years by all volunteers and staff, and I have retained that use throughout this book in referring to those men and women who were in charge of country programs.

any kind, although host governments everywhere gave
Peace Corps staff such privileges. Peace Corps staff would
not receive post differentials (so-called "hardship" allowances, sometimes amounting to twenty-five percent of
base salary) or cost-of-living allowances that embassy,
AID, and USIS employees were entitled to. Peace Corps
would not have the rest and rehabilitation travel privileges
which were often available to other foreign service
personnel.

All of these decisions we thought to be consistent with
one Peace Corps aim of presenting a new American image
overseas, of combating "Ugly Americanism." We also believed that such a living style would help break down
barriers between Peace Corps volunteers and staff and
the people of the countries with whom they worked.

These ideas were perhaps naïve. They certainly caused
problems and produced guilt feelings within the Peace
Corps, which I will discuss later. They undoubtedly made
unhappy many embassy and AID people who felt threat-
ened by them; and they opened the Peace Corps to a
general charge of posturing, hair-shirtism, and phoniness.

Yet these ideas were appropriate to the time, to the
rhetoric of the New Frontier, to the national feeling that
a different approach was needed to replace our sterile
efforts overseas. In any case, the Peace Corps would
have been a very different organization without this philosophy and, I believe, a considerably less vital one.

If the philosophy was naïve, it was still explicitly stated
by a great historian. Writing in the New York *Times
Magazine* of November 13, 1960, in an article entitled

"If We Are to Be the Wave of the Future," Arnold J. Toynbee said:

Present-day America's unprecedentedly high material standard of living is her most serious handicap in her waging of the cold war. This may sound like a paradox to Americans who think of this abundance of material goods as being the sovereign recommendation of the present American way of life. Yet, in its competition with Russia, America's high material standard hits America in several ways.

To begin with, it tends to set apart Americans on missions abroad from the people among whom and for whom they are working. Many present-day Americans cannot bring themselves to eat the food and live the life of the "natives." They would find expatriation intolerable if they did not carry the American apparatus of material life along with them. The symbol of this is the PX. And the PX is a strong point for communism in the cold war, because it advertises that there is a great gulf fixed between Americans and the world's ordinary human inhabitants.

The gulf would vanish if America could be represented abroad today by the generation of men and women who won the American West. Those Americans were the wave of the future in their day because they lived as hard as the average human being, and sometimes a good deal harder. If they were with us still, they would be able to live and work among the ordinary people of the world in these ordinary people's way, and that would win the ordinary people's hearts.

Can the pioneer generation of Americans be brought back to life? I believe it can because I believe its tradition is still alive. The virtues of this deep-rooted American tradition are the basic virtues: independence of mind, initiative, courage, vigor, hardiness, generosity. These virtues can be counted on to win a watching world's adherence because they are the virtues the world most needs.

It is interesting to note that this article was written while the Peace Corps was still only campaign rhetoric; also it deals not with the Peace Corps per se—which isn't mentioned in the article—but with America's problems in the cold war. Those of us in the Peace Corps did not like to think that we were in any way a part of the cold war; but in every word he wrote, Arnold Toynbee was talking our language.

The first Nigeria Peace Corps group of thirty-seven arrived in Lagos by Pan American jet on September 26. They actually were not volunteers but rather still trainees. Harvard had worked out an arrangement with the University College of Ibadan in the Western Region that after eight weeks at Harvard the trainees would move to the University College for an additional three months' training.

I had been a bit doubtful about training taking place in the country of service, but Harvard was very interested in establishing a university-to-university relationship with Ibadan. Besides, they argued plausibly, volunteers could be better prepared in Nigeria for life in Nigeria than they could be in Cambridge, Massachusetts. I also felt that five months was too long a training period for volunteers eager to get on the job and too large a slice out of a total of two years' service.

But the Harvard people maintained that not even five months was time enough to make finished teachers out of raw college graduates (of course it wasn't) and that if their institution was to be associated with the project, it had to be done right. Harvard was very hard to argue with, in those days, at least, and the five-month training program was approved. The programs for the volunteers training at UCLA and Michigan State began in late September and lasted about three months. Twelve weeks became the norm for most Peace Corps training programs.

The trainees passed quickly through Lagos—I remember being very much aware of how young they looked —and settled into their routine at Ibadan. The training was conducted by a joint Harvard-University College staff, and Peace Corps, except for our new associate rep in Ibadan, Murray Frank, had little to do with it.

Bill Hintz and I continued our work of getting ready. The problem of what kind of transportation, if any, volunteers were going to have was extremely perplexing. We had to arrange for a survey of health facilities throughout the country. Some church-supported schools (which make up the great majority of secondary schools in Nigeria) were suggesting that it was important that they should have a Methodist volunteer or a Christian or a Seventh Day Adventist.

This worrisome matter took many hours to sort out, but the Peace Corps' position on it was firm to the point of bluntness: Volunteers would not be assigned by religion. We did not ask a volunteer his religion, and any school that insisted on religious screening should forget about having a volunteer teacher. All Nigerian ministries supported this position without equivocation. Once the Peace Corps' point of view was made clear, schools quickly dropped the issue.

Sorting out relations with our embassy was also time consuming. I would in no way want to minimize the help we received from Ambassador Joseph Palmer, his deputy Jerry Greene, and from others of our diplomatic colleagues. They took the lead in our early discussions about the program approval and their contacts were invaluable. We received major help from them in arranging staff housing and in preparing for and handling emergencies that inevitably arose. Of course they dispatched all of our cables and official mail.

But embassies everywhere, I have learned, are always looking for ways to add to their staffs; seldom do they think they have enough people to do the work asked of them, and in some cases they are right. Our embassy in Lagos presented us with a list of additional staff members they felt they urgently needed to take care of the extra work that would be required by the presence of a Peace Corps program in Nigeria. The list included the following:

Personnel Officer
Assistant Administrative Officer

Consular Assistant

Accounting Assistant

Communications Clerk

Clerk-Stenographer

Foreign Service Local Disbursing Assistant (2)

Foreign Service Local Mail Clerk

Foreign Service Local Chauffeur

In addition, because of Peace Corps business, the embassy felt that it needed two additional passenger-carrying vehicles and additional office space and housing.

At the time of this request the Peace Corps staff in Nigeria totaled three persons.

The final allocation of Peace Corps money to the embassy for administrative support would have purchased but a fraction of their requested help. Nevertheless, I was awed by the dimensions of what my embassy friends considered their rock-bottom needs. It was a valuable bureaucratic lesson but one that the Peace Corps' parsimony gave me little opportunity to apply.

In early October I made a trip to UCLA with a group of Nigerian education officials to review the program and become acquainted with the trainees. Afterward, I flew to Washington for my first visit to Peace Corps headquarters. I arrived on Saturday, October 14, and as it turned out transacted very little business during my brief stay there.

On Sunday the wire services from Lagos carried a story about a Peace Corps trainee at the University College of Ibadan who had dropped a postcard in the street. The trainee's name was Margery Michelmore, and she and the Peace Corps were in trouble.

The "Michelmore Postcard Incident" was the Peace Corps' first great crisis. It focused the white, hot glare of worldwide press, radio, and television attention on the infant organization. It made headlines for days in the United States and for weeks in Nigeria. It proved for Peace Corps critics that immature young Americans overseas would do nothing but get the U.S. in trouble. It provided glorious ammunition for Moscow and Peking. It left in its wake a shaken and sobered Peace Corps.

Margery Michelmore looked like a top-flight prospect for the Peace Corps. She was twenty-three years old, a magna cum laude graduate of Smith College. She had gone to work as a researcher for *Reader's Digest* magazine upon graduation and had resigned to serve in the Peace Corps in Nigeria. The training staff at Harvard rated her one of the best of the group.

On the morning of October 14—as best Margery or anyone else has ever been able to figure out—she mailed a number of postcards at the porter's lodge in her hall at the University College of Ibadan. Apparently, however, she dropped one of the cards in the street; she of course could not be certain. By lunch time the mimeographed text of her postcard was being circulated all over the campus. The postcard was written to a friend in the United States. In it, she apologized for not writing a letter but said she wanted the young man who received the card to see the fascinating city in which she was living. She felt that, with all her training, she, and others with her, really had not expected to find the squalor and primitive living conditions she saw as existing all around her; the word "underdeveloped" took on new meaning. She described the people as living in the street, cooking in the street, selling in the street, and even going to the bathroom in the street. Margery felt that the experience of being a foreigner in an African university was an exciting one, commented on the Lumumba riots which had taken place the previous year and asked the person to whom she was mailing the card to please write.

The Nigerian students reacted instantly and with a vehemence that shocked the Peace Corps trainees. Within a few minutes after the circulation of the mimeographed postcard text, small riots started in the men's residence hall where the male trainees stayed. Groups of students began to roam about shouting such slogans as "Yankees go home!" and "Imperialist agents unwelcome!" Trainees found similar messages written on the doors of their rooms; and within a few hours the announcement was made that all Peace Corps people were banned from the student union, where they had previously been welcome for soft drinks and conversation.

Many students refused even to speak to the Peace Corps trainees, and in some halls they were segregated at supper that evening. If a Nigerian student sat down with a trainee, he was shouted at and ridiculed by his fellow students. A mass protest rally, to which all white students (including British and European) were barred, was announced for eleven-thirty the next morning.

Margery was quite broken up over what she had done and caused but quickly pulled herself together and did what she could to relieve the situation by writing an open letter of apology and offering to resign from the program. The letter was mineographed and distributed in all residence halls before dawn on Sunday morning.

All of the Peace Corps trainees were deeply concerned, not so much for their physical safety but for their future as volunteers in Nigeria. They were also bewildered by the violence of the reaction on the campus. On the surface Margery's postcard had not seemed all that heinous. It was thoughtless, immature, and exaggerated; but could any reader not see that she was trying to dramatize her experience? The answer was "no." The students saw only insult to them personally and to their country by a white foreigner.

This was the trainees' and the Peace Corps' first face-to-face encounter with the deep sensitivities of most people of the underdeveloped world, particularly those who have recently thrown off colonial rule. If a Nigerian student attending Smith College in the United States had written an exaggerated description of the decay in Appalachia or the squalor of Harlem, she would probably have been congratulated by the Smith students. But now the Peace Corps trainees knew in a way they had not learned from lectures at Harvard or what they had casually observed since coming to Africa that the University College of Ibadan students were not Smith students and Nigeria was not America.

The trainees reported that, while pressure was mostly directed at the whole group, they had seen at least one sign that read "Margery must go. The rest may stay." And a number of students had expressed the same sentiment. They also reported that most of the Nigerian students

with whom they had established some real degree of
friendship had not deserted them. Some had even expressed sympathy for Margery, yet they had been hurt
by her card. Moreover, they seemed to be questioning
whether the other trainees saw them and their country
as Margery described it in her postcard but had simply
hidden their true feelings. Only a very few understood
that Margery had not been trying to write a fair and accurate description of Nigeria and Nigerians.

In this postcard message of a hundred words was
grist for a thousand seminars and discussions in Peace
Corps training programs of the future—if, indeed, the
Peace Corps had a future.

The Nigerian newspapers Sunday morning carried the
postcard story in blazing headlines, and editorial comment was bitter. Most newspapers enjoined their readers
to attend the mass rally set for that morning. The rally
took place as scheduled, and press reports the next day
estimated the attendance at over a thousand. In fact
fewer than two hundred persons were present, and reactions around the campus indicated that tempers were
subsiding.

Nevertheless, the rally was well managed and produced extreme resolutions. One called for the boycott of
all Peace Corps volunteers (the fact that they were
trainees and not yet volunteers was never noted by anyone anywhere during this incident) as long as they were
on the University College campus. Another, more sweep-
ing, called for the expulsion of the Peace Corps from
Nigeria.

The pressure on Margery at University College was unbearable, so she was driven to Lagos, where she and all concerned might with less emotion consider her future. She felt that she should resign from the program, that her future presence at the college would make her ineffective as a volunteer anywhere in Nigeria. There was general agreement with her analysis. The ambassador and his advisers, however, did not want to give the impression that the embassy had panicked and spirited her out of the country in violation of her rights. Shriver and his advisers—I include myself—did not want the American public to get the impression that the Peace Corps had abandoned its first volunteer in trouble. So Margery—who now more than anything else wanted to go home—stayed in Lagos, with Jerry Greene and his wife while the storm raged around her.

In the United States the Peace Corps was now front page news and the subject of much more editorial comment than it had been when the agency was born. In general, sympathy was expressed for Margery and her personal ordeal. But the burden of editorial and press comments that poured into the Peace Corps office was that the Peace Corps idea had now been exposed for what it was: a dangerous, unworkable exercise in do-goodism and, as one writer called it, "the most dangerous experiment since the children's crusade." Former President Eisenhower, at a Republican party fund-raising function, took note of the incident by commenting that there seemed to be "postcard evidence" that the Peace Corps was an unsound idea. He then suggested that Peace Corps volunteers be sent to the moon since that was an underdeveloped country and there would be less chance of creating problems there.

There was, however, some significant rallying to the defense of the Peace Corps. James A. Wechsler, in his New York *Post* column of October 18, wrote:

. . . Nothing in the card was sinister. It contained the instinctive expression of horror of an affluent American girl in her first direct encounter with the gruesome squalor of Nigeria (which might have been East Harlem). She was neither patronizing nor self-righteous in her comment; yet whoever found the lost card managed to stage a big production. Like many other people, the Nigerians need and want help; but they do not like to be told how desperate is their need. The demagogues in their midst exploited the incident.

. . . The most serious aspect of the episode is not its disclosure about the sensitivity of Nigerians. It is what it reveals about our own condition. For by and large—to judge from the clippings and reports reaching Peace Corps headquarters here—this incident has provided a cruel field day for the know-nothing U.S. press. It has been proclaimed as proof that the adventurous spirit of idealistic young Americans is doomed to frustration and disaster.

. . . The early press reaction to the Nigerian episode provokes more question about us than it does about the Nigerians. Why is there so much desire to burlesque the Peace Corps? Why does so much of the press relish this episode as sure evidence that any adventure in idealism is a capricious and futile effort? In such matters it might be said—if much of our press truly reflects us—that we are a backward, primitive, underdeveloped people.

The New York *Times* commented editorially that "compassion and understanding will have to operate in two directions if the Peace Corps is to succeed. The countries to which units go must be mindful that youth is often brash; and our earnest young volunteers will need a heightened consciousness that they arrive as ambassadors whose every word and act is subject to distortion by anti-American elements." The editorial wished Margery a "fruitful new assignment" in the Peace Corps.

The New York *Herald Tribune* pointed the finger at Harvard for not preparing Margery for the squalid conditions of Nigeria. "What, in Heaven's name," it asked, "was going on in those indoctrination classes?" The *Post* also commented that the whole business seemed to have been very carefully and well planned and that "its resolution calling for the expulsion of the Peace Corps followed the Communist line even to denouncing Corps members as 'agents of imperialism.'"

The American press was quite preoccupied with the possibility that the incident was Communist inspired and engineered. Writers cited much the same evidence: the mysterious circumstances surrounding the loss of the postcard, the speed and skill with which public sentiment was whipped up, the rally with its stereotyped resolutions and language.

The facts, I believe, are quite otherwise. There was on

the Ibadan campus—as on most African, Asian, and Latin campuses—a group of intensely nationalistic students. They were very suspicious of all United States foreign policy and actions, including the Peace Corps and its motives. As best we could determine, a member of this group found the postcard and quickly rallied his companions to take advantage of it. Their motive certainly was to damage the Peace Corps and the United States, not because they were Communists but because they were Nigerians, full of national and racial pride and distrustful of what they considered "neo-colonialism" in any form. Once they had made the postcard public, the reaction of hurt and indignation was quite genuine. A sensational press fanned the flames of this indignation, but it needed no engineering.

After a few days in Lagos Margery returned to the United States, entirely of her own volition. She worked with the Peace Corps in Washington for a while and then returned to Massachusetts. She remains to this day the Peace Corps' most famous volunteer alumnus, though in fact she never graduated from her trainee status.

Although I am sure she could take scant satisfaction in the fact, Margery Michelmore made a valuable contribution to the Peace Corps. Her woes in Nigeria became a classic case history in the sensitivities of emerging nations for all future generations of volunteers to be aware of and profit from. Furthermore, the incident focused a greatly heightened press and public attention on the Peace Corps. From that time everything we did was news, and we did enough things right that we could stand the attention.

Happily, the episode seemed even to have some beneficial effects for the group of trainees at Ibadan. After the furor died down, they reported that some Nigerian students who had previously paid no attention to them made an effort to become acquainted. And those with whom they had been friendly unburdened themselves about some special problems or doubts that they had. It had seemed to some of the Nigerians that the smiles of the Americans had been a little over-friendly and perhaps hypocritical. Why did the Peace Corps people not share Nigerian food with the other students but instead eat specially prepared "European" food? And was it not true that the Peace Corps was really a propaganda scheme rather than a sincere program of service? As much as they could appreciate the honest motives of individual volunteers, some of the Nigerian students said, they still could not help but believe that the volunteers were dupes of the neo-colonialist policies of the United States Government.

Getting such feelings out into the open for frank discussions was a very good thing. Many evenings throughout the rest of the training program were devoted to the trainees and students talking about these ideas. The trainees probably learned more about Nigeria and Nigerians from these sessions than they did from their formal classes. Many felt that their friendships were now on a real and honest footing.

The volunteers who had trained at Michigan State arrived in late November without incident and to a generally favorable and subdued press. The Michelmore episode seemed to have used up most of the writers' emotional energies. The prime minister received some of the group and made a very gracious statement about the Peace Corps. The Nigerian leaders in every way conducted themselves with dignity and restraint throughout the postcard turmoil. They consistently passed up their many opportunities for demagoguery and kept the program quietly on track. The principal of the University College, Dr. K. O. Dike, was a particularly wise and courageous administrator throughout the trouble.

My last clear memory of the Michelmore case is associated with the arrival of the UCLA volunteers three days after Christmas. At the orientation in Lagos they received from the Nigerian government welcome kits containing maps and pamphlets of useful information. The kits also contained a few postcards with attractive Nigerian scenes.

Immediately upon discovering the postcards, one of the new volunteers came hurrying up to me. "What are they trying to do," he asked indignantly, "trap me?"

I made a mental note to write to our Washington training division about over-zealous application of the postcard incident.

I have written in detail about the birth and beginning of the Peace Corps program in Nigeria not only because it was my own experience but also because the problems we faced and the activities that consumed our days were much the same as those of the men and women who started Peace Corps programs in other African countries and in Asia and Latin America. The specifics in each country were different; the order of staff priorities varied; though similar in some ways, countries and peoples were vastly different in others. But the broad patterns of what had to be done to get a Peace Corps program underway were remarkably similar. Even our troubles at Ibadan were different only in degree; every volunteer and staff member everywhere encountered the realities of nationalism and the sensitivities of national and racial pride.

By the end of 1961 just over five hundred volunteers had received training and reported for duty in nine widely scattered countries. Several hundred more were in training for other countries. While most of the volunteers were teaching in schools in Ghana, Nigeria, and the Philippines, a respectable variety of activities was still present in the first year's program: Volunteers were working in community development on St. Lucia, in rural public works in Pakistan, and at road surveying in Tanzania.

It was a mix of countries and jobs in which the Washington planners took more than quiet pride. Starting with nothing but an idea, they had put the Peace Corps in business on three continents in less than a year.

CHAPTER TWO

The Year of the Volunteer: 1962

The Peace Corps Act, drafted chiefly by an able young
Peace Corps staff lawyer named Roger Kuhn, made its
way through congressional committees during the spring
and summer, passed both houses by an impressive majority, and was signed into law by President Kennedy on
September 22, 1961. The act gave the Peace Corps thirty
million dollars and one year to show what it could do and
tied astonishingly few strings to how it was to do it.

In a statement of purpose the Congress declared that it
was the policy of the United States and the purpose of
the act "to promote world peace and friendship through
a Peace Corps, which shall make available to interested
countries and areas men and women of the United States
qualified for service abroad and willing to serve, under
conditions of hardship if necessary, to help the peoples
of such countries and areas in meeting their needs for
trained manpower, and to help promote a better understanding of the American people on the part of the
peoples served and a better understanding of other peoples on the part of the American people."

With that very general but highly important bit of pol-

icy direction, Congress authorized the President to build
programs that would carry out the purposes of the act,
"on such terms and conditions as he may determine." The
act specified that volunteers would have to be "qualified,"
that they must be citizens or nationals of the United
States, and that persons who wanted to be volunteers
must be given no political test nor be discriminated
against on account of race, color, or creed.

Beyond those limitations everything was left to the
Peace Corps. The act did not attempt to spell out what
it meant by "qualified." It did not specify any particular
skills volunteers had to have; it did not name special
kinds of programs to be undertaken, such as teaching,
health, or agriculture. It did not set age limits for volunteers, specify how long they should serve, or try to dictate how they should live and be paid overseas. It did
not restrict the countries in which they might serve
abroad. In every way, Congress left the Peace Corps Act
about as open-ended and unrestrictive as a young, free-
swinging organization could possibly want. A less charitable view expressed by some was that Congress preferred to let the Peace Corps hang itself rather than take
responsibility for telling it how to do so.

The overriding question as the Peace Corps began its
first year of overseas operations in 1962 was how would
the volunteers perform? Would they make it? Everything
depended on that, of course, and the Michelmore episode
had not helped anyone's confidence. For all the brave
talk at Peace Corps headquarters, no one really knew
what to expect. Many ambassadors were privately hor-
rified at the prospect of hundreds of soft, young Ameri-

cans scattered throughout the countries they were
responsible for; they also had counseled small, pilot
beginnings. My friends in AID, with the best of intentions, assured me that I could come back to work there
any time.

And despite their need for teachers, not every education official was eager to get Peace Corps volunteers that
first year. Hector Jelf, a tough, plain-talking Englishman
who had been permanent secretary of the Ministry of
Education in Northern Nigeria for many years, told me
quite bluntly at our first meeting that he would prefer to wait a year and see how the volunteers did in the
other two regions of Nigeria. Jelf told me that the care
and feeding of expatriate teachers had always been one
of his biggest headaches and that he had had particular
trouble with Americans he had recruited through private
U.S. organizations.

"They have no idea what it's like to live and teach in
an African school," he said. "I hired five last year and four
of them were gone before the second term was well
underway."

Jelf finally asked for some volunteers but chiefly because his Minister of Education didn't want the Northern
Region to be the only one left out of the new Peace Corps
thing.

There was nothing new about Americans living in
Africa, Asia, and Latin America. Embassy, AID, U.S.
Information Service, and private business people had
been doing it for a long time. But they were older professional people; they lived in the capital cities with their
families, in excellent homes; all the trappings of Ameri-

can life were shipped in to them. Thousands of American missionaries were living and working in the hinterlands of developing countries, but they also were older, had families, had been prepared for that life as a career, had built good comfortable homes, and, most especially, were sustained in their efforts by their religious faith.

By contrast, volunteers would be mostly young and inexperienced. They would have a few weeks of language training instead of the two years that most missionaries received. They would live in remote locations in whatever housing was available. They would not have the good material things of American life shipped in nor a large American community to relax with in the evening. And it wasn't at all clear what many of them would be working at.

At an embassy cocktail party in Lagos a week before the first group of volunteers arrived, I couldn't find anyone who, after three Martinis or four Scotches, would give the Peace Corps more than three months before it fell on its face. The sober ones—there are many, folklore to the contrary—remembered that they were talking to the poor guy who was holding the Peace Corps bag. They told me they were sure the kids would do great.

Arrival and Departure

I never called Peace Corps volunteers kids, but I did think of the early ones as Mr. Kennedy's boys and girls because they truly were. They had many motives for joining the Peace Corps: a yearning for adventure, postponing a career decision, a desire to get away from college boredom before going on to graduate school. Some simply wanted to take a look at the world; others sought to delay military service (though this was not often a motive in the early years).

But in almost every case an additional motive was present: They wanted to make some kind of contribution to a better world in a personal, individual way. And for many, perhaps most, this motive was connected with their affection for Kennedy and with the things he had said about building a stronger and better America through helping the poor countries of the world. I think it probable that John Kennedy was the last American President who was or will be loved by his people in this century. The lovelessness and divisiveness of Vietnam, poverty, urban decay, and racial hatred will preclude presidential affection as a national emotion.

But a great many of the pioneer volunteers had a deep feeling for Kennedy, and they felt they were answering his call to national duty in a new and constructive way that he had made possible. As one of the first Philippines volunteers put it, "He made being an American an exciting idea."

Though their mission was peace and not war, the Peace Corps volunteers of the Kennedy years may have been among the last of the old-fashioned patriots.

Volunteers disliked talking about why they had joined the Peace Corps and resented the eternal probing of the question by friends, reporters, psychologists, and strangers at parties. Motives that were complex, highly personal, and often not fully understood by the volunteer came out sounding like pious clichés. A volunteer going to Africa wrote:

". . . we held to a sharply restricted view of our role as Peace Corps teachers. . . . Probably we were sensitive to public criticism of the Peace Corps as opening the floodgate to youthful, naïve idealism. In any case, we struck the exact opposite pose. We were 'hard-headed.' We were 'realistic.' First and last, we aimed to succeed simply as teachers."

Whatever the motives, the testing of them lay in hundreds of places with names like Abeokuta, Chimbote, Oyo, Kakinada, and Fusagasugá, names that registered strangely on the American ear and sent thousands of parents hurrying to the atlas. But before the volunteers went to their individual "sites," they arrived in a group at the capital city for orientation. The arrival of a new group of volunteers was always an exciting moment for those most closely connected with the Peace Corps, but the novelty made the arrival of the first groups exciting for everyone.

A typical group would have from thirty to fifty volunteers, about twice as many men as women, two or three young married couples, and two or three persons in their fifties or sixties. The great majority would be in their early twenties. The early groups would have a few blacks— sometimes three or four—but by 1965 it was more likely to be one or none. While the ratio of men to women in the Peace Corps has throughout the years stood at about six men to four women, some special groups such as agriculturalists or nurses would be all or heavily male or female. Non-teaching groups would occasionally contain a volunteer under twenty—usually a young man with a farm or mechanical background—but that was rare.

The volunteers would climb off the big Pan American or TWA jetliner (the American companies were terribly unhappy when we used a foreign carrier, as we sometimes did) in an almost zombie-like state from their long flight plus a round of farewell parties at home that had left them sleepless for nights. They were herded through immigration and customs, put on a chartered bus, and driven to a second-rate hotel, a school dormitory, or a government hostel. There they were assigned a room, given a welcome kit, issued some "walk around" money, and perhaps left alone for a few hours to sleep or rest— depending upon what time of day or night they arrived.

If the volunteer didn't feel like a new recruit at boot *141819* camp, it must have been because he was too tired to feel anything. For the first few years the Peace Corps even assigned "escort officers" from the Washington staff to muster the new volunteers at the U.S. international airport from which they were leaving and *accompany* them —these men and women who were going to spend two years in the African bush or an Andean village—on the flight to their country of assignment. Finally, sometime in 1964, the absurdity of the escort officer idea became so obvious and the fact so patent that it was being used solely as a means of rewarding a deserving Washington staff member with a trip abroad that it was dropped.

It always seemed to me that the Peace Corps should have been able to devise a better arrival system—like giving a volunteer an airplane ticket at the end of training and telling him to show up at the Peace Corps office in

Bangkok or Bogotá on a certain day. But the savings in group travel and the convenience of having everyone arrive at the same time for orientation seemed to outweigh the psychological problems of treating arriving volunteers like a cross between an army battalion and a student group on a study tour abroad.

The volunteers did not seem to care much, and I suppose that is why the system was not changed. They sat with drooping eyelids through official welcoming speeches and the embassy country team briefing. They listened with intense interest to anything the Peace Corps staff could tell them about their specific assignments and were reasonably attentive to the Peace Corps doctor's lecture on health precautions.

They really came alive, however, in the few hours during orientation when they were mercifully let loose on their own. Here was their first chance to see the people and country that they had been talked to about in training for the past three months, and they plunged in with intense interest. They visited coffee shops and bars, roamed the streets and tried out their woefully inadequate language on fish sellers and traders in the open markets, haggled with taxi drivers over the fare. Even buying a postage stamp was an adventure.

They were neatly, if casually, dressed, though in later years there were problems of appearance. While they all had cameras, they were reluctant to use them because they didn't want a tourist label. They ate and drank in cafés where foreigners had never been seen before, kicked soccer balls with schoolboys, and altogether made it clear that a new brand of American had come to town.

The volunteers were always bursting to get to their jobs yet understandably nervous about what lay ahead and a little sad to cut the cord with their training group. In mixed groups a romance or two had usually budded during training, and the luck of the draw seemed almost always to see them assigned at opposite ends of the country. Only in rare cases, however, did the young man and woman ask for a more geographically favorable assignment. Romance or not, they wanted to do the job they came to do.

And the moment arrived when the group went their different ways, some by Jeep, some by train, bus, or plane. Never did they have an escort officer, though someone at the other end had been informed when they would arrive (or at least a telegram had been sent); and sometimes a headmaster or agricultural officer would come to the capital to collect "his" volunteers and take them back with him. Everybody liked that arrangement. It gave the local official a chance to come to the big city, and the trip back provided a chance to get acquainted in an informal, leisurely way.

The Peace Corps Volunteer as Teacher

In the Peace Corps' first year overseas almost sixty-five percent of all volunteers were classroom teachers. The percentage dropped in succeeding years as other kinds of programs were added; but as late as 1966 over fifty percent of all volunteers were teachers, and in 1970 teachers still made up by far the largest single job category. I have explained Washington's reasons for encouraging volun-

teer teacher programs: Teaching enabled the Peace
Corps to make a fast and big start. It provided a structured job and clear-cut responsibilities for volunteers. It
seemed the task best suited to a young college graduate
whose chief credential was his new college degree. Furthermore, most African countries were short of degree-
holding teachers in almost all subject matter fields, and
native-speaking English teachers were scarce everywhere.
In short, teaching—particularly in secondary schools—
seemed like a Peace Corps natural, if there was such a
thing.

In the distance between romantic conception and reality it is possible that the early Peace Corps teachers had
a greater adjustment to make than their fellow volunteers
in other kinds of programs. Everyone who volunteered
for the Peace Corps expected rugged living conditions
and was prepared "to serve under conditions of hardship,"
as the Peace Corps Act put it. The early newspaper con-
jectures, written out of imagination because there was yet
no reality, pictured the volunteer laboring with shovel
and trowel in rain forest villages and going home at sun-
down to cook and sleep in his lantern-lit mud hut. Even
when the reality was known, writers and most of the
Peace Corps' public information output continued to feature the work and lives of those volunteers who most
nearly fitted the original conception, the "mud-hut
image" as the volunteers themselves dubbed it.

Peace Corps volunteer teachers did not live in mud
huts.[1] In most African countries (and usually elsewhere),

[1] I knew some volunteer teachers who lived in mud huts and I hope,
if they read this, they will not write me accusing letters. In a program that

when the volunteer arrived at his school, he was taken to a house on a school compound often located three or four miles from a good-sized town or city. Sometimes, however, the school was much more isolated than this. The compound was hot, dusty, and treeless, the school a drab stone or adobe structure. But the house was much better than he expected: living room, two bedrooms, kitchen, bathroom, sometimes a dining room. It was simply but adequately furnished and (again in Africa) the Peace Corps had frequently supplied a refrigerator. Of course there was electricity. Usually two volunteers assigned to the same school shared such a house, though sometimes it was occupied by only one.

The volunteer discovered that the headmaster or even the Peace Corps had lined up a cook for him, a cook who in most cases would also double as a houseboy or steward. Coming from a servantless society, the volunteer's egalitarian sensibilities were often outraged, and having a servant certainly did not fit his Peace Corps image. But there were advantages, both in health and time saving— the volunteer had never cooked in his life and the food market was usually miles from the school. Besides, all his fellow teachers, native-born and expatriate, had servants, as did everyone in the country with any money or status. And as everyone explained to the new volunteer, he wouldn't accomplish anything by not having a cook ex-

---

involved thousands of individual situations in sixty countries over the better part of a decade, there were certain to be exceptions—often many— to any generalizations that can be made about any aspect of Peace Corps life or programs. The reader should know that, and I assure my Peace Corps friends I have not forgotten it. But to avoid being tiresome, I will refrain from saying "Of course, there were exceptions" every time I introduce a new subject.

cept add to the country's unemployment problem. The volunteer was uncomfortable with the idea for a while but soon became accustomed to it.

The first few days at the school were interesting, even exciting, as the volunteer met his headmaster (who might be an expatriate), was assigned his classes, became acquainted with his teaching colleagues, and went to town to buy some things for his house. Getting to town was a problem because he didn't have anything with wheels yet and there was no public bus service. The Peace Corps had given him money for a bicycle, which was one of the things he would buy in town. One of the Nigerian teachers gave him a lift in his car and expressed his astonishment that the volunteer was going to buy a bicycle.

"You can't ride it in this sun or when the rains come," he said. "Surely the Peace Corps is going to give you a car."

But the Peace Corps wasn't.

The volunteer had expected to reach his school just in time for the start of classes, but, for reasons he never fully understood, school opening was delayed two weeks, and then came a religious holiday that somehow stretched into a week. During this time the volunteer worked on his course notes and talked to the few teachers who were around the school. They spoke English of course but the range was limited for some, and even more limited for both were topics of conversation that they could develop beyond superficial levels.

The volunteer had discovered that there was a little club in town where one could get a cold beer and be invited into a good game of bridge. But he had not seen anyone but Englishmen and a few other foreigners the one time he had been taken as a guest. The volunteer decided that he had not come into the Peace Corps to join an expatriate club, so he didn't apply for membership. He stayed in his house at night and began to read a lot from the very good foot locker full of paperback books with which the Peace Corps had thoughtfully provided him.

The volunteer was pretty tense and jittery by the time classes started, but he thought he would be all right once he started working with his students. For the first few days they had real problems understanding each other; that finally improved, but the volunteer was dismayed at the low level of English comprehension that his fifth form students had. The volunteer had learned a little bit of Yoruba in his training program but—how were such things possible?—he had been assigned to a Hausa-speaking area.

The main trouble, however, was the way everyone was expected to teach. For every course there was an extremely detailed syllabus covering everything the student was expected to know in order to pass a standardized nationally administered final examination. Whether the student received his school leaving certificate and thus became eligible for university entrance or for employment with the government depended entirely on whether he passed the examination with a good mark. Under this system the good teacher was the one who could cover the syllabus material most carefully with the least deviation and coach his students to parrot back answers to the syllabus questions whether or not they understood at all what the answer meant.

When the volunteer tried to get his students to think about what an answer really meant or how it was logically arrived at, they would become restless and inattentive. When he tried to introduce material not in the syllabus, they would become quite unhappy. The bolder students would even speak up to tell him that he would cause them to fail the examination if he did not concentrate on the syllabus. What they most wanted him to do—and what all "good" teachers did—was carefully and slowly dictate answers to syllabus questions, which they would copy word for word into their notebooks. These notebooks would then become their golden treasure in studying for the examinations.

The volunteer had never taught before, and he quickly discovered how much drudgery is connected with teaching. Working up the syllabus answers was very time-consuming and grading test papers and marking compositions was plain hard work. Sometimes he would discover that he had spent two hours trying to straighten out the grammar, syntax, and thoughts on one paper and then in a panic stay up half the night racing through the forty other themes in the stack to have them ready for class the next day.

There were the good parts. He developed a special relationship with a few of his students, who seemed to know why he wanted to go beyond the syllabus. Often at night they came around to his house and talked. They asked him about America, about going to college there, about American girls, about his home. Sometimes the questions were hard to answer, questions about Little Rock and Birmingham, questions about things they had heard on the short wave Radio Moscow broadcasts or read in one of the Nigerian newspapers that headline all racial news from the U.S. After a particularly good session one night, he discovered that his alarm clock was missing. He was only mildly depressed; it had still been a good evening.

One of the best times came on a holiday when one of his students asked him to come home with him. They traveled by lorry to a village about a hundred miles away, and there the volunteer felt that he was finally in the "real" Africa. He met his student's parents, slept in their hut, watched the holiday dances, and ate the fiery chicken that had been prepared especially for him. If he could only have spoken with these people directly instead of through the laborious translations of his student, it would have been great.

But the days were made up mostly of the dreary classroom routine, the tedium of paper marking, the heat, and the monotonous food. His cook, he discovered, was an unemployed roof thatcher who had washed dishes for a while at the club in town.

Sometimes at night before going to sleep the volunteer could actually smell a steak cooking on a charcoal grill. He could hear the faint hum of an air-conditioner and feel the soft coolness. He would think about the girl he had dated casually during his senior year, and he remembered the car he had passed on to his younger brother. He wondered how the Celtics were doing.

He also wondered what the hell he was doing in this place. What was he doing in the classroom that lots of

Nigerians couldn't do as well or better? Where were the young minds whose horizons he was supposed to widen? Where were the deep and lasting friendships he was supposed to form? It was true that he had begun to reach a few students and there was one teacher that he now had some good talks with, but those things seemed a pitifully small return on his expectations of six months ago. He had heard from some of the others in his training group, and he knew they felt the same way.

One day the volunteer received a telegram from a staff member in Lagos saying he was coming to visit him later in the week. The volunteer was pleased. He had expected a staff visit long before this, and he wanted someone he could really talk to about his growing feelings of futility. He might even ask for a transfer.

The staff member had said he would arrive about noon, and the headmaster had prepared a special lunch. At dark on the day of the expected visit, the staff man still hadn't arrived. For dinner the volunteer had his cook prepare the one thing that came out fairly well: fried fish and french fries. About eight o'clock the headmaster brought another telegram to the volunteer's house. It was from the staff man and it said: "Regret must postpone visit. Washington urgently requires documents for new program. Will reschedule trip soonest."

The volunteer ate the fish and potatoes and drank some of the beer he had laid in for the visit. He found a mystery novel in his book locker and went to bed. The next morning he went to class and dictated material on the syllabus questions. The subject was *The Vicar of Wakefield*.

The above picture of the first months of a Peace Corps

teacher on the job is of course a composite, but I think that every volunteer teacher, no matter where he taught, will recognize some elements as fitting his particular picture; and for most volunteer teachers in Africa, and many in Asia, I believe the majority of the pieces will fit.

On my first round of visits to volunteers in 1962 (during my years overseas I sent some regret telegrams also), I found at one place or another every one of the conditions I have described. One volunteer in a particularly isolated school was half dead with loneliness and homesickness. We talked almost all night and every half hour or so he would say, "I'm not going to be the first one to quit." He didn't quit at all.

Occasionally a touch of the absurd lightened the journey. I dropped in unannounced on one volunteer and found him on his hands and knees scrubbing his living room floor. His houseboy was stretched out on a couch looking at the pictures in a copy of the *Saturday Evening Post*.

When the volunteer saw me, he grinned and said, "I'm teaching him the dignity of labor."

"I think you have thoroughly convinced him of the joys of the leisure class," I said.

This volunteer, amazingly young and naïve in some ways, was nonetheless a good teacher whose students did well on their examinations. During his time there, he managed to set up a library that really functioned, a noteworthy achievement in a system where headmasters almost always kept books severely under lock and key for fear they would be lost or stolen.

The most incredible episode in all my years in the

Peace Corps involved a volunteer teacher. One morning I received a frantic phone call in my Lagos office. The caller, whom I never identified, shouted that one of the volunteer teachers assigned to a school near the city had been bitten by a green mamba, an extremely venomous West African snake. I rushed to the school and found the volunteer waiting at the roadside with two of his twenty-one students and the dead snake. As we drove to the hospital, I got the story. The volunteer, who was wearing shorts, had gone to his house between classes and just as he entered his living room had been struck on the leg by the snake. The volunteer ran to the kitchen, picked up a butcher knife, and killed the snake. He then took his snake bite kit, which we had issued to all volunteers, and walked to his next class. He told his students what had happened and then said, "If you ever get bitten by a poisonous snake this is what you should do."

He proceeded to take the razor blade from the snake bite kit, cut the proper cross over the wound made by the snake's fangs, and draw out the blood with the suction cup. He explained that if the victim did not have that kind of equipment, he could suck out the blood and spit it out, or have someone else do it for him. The students told me this story in awe, and I am sure I looked awestruck as I listened.

At the hospital the snake was positively identified as a green mamba, and the volunteer was given an injection of anti-venom. He had no trouble from the snake bite but a few days later collapsed and nearly died from a violent reaction to the horse serum used in the anti-venom. Happily, he recovered completely.

Many volunteer teachers over the years found that one positive contribution they could make at their schools was the introduction of more imaginative teaching methods into a classroom dominated by lectures and the dictation of notes. I don't believe, however, that anyone ever used the demonstration method quite as dramatically as the snake-bitten volunteer from Lagos.

Teaching was supposed to offer volunteers well-structured, clearly defined jobs, but almost anything could go wrong and usually did for about fifty percent of a group. In some cases a headmaster had no confidence in the Peace Corps in general or in his particular volunteer and gave him as little as possible to do. Sometimes a volunteer was assigned to a school with an oversupply of teachers (probably because there was a house available) and he was underemployed. At other times a headmaster had been expecting a biology teacher and an English teacher showed up because that was what was available.

Whenever possible errors of this kind were corrected by transfers to other schools, but the problem took time to spot and the solution even longer to work out, and volunteer morale suffered badly in such cases. Usually a volunteer did everything he could to make these bad assignments work. He tried to run the library, start a science or drama club, organize field trips, coach sports, tutor slow students, clean up the chemistry lab, or give special help in English no matter what his subject was. I had the highest admiration for these young people who took a bad deal and did their level best to make it into something worthwhile. In my judgment, and I hope in theirs, they frequently succeeded.

The volunteers with full teaching loads usually devoted as much of their time as they could to these special activities or approaches to teaching that had largely been missing from their schools and in so doing frequently made the educational climate of their school a little better than it was before they came. When all was considered, however, the good Peace Corps volunteer teacher made his essential contribution by giving his students the example of a teacher who had a human concern for the well-being of his students, who took an interest in them as individuals, and who considered that their problems were important and worth listening to. Some critics have maintained that this posture of human concern is inappropriate for the harsh realities of life in Africa and Asia. All I can say is that I do not agree with them.

Tai Solarin, a Nigerian headmaster and highly regarded newspaper columnist, did not agree either. Solarin, who wielded a sharply barbed pen and was quite cosmic in his criticisms, wrote in one of his columns: "I believe in my heart of hearts that a lubrication of our teaching force with the Peace Corps is a greater service to this country than Britain did in a hundred years with all the epauletted and sword-carrying Governors who ever ruled this country."

After the first term in 1962, I saw Hector Jelf, the Northern permanent secretary who had lost four out of five Americans the previous year. "I won't say your Peace Corps volunteers are the greatest teachers I ever saw," he said, "but I will say they stay on the job."

His roster showed that not one volunteer had resigned

from his post during that term, and his roster was quite correct.

A View from America

In the summer of 1962, when I had been with the Peace Corps program in Nigeria for a year, my wife and I decided it was time that we returned to the United States for a while. We had lived in various parts of Africa for six years, and I thought working with the Peace Corps in Washington for a year or so would give us a chance to get our roots back in native soil and provide me with an interesting change of perspective on our precocious new agency, of which I felt at least a godfather.

When we reached Washington in September, I found the staff still in a lather of activity and excitement. Other agencies I visited—State, AID, USIS, HEW—seemed almost tomblike by comparison. Nineteen sixty-two had become a year of wild and uncontrolled growth for the Peace Corps. By the end of 1961 we had volunteers in nine countries. In 1962 programs were developed in and volunteers sent to twenty-eight new countries. In addition, most of the 1961 countries received more volunteers. Here is the 1962 line-up of countries in which programs were started:

Africa	East Asia-Pacific	Latin America	North Africa-Near East-South Asia
Sierra Leone	Malaysia	Bolivia	Afghanistan
Cameroon	Thailand	Brazil	Ceylon
		British Honduras	
Ethiopia		Dominican Rep.	Cyprus

Africa	East Asia- Pacific	Latin America	North Africa- Near East- South Asia
Ivory Coast		Ecuador	Iran
Liberia		El Salvador	Nepal
		Honduras	Tunisia
Niger		Jamaica	Turkey
Senegal		Peru	
Somalia		Venezuela	
Togo			

Most of the programs started with small groups of from twenty to fifty volunteers. The initial contingents of a few countries were less than ten, and only one—Ethiopia with 281 volunteers—was relatively large. The Wiggins theory of dramatically large programs focused on unified problems in carefully selected countries was clearly not being implemented. There had emerged in the staff strong opposition to massive programs in individual countries, at least until more operating experience was gained. It had also become clear that, while many countries were well disposed to try the Peace Corps, few if any were prepared in the beginning to lower the floodgates to thousands, or even hundreds, of young untested Americans. It is also true that when the Peace Corps idea moved from theoretical papers to the reality of sending volunteers overseas, neither Wiggins nor anyone else on the Washington staff could do more than guess at how big programs could actually be or what the level of acceptance would be by receiving countries.

The importance of bigness and the fast, dramatic start still prevailed in Washington, but in 1962 "big" came to mean getting the Peace Corps started in as many countries as possible. There seemed to be no conscious shift of strategy; it just happened that way. But Shriver, Wiggins, and Wiggins' regional directors still had every intention of building large individual country programs wherever possible. Wiggins had once argued that a small group of volunteers in a country might be more a nuisance than a help. We would now find out.

Finding overseas staff to start twenty-eight new programs in one year was an almost impossible task. The Peace Corps frequently robbed itself to start a program or bolster a growing one. My Lagos colleague, Bill Hintz, for example, made quick jumps (with his family) from Nigeria to Liberia to the Philippines. Other overseas staff played the same kind of country musical chairs. Washington staff were frequently sent out to start a program or run one temporarily while a permanent representative and staff were recruited.

I had been in Washington but a few days when Shriver called me in. He started talking about India and its importance and how he felt the Peace Corps might do some of its best work there. I wondered if Sarge had got me mixed up with someone else. Then he told me that after a long search and breaking down a great deal of resistance on the person's part, he had finally got the man he wanted to be the first Peace Corps representative in India. The man's name was Charles Houston. He was a medical doctor; he had done pioneer work on the development of a mechanical heart; he was a well-known mountain climber who had been in the assault party on the mighty Himalayan peak K-2. Houston had written a stirring account of the climb in his book, *K-2: The Savage Mountain*.

Sarge's eyes glowed as he described what was obviously his vision of the perfect Peace Corps rep for a major country: a man of proven professional ability, a man with a questing scientific mind, a man of adventurous spirit, an articulate man. "But he doesn't know item one about government or administration," Shriver said. "That's why I want you to go to India with him and be his deputy."

I tried to tell Sarge about our plans to buy a place in Washington and get to know the country again, but he kept talking about India. The first volunteers, twenty-six of them, had gone there at the very end of 1961. A new group of fifty would be arriving in October. This was September and the program still didn't have a rep on board and had not had a single permanent staff member. The programs had been put together by Washington staff on flying visits, and an AID officer had been acting as rep in such time as he could spare for the Peace Corps. When he could help no longer two Washington staffers went for short periods as acting reps. The volunteers had been in India the better part of a year and had yet to see anyone they could think of as their rep or their staff.

Sarge talked on about India, the possibilities for Peace Corps there, Nehru's interest in the Peace Corps idea. Half an hour later I left his office, called my wife, and told her that Shriver wanted us to go to India. She was silent a moment and then said, "I haven't even unpacked. If you want to go, I'm ready."

And so it was decided.

The next day I met Charlie Houston, and we compared notes on Shriver's persuasiveness. Charlie had just bought a lovely home in Aspen, Colorado, where he practiced. A foundation had recently given him additional funds for his work on the mechanical heart. But Shriver had prevailed. Later at lunch with a few other people, the conversation turned to mountain climbing and the Himalayas, and someone asked Charlie if he thought the abominable snowman really existed.

"I know he does," Charlie said morosely. "He lives in Washington, and his name is Shriver."

In the short time I was in Washington before going to India, I heard something about the other programs that, like Nigeria, had got an early start. In the Philippine program, the Peace Corps' largest in 1962, over four hundred volunteers were serving as teachers' aides. In this capacity they were assigned to schools not as classroom teachers but as resource persons who would work with Filipino teachers in improving their teaching methods, in better pronunciation of English, or in any other way that seemed feasible. It was a fuzzy, nebulous concept and early reports were that the volunteers, while trying hard to make the idea work, were in a great many cases badly underemployed and becoming increasingly bitter about what they called their "non-jobs." Very few, however, were giving up.

In Latin America the emphasis was almost entirely on something called community development. In this kind of program, a volunteer would live in a village or *barrio* (city slum) and try to encourage community interest in bettering itself through group effort in building a school or health clinic, constructing a road or improving streets, or starting a recreational or feeding program for children. The concept was a highly sophisticated one calling for a

deep understanding of the Latin people and their social
and political structures. It also called for good Spanish
and advanced skills in the techniques of motivation and
organization. Some stories reached Washington of volunteers hard at work and the beginnings of success, but
there were also ominous rumbles of underemployment
and of bewildered volunteers literally roaming the high-
ways of Chile and Colombia looking for something to do.
Washington was moving too fast to examine either the
good or bad stories very carefully.

The program of surveyors, engineers, and geologists in
Tanganyika looked good. The engineers were right in the
middle of all major road construction in the country. The
surveyors worked with the engineers on harbors, water
lines, drainage systems, and sites for airports and bridges.
The geologists mapped seventy-five hundred square miles
of rugged territory for mineral surveys. The work was
"Peace Corps" in its most romantic conceptions, and it is
small wonder that the National Broadcasting Company
chose that program for an hour-long special color television feature on the Peace Corps in December 1962.

The New York *Times* was high in its praise of both the
television show and the Peace Corps it portrayed. The re-
viewer commented, ". . . An almost story-like quality
. . . expertly done. . . . The effect was not unlike those
interesting war tales that show random groups of Americans thrown together—the Princeton man, the Boston
Irishman, the Bronx boy, the Southerner, the Westerner.
In this case, however, they were all personable, educated
and thoughtful. The nation can be proud to have them
as its representatives. They told with sincerity, humor and

perception their reasons for joining the Peace Corps and, later, how the actual life of Tanganyika had matched their idealistic preconceptions. . . ."

Gerald Green, the producer of the film, made clear that NBC hadn't set out to make a promotional film for the Peace Corps. "We were more and more impressed by what we found," he said, "and we think this is an honest reporting job on a remarkable group of young men."

Mid-1962 really began America's love affair with the Peace Corps. Papers across the country carried features about the exploits of local volunteers. One story told how a volunteer in Pakistan led one thousand villagers in building dams and culverts that saved a $750,000 rice crop from floods. Another told of how a volunteer revolutionized the economy of a Brazilian village by persuading the farmers to pool their oxen in a cooperative. Yet another recounted how sixteen Philippine volunteers had organized a month-long summer camp, called "Camp Brotherhood," for six hundred indigent boys.

Newspapers and magazines loved human interest stories such as the one about a volunteer who spent hours trying to get an expectant mother of the Gogo tribe to the hospital and ended up carrying out the successful delivery himself, or the account of a volunteer group that adopted a leper colony in West Pakistan. The press particularly liked stories that showed how volunteers were getting rid of the Ugly American image such as the volunteer in Sierra Leone who played saxophone every Saturday night with a local high life band in Freetown and the Tanganyika volunteers who played a hilarious game of

American baseball with Tanganyikans to everyone's delight at a charity benefit.

On March 1 sixteen state governors proclaimed Peace Corps day. In June the New York *Times* carried a highly favorable full page story on how the volunteers were doing overseas, and earlier the *Daily Princetonian* devoted an entire issue to the Peace Corps and lamented the fact that Princeton was lagging far behind other major universities in the number of volunteers in service. Late in the year a musical comedy starring Judy Holliday and based on the adventures and misadventures of a Peace Corps nurse went into rehearsal (it closed after five weeks' run on Broadway). And the final evidence that the Peace Corps had arrived came when Harvard's Hasty Pudding Society chose it for lampooning in their spring production.

Volunteers Outside Classrooms

The first group of volunteers who went to India at the very end of 1961 was supposed to deplane at New Delhi but, because of bad weather, had to overfly that city and land at Calcutta some eight hundred miles to the east. As they drove into Calcutta from the airport, the volunteers were astonished to find hundreds of thousands of people lining the streets. They couldn't believe that a crowd of such size had come out to see the first Peace Corps volunteers. And they were right. When they reached the American consulate, they discovered that a high Soviet official had been just a few minutes behind them also coming from the airport.

The volunteers made their way back to New Delhi by

train, and there they did receive a suitable welcome in the form of lunch with Ambassador and Mrs. John Kenneth Galbraith and later, in the state of Punjab where they were to work, a round of teas and orientation meetings with state officials. The first India group was what the Peace Corps came to call a "shopping list" program, one that scatters volunteers into a wide variety of jobs. The volunteers of that small India 1 project (all Peace Corps projects are numbered in sequence in each country and volunteers ever after identify themselves as India 1 or Thailand 5 or Brazil 10) had been recruited for work in agricultural extension, farm management, dairy cattle upgrading, poultry development, farm machinery maintenance, industrial consulting, vocational education, rural housing, and rural youth club development.

The volunteers of India 1 all had experience or education appropriate to their assignment when they came into the Peace Corps. The agricultural volunteers, for example—about two-thirds of the group—had lived and worked on farms, and some had agricultural college training in addition. The shopping list type of program quickly went into disfavor in Washington, and such a concentration of agricultural skills became an immediate rarity. I will discuss the reasons for both these facts in the following chapter.

When Charlie Houston and I arrived in October, the India 1 volunteers had been in the Punjab for ten months. They were all settled into work, some of it excellent, but for most there had been months of rough, trial-and-error adjustment, which they had managed largely on their own. Washington's inability to get any permanent staff in place had precluded much help from that source; and, as they were the first Peace Corps volunteers to appear in India, Punjab officials had been very uncertain about how to utilize them.

They did, however, receive strong support from Mr. A. L. Fletcher, the dedicated and resourceful Financial Commissioner for Development in Punjab State. It was Fletcher, in fact, who petitioned the central government in New Delhi to request volunteers for the Punjab. Throughout the volunteers' months of adjustment, Fletcher, who carried a heavy load as a most senior civil servant, still found time to be concerned and helpful, and he assigned an experienced assistant to be his liaison with the volunteers. One of the early lessons I learned was that there was little hope for the success of a Peace Corps program without active interest on the part of host officials high enough up in government echelons to make their interest felt.

Nevertheless, almost the entire burden of initiative lay with the volunteer to create a viable job for himself. The agricultural extension volunteers had a particularly unenviable task. They had to learn quickly about farming conditions in the Punjab, but with their backgrounds, that was the easiest part of the assignment. The basic extension aims were to encourage the proper use of fertilizers and the institution of an effective double crop and triple crop system that would not only lead to maximum productivity but through proper rotation would build up the soil.

Perhaps the greatest problem was that farm extension is the work of a lifetime and not of a short two years minus learning time. The volunteers were not only strangers to the Indian farmers but, in a country where age is respected, they were young strangers. Their command of Punjabi was severely limited, though they did make gains in the narrow range of the language of farming. But the months melted away, and a volunteer was lucky if he had convinced two or three farmers to buy fertilizer or try a new hybrid seed or introduce a new crop into his rotation. When success did come, it was almost always with a well-to-do farmer who could afford to experiment. Reaching the poorest farmers was almost impossible.

Most of a volunteer's hours and days were spent in pedaling his bicycle over the hot and dusty (and sometimes cold and muddy) Punjab plain either to talk to a new farmer or to look in and offer encouragement or help to one of the few who were trying something different. It was not much to be pleased with, and the volunteer knew that he would be gone from India before he had really been there long enough to get anything established. Still, he had seen a lot of people, maybe planted some ideas; and a few new practices he had helped start would be seen by other farmers.

The two volunteers who came as industrial consultants had an even shakier start. There was no defined routine or fixed duties, and no one seemed to want to consult them. One of the volunteers finally promoted some tools and a few rupees for materials from various aid agencies and started a toy factory on his own. His idea was to bring a few unskilled and unemployed men into the operation, train them, and hopefully give them a source of income. After training, his small crew began to turn out some rather attractive wooden toys and puzzles, which the volunteer loaded up every two weeks or so and personally peddled to the shops in New Delhi. The factory survived precariously until the volunteer left India and then, unhappily, expired.

The other industrial volunteer, after several months, was finally asked to do a time and motion study of a moribund peanut oil factory, only to discover that there was no motion and a world of time. After that he began helping villagers raise chickens. A volunteer recruited to help raise the quality of dairy herds found no program and in fact no herd in his area except a small one belonging to a former maharaja. He joined the industrial volunteer in poultry work.

Two volunteers of India 1 who had come to work in poultry production had found immediate receptivity among the villagers and were overwhelmed with work. The one eighteen-year-old in the group was running the farm shop at a training center for village level extension agents; he had a skill developed on his father's farm and he was making excellent use of it training students and keeping the school's farm equipment in good condition.

One by one the other volunteers in the group found their thing to do, as often as not something unexpected. Two of the volunteers who had come to work in rural housing, an architect and a town planner, designed and helped build a base camp for skiers in the upper Kulu Valley; it became a good tourist attraction. At the time I arrived in India, they were designing a sports stadium for Chandigarh, Punjab's capital.

The first volunteers I visited in India were four young men living at a *gram sevik* (village level worker) training center near the town of Nabha in the southern part of Punjab state. Two of the volunteers were Sean Doherty, the industrial consultant, and Bill Donovan, the dairy man who had gone into poultry work. The other two were Tom Kessinger, who was organizing rural youth clubs, and Ken Sherper, an experienced agriculturist, who was working effectively in farm management at the school. I had heard that Bill and Sean had got quite a bit going in poultry, and I was particularly interested in how they had been able to do it; apparently they had known little or nothing about chicken raising before coming to India.

I arrived at their house in the early afternoon and had been expecting, or at least hoping, that one or all would be there; but the door was securely locked, with no indication of where they might be. A kind Punjabi lady who lived next door saw me standing there and invited me in for tea. She told me enthusiastically about what fine young men her volunteer neighbors were and about how hard they worked.

After about an hour Bill and Sean rode in on their bicycles, and Tom arrived a few minutes later. Ken was away on a trip, I learned. They professed surprise at seeing me. I told them I had sent my itinerary, but they said they had not seen it. They were courteous but reserved and not very communicative. They asked me a few questions about Washington and about the teacher program in Nigeria. But the largely unspoken message that came through quite clearly was, "The hard part is over and now the staff shows up."

I told them I was very interested in their poultry work, and we set out in my Jeep to see some of it. Tom came along because a number of his youth groups had started poultry units as a means of raising money for their clubs. As we drove to the first village, their enthusiasm for their work overcame their reserve and they began to talk. They had got into poultry because they had discovered great interest in chicken raising among the farmers in the villages around Nabha. The manager of the state poultry farm in Nabha, a good man, was totally occupied with the farm and unable to provide extension help to the villagers. He had asked the volunteers if they would help.

Bill, Sean, and Tom learned about chickens from the farm manager. They visited the two qualified poultry volunteers, Justin McLaughlin and Frank Ziegler, who were working successfully in other parts of the Punjab, and learned from them. They learned of a poultry expert, William Stopper, on the AID staff in New Delhi and went to him for information. Stopper not only gave it but helped them work up a handbook on chicken raising, designed for use by farmers with small flocks and printed in Punjabi.

"We're no kind of experts," Bill Donovan said, "but we know enough now to help a Punjabi farmer raise two or three hundred layers the right way." At that time they were working with twenty youth club units and twenty-four individual farmers. "And we've got a backlog for more," they said.

We visited half a dozen of the farmers that afternoon, and I learned a lot about poultry in the Punjab myself.

The poultry units were all very much the same, small, oblong buildings with brick or adobe walls, screened on the long sides, with peaked thatch roofs. The floors were covered with from eight to twelve inches of rice hulls or straw. Every four to six months this "litter" would be cleaned out and replaced; it then made excellent fertilizer.

This method of chicken raising was called the "deep litter, close confinement" system. It made possible the proper feeding and sanitary control of the birds and provided the best available protection from predators. It was as different as day and night from the tradition of letting the chickens run free, forage for themselves, and take their chances with disease, hawk, and mongoose. The latter approach to keeping poultry was no expense or effort, but the net result was an egg now and then.

I learned about the economics of the deep litter, close confinement system. "It costs about three hundred rupees[2] to build a house like this," Sean said. "Day-old chicks are a rupee apiece. Say a farmer starts with three hundred chicks and twenty-five percent die; that's about the average mortality. He sells off the cocks when they're about three months old and recovers his purchase and feed price on them. He ends up with about one hundred layers which cost him fifty rupees per bird per year to feed and maintain. If his birds average 250 eggs a year per bird and he sells them for twenty-five pice[3] per egg, he will end up with a net profit per bird of twelve rupees. It isn't a fortune but it's some cash in hand he didn't have

[2] At that time the rupee was equivalent to about twenty-one cents American money.

[3] At that time, about five cents.

before. Also, even though the house is good for about ten years, the average farmer writes it off upon completion of construction. He still makes money, nine hundred rupees in the first eighteen months."

Although an industrial consultant might be expected to be glib with figures, I guessed that Sean had been over that particular set many times before. "It does take some rupees to get started," I said.

"That's right," Bill answered. "We haven't found any way to work with the poorest people, the Harijans.[4] We work with the farmers who have a little bit and help them make a little bit more. We don't see anything wrong with that."

I thought about it. "Neither do I," I said.

It was a joy to see the volunteers with the farmers. They talked in a combination of broken Punjabi, an occasional word of English, and some sign language. They discussed sanitary conditions of feed boxes and waterers. They talked about feed and about debeaking some of the bigger birds who were beginning to peck their sisters. I learned that a good feed supply was a major problem. The volunteers had promoted a fifteen-hundred-rupee grant from AID and had gone into the feed business themselves. They mixed a good, reliable feed formula and sold to the farmers for cost, turning the money collected back into more feed.

"We want them to take over the business and start a feed cooperative," Sean said, "but they've been burned on

---

[4] Landless people or so-called untouchables, before that caste was abolished by the Indian constitution.

co-ops too many times in the past; they'd rather buy from us. But they will take it over in time."

At every stop we had to go into the farmer's house and have tea. There was an easy informality among the farmers, their families, and the volunteers that I could not imagine had ever existed with any other outsiders, even agricultural officials of their own government. I doubt that they understood much in the abstract sense about the Peace Corps, but it was clear that they liked and trusted these young men who worked with them, shared tea and food with them, and even joked with them in fractured Punjabi. I remember afterward writing to Sarge that I had just seen the Peace Corps of his dreams.

That night we bought some beer and sat around in their house talking. They had a comfortable little place: sitting room, two bedrooms, and a kitchen. The latrine and a place to wash were in the back in a small enclosed patio. I learned that the luxury of a house was recent. When they had first arrived in Nabha, they had lived in a tent for several weeks and then had moved onto a porch of one of the training school buildings for more than two months.

"This house looked like a little bit of heaven," Tom Kessinger said.

We talked all night about poultry in India. They had a vision that it could be a big thing, help in a protein starved land, be the basis of agro-industries, cash for farmers, and purchasing and marketing cooperatives that would employ people and save farmers money.

Then they started to go over the problems. Good chicks were hard to get in quantity. Theft was a constant threat.

Disease or a mongoose could wipe out a flock overnight. There was social prejudice against raising chickens. A good feed supply was an unending headache. There were few real egg markets. People wouldn't eat eggs in hot weather. There were no storage facilities.

"How can poultry be a big thing with all those problems?" I asked.

They looked surprised.

"Because they can be solved," Bill said.

"Because you can still make money at it," Sean said.

All day I had been pondering why Peace Corps volunteers should be spending their time at something Indian extension agents could do as well or better. I decided that Bill and Sean had just given me the answer.

The next morning as I got ready to leave, I noticed a familiar-looking piece of paper in the trash box in the kitchen. It was my trip itinerary, which someone had used to wrap potato peelings in. I laughed. I didn't know whether Charlie Houston and I could ever do anything for this bunch of volunteers, but they now knew that we would help if we could. I knew they had helped me a great deal, and I felt we were friends.[5]

[5] I sent to Bill Donovan for help on the accuracy of figures the part of this chapter concerning him and his two fellow volunteers. He sent back the corrected pages with the following note:

Dear Brent:

Luckily, Tom Kessinger was in town while I had your draft and I invited Tom and Sean over for dinner. We went through the draft in some detail, argued over what the figures should be and came up with the ones listed.

General comments from all of us:

1. Too romanticized. It was a grubby business at that point and we weren't at all sure that it would work.

2. We weren't getting along personally at all at that point. We

I encountered some other examples of staying power in the first group of India volunteers. On that same first trip I made, I visited Martin Ross, a volunteer living alone in a small village in which he was the only outsider. He was doing crop extension work and also had a demonstration plot where, at that time, he was raising sweet potatoes. I remember very clearly that we had a lunch consisting of sweet, hot tea and bananas and then walked three miles in the midday heat across the fields to look at his sweet potatoes.

---

fought constantly and damn near ruined the whole project in very real but very petty bickering and fighting.

3. A sequel to our thoughts and pie-in-the-sky philosophizing about poultry being the basis for agro-industry: In 1963–64 the Punjab government removed poultry from the Department of Animal Husbandry and put it under Industry! Several other states, I believe, followed suit.

In essence I think (stress on the I) that what doesn't come across to me is the sweat, fear, tragedies and errors of judgment that we made and felt and lived with—or refused to live with.

Were we "conning" you? I suspect so. We were an achievement and approval-oriented group of people who presented you with what we thought you would like. That's strong but I believe it is true.

We did the same thing to a lot of fat farmers and then shook with fear until the thing finally worked. The miracle is that it did work.

The question is was it right? I don't know the answer, but I suspect it was wrong.

Bill Donovan

If they weren't conning me, I'm sure they put on a good show for me that day, and I'm very glad they did. In the next chapter I go into some detail on what developed from their early poultry work in the Punjab.

I am not sure I agree that what I have written about these young men is too romanticized; I certainly agree that it lacks "sweat, fear, tragedies and errors of judgment" vividness, but that is a task for former volunteers who have lived the experiences and felt the emotions, and fortunately a few excellent volunteer memoirs are now in print.

Of one thing I am quite sure: What they did was not wrong. The farmers they worked with, while not the wretchedly poor Harijans, were still far from being well off and could certainly use the extra income. More importantly, these farmers helped to make poultry raising "respectable." In India, this respectability is crucial if an activity is to spread to lower social-economic groups.

Marty was pleased with his crop, which he said was just about ready for harvesting. He dug down in the ground to show me a specimen. There was nothing there. He dug in another spot and came up empty-handed. He tried again and again with the same result. Someone had done the harvesting for him the night before and had carefully replaced the vines over the ground.

Marty stood there a minute, thoughtfully, with his head down. "Well," he said, "they are all hungry." As we walked back to his one-room house, he managed a smile and said, "Anyway, the word will get around about how big and sweet those potatoes are, and that's why I raised them."

Marty was still in the village when his two-year assignment was up.

Two extension volunteers in India 1 took over the management of a farm on *panchayat* (local government) owned land. Their purpose was, again, demonstration. They introduced a new variety of wheat, fertilized and cultivated it well, and it grew magnificently. Farmers in the area came around to admire it, and the volunteers explained how their crops could be the same.

Just a week before harvesting, the sky blackened and a violent hailstorm beat the volunteers' wheat into the ground. Only a fraction of it could be salvaged. In one of those inexplicable freaks of nature, their wheat field was the only one in the area to be hit. The farmers were even more impressed by that fact than they were by the quality of the wheat.

The next season the volunteers planted wheat again. Although their two-year tour was up, one of them stayed on for three months to take care of the wheat and harvest it. This time it did not hail and the crop was bumper.

By the end of 1962 one fact had been very clearly established: If the Peace Corps ever came to an unhappy or premature end, it would not be because volunteers could not survive overseas. Not only could they survive, some of them could take a non-programmed or mal-programmed assignment and make something decent out of it. I have given examples from two countries, but they were repeated everywhere the Peace Corps had programs. Perhaps the greatest feats of individual initiative were performed by some of the volunteers in Latin America in those very vague assignments labeled community development. Not all volunteer assignments were bad or fuzzily conceived, of course, but many were. Not all volunteers with bad assignments could work into something worthwhile, but a surprising number could. A sense of commitment, a dedication to Kennedy, and simply a dogged determination not to quit were also very much present in that first year overseas. The attrition, or early termination, rate for volunteers was more than fifty percent lower than for any succeeding year.

The year 1962 proved very little about the value of the Peace Corps or the merit of the Peace Corps idea. It proved a great deal about the durability of young Americans spilled rather haphazardly into the cities and villages of Africa, Asia, and Latin America.

CHAPTER THREE
Growing Pains: 1963–66

The Peace Corps did not stop to catch its breath in 1963, and after that sheer momentum prevented its doing so for the next three years. Nine additional countries[1] received volunteers in 1963, bringing to forty-six the total on the Peace Corps roster. Only two new countries—Kenya and Uganda—were added in the next two years (the Peace Corps was running low on likely clients), but volunteer numbers streaked upward. At the end of 1962 slightly more than four thousand volunteers and trainees were in service. The year-end strength for the following four years looked like this:

1963:	6,988
1964:	9,391
1965:	11,826
1966:	13,999

From a dead start of zero volunteers in late 1961 to fifteen thousand (peak 1966 strength) five years later had taken a total agency commitment to growth that had dominated all other thinking.

[1] Gabon, Guinea, Malawi, Costa Rica, Guatemala, Panama, Uruguay, Morocco, Indonesia.

The Peace Corps naturally grew in fiscal size also. In 1961, start-up costs had been financed by funds already available to the President. Beginning in fiscal year 1962, the agency depended on annual congressional appropriations as did any other government bureau. The fiscal growth naturally paralleled the increasing volunteer strength, but Shriver took great pride in the fact that cost per volunteer decreased as the Peace Corps grew in numbers.

Fiscal Year	Budget Appropriation	Cost Per Volunteer
1962	$30 million	
1963	$59 million	$9,074
1964	$95.56 million	$8,214
1965	$104.1 million	$7,809

The cost per volunteer represents the average yearly cost to maintain one volunteer overseas; the figure includes everything: transportation, training, readjustment allowance of seventy-five dollars per month, and overseas and Washington staff costs. The decreasing volunteer cost was possible because some expenditures such as Washington and overseas office rentals and Washington staff size— were kept relatively constant at 1963 levels in the face of rapid volunteer growth.

Shriver was especially proud of the fact that the size of the Washington staff stayed the same between 1963 and 1966—roughly 650 persons—even though the number of volunteers doubled during that time. In his congressional budget hearing Shriver used such figures effectively to demonstrate that the Peace Corps was not succumbing to the normal Washington bureaucratic growth tendencies or the pressures of Parkinson's Law. Shriver also took great pleasure in turning some of the Peace Corps' annual appropriation back to the Treasury. He did so every year, with well-publicized flourishes; in 1964 he returned a cool twenty million.

Shriver stoutly maintained that these returns to the Treasury were made possible by sharp Peace Corps economies and efficient practices all the way from Washington to Ouagadougou. Congressman Otto Passman, long a bitter foe of the Peace Corps, was always furious that Shriver took credit for giving back such big chunks of the Peace Corps annual budget. Passman loudly maintained that such turn-backs merely proved that the Peace Corps did not know how to figure out what its annual costs would be. It simply asked for more money than it could spend and then looked virtuous when it turned some back, the congressman insisted. Shriver blandly and smilingly assured Mr. Passman that that was not the case at all. Other congressmen, grateful to see any federal agency return money rather than ask for a supplemental appropriation, praised Shriver.

Though it galls me to admit it, Passman was essentially correct. In those years of rapid growth, the Peace Corps was never able to estimate very accurately the total number of qualified persons it could get into training in any given year. The variables for accurate prediction were simply too great. With requests for volunteers pouring into Washington from overseas, the inevitable tendency of the planning staff was to be optimistic about the number of qualified new volunteers that could be recruited. Budget requests were made on the basis of these optimistic guesses; when total recruitment fell short by from one to several thousand, substantial chunks of money were unused. The Peace Corps could, of course, have spent a good deal of the surplus money in many attractive ways—increasing volunteer living allowances, buying more vehicles for overseas use, increasing travel budgets—without calling down congressional suspicion or ire; but Shriver never considered such an alternative. While old-line government hands would have been embarrassed to hand back large amounts of money as a reflection on their planning ability, Shriver did so with jaunty confidence and—except for Passman—received bouquets for this action.

It is also probable that Shriver had an eye to Congress and to the Peace Corps' youth image when he made a key staff appointment in February 1963. To the surprise of many Peace Corps people, Shriver chose Bill Moyers as his deputy when Paul Geren resigned to return to the foreign service. Warren Wiggins had in numerous ways seemed the logical choice; but at that stage in the agency's history, Shriver clearly felt that Moyers' legislative experience and connections, as well as his close tie to Vice-President Johnson, would make him the most valuable deputy director. Also, while Shriver consistently got productive results by mixing able, energetic outsiders with experienced government career men, he tended to put the most important policy-making jobs, both in Washington and overseas, in the hands of staff whom he selected from outside government. Major exceptions were areas of government finance and in building the overseas program, where Shriver placed great confidence in Wiggins.

Attractively youthful in an agency that depended for its life on the support of young people, Moyers at twenty-eight was by far the youngest man in a New Frontier position of such importance. He served ably as Shriver's deputy, promoting new country growth and supervising congressional relations and presentations with great skill. He also supported Shriver's policy of rapidly expanding volunteer numbers, but he did show some serious concern about the quality of volunteers' jobs overseas. Moyers' tenure as deputy was short, however. After only eleven months in the job, he was called to the White House when Lyndon Johnson became President, and he never returned to the Peace Corps.

The Lost Leader

A shudder went through the Peace Corps on November 22, 1963, when news of President Kennedy's assassination was flashed around the world. Of all New Frontier programs, the Peace Corps had drawn most heavily on his charisma and his image. I think that almost every volunteer felt that in Peace Corps service he or she was giving the most tangible and symbolic response to Kennedy's challenge to "Ask not what your country can do for you—ask what you can do for your country." Kennedy had visited volunteers in Latin America; he had talked with the assembled Peace Corps staff in Washington; he had new groups of volunteers to the White House whenever possible before they went overseas.

Kennedy's popularity in developing countries was enormous, and volunteers basked in the esteem in which he was held. Volunteers in the Philippines told of how small children would try to attract their attention by standing outside their houses and shouting, "Ken-ne-dee! Ken-ne-dee!" People throughout Africa, Asia, and Latin America felt genuine grief at Kennedy's death. Volunteers from every country reported that for days after the assassination they were visited by friends and even by strangers who simply wanted to make a personal expression of their sadness at the President's death. Volunteers everywhere, often the only Americans in an area but always known as symbols of one of Kennedy's dreams, were the recipients of touching and entirely spontaneous expressions of sympathy from thousands of humble people throughout the world.

One volunteer in India told me that a farmer with whom he had been working for a year heard the news of Kennedy's death on the village radio. The farmer walked ten miles through an unseasonable rain to the volunteer's home to make sure that his young American friend had heard the tragic news and to express his sorrow.

Hundreds of volunteers and former volunteers wrote letters to Shriver, to their country reps, their home town newspapers rededicating themselves to Kennedy's goals and ideals. "If a man lives on in his creations, then let the Peace Corps attempt to be the measure of this man," wrote a former volunteer from Sierra Leone. Another wrote: "President Kennedy had the foresight to establish an outlet for grass-roots, nonprofessional, international idealism—for *people* in our country to go out to other lands and work with and learn from other *peoples*. A strongly felt personal concern on the part of all people for fellow human beings everywhere was one goal towards which we were striving. . . . We have made a beginning; now we must continue."

One volunteer recounted that he had met Kennedy twice, once when the President had greeted the volunteer's group before they left for Colombia, a second time when President and Mrs. Kennedy had visited Colombia. On that occasion the people of the volunteer's village had given him a letter to deliver to Kennedy; the villagers were firmly convinced that the President had personally sent the volunteer to their village to help them and they wanted to thank him. The volunteer concluded: ". . . John F. Kennedy embodied my ideals and gave me an opportunity to play an active part in our struggle for world peace and justice. I thank him for this and for my rededication that comes as a result of his death."

In the Peace Corps the death of the man who gave it life and identity brought forth an emotional response for which no one felt embarrassed.

Volunteers had been serving overseas less than two years at the time of Kennedy's death, but in that time the program had become so firmly established that it moved on with a pause of respect and affection but without the slightest faltering from the course on which it was set. About seven thousand volunteers were serving overseas when Kennedy died. That number would more than double in the next three years.

Shriver was still at the Peace Corps helm; and when

the new President called Bill Moyers immediately to the White House, Shriver did then name Warren Wiggins acting deputy director. President Johnson made the appointment official in April 1964, and Wiggins became the third deputy director of the Peace Corps.

As deputy Wiggins was in a stronger position than ever to create and carry out agency policy; and his position was strengthened even more when, in September 1964, President Johnson gave Shriver the additional job of running the Office of Economic Opportunity. His new duties were so demanding that Shriver spent only two days a week at the Peace Corps, relying increasingly on Wiggins to be in effect the operational head of the agency. To the end of his time as director, however, Shriver made or approved all policy decisions. And if he and Wiggins were ever seriously at odds over such basic policy matters as size, direct administration of overseas programs, and Peace Corps image, the conflict was never apparent to those of us down the line.

The Rise of the BA Generalist

The developing countries first saw the Peace Corps as a source for filling their manpower shortages in technical fields. The earliest Nigeria requests revealed this hope of highly skilled help. In India at one time in 1963 we had from the state of Uttar Pradesh alone a request for 250 volunteers with professional training and experience in agriculture, engineering, industry, health, and education. Almost all country representatives had similar requests, and it was always our delicate task to explain that the

Peace Corps could not supply such persons in any sugnificant numbers.

The misunderstanding about what the Peace Corps could provide stemmed partly from the developing countries' desperate need—they wanted to believe the Peace Corps could help—and partly from the desire of the early Peace Corps negotiators not to be too discouraging until the agency had a better idea of just who was going to volunteer and in what numbers.

Certainly, however, Shriver, his key staff, and President Kennedy himself had always visualized the Peace Corps primarily as an organization in which young Americans could serve usefully overseas and in which older, professionally experienced people would be welcome to the extent they were available. The President's executive order establishing the Peace Corps had clearly stated that it would undoubtedly be made up chiefly of young people just completing their formal education.

The Peace Corps could no doubt have built a small program of five hundred to one thousand volunteers a year that would have been made up of persons with training or experience or both in agriculture, health, industry, teaching, and other fields. The result would have been a few volunteers programmed into carefully selected jobs in a number of countries (or concentrated in a few). Though some staff members and outside advisers argued for that approach, it was never seriously considered. The President's commitment was to youth, and Shriver's commitment was to a Peace Corps large enough to give many thousands of young Americans a chance to serve overseas.

With its focus on youth and size, the Peace Corps inevitably turned to America's colleges and universities for the great majority of its volunteers. The segment of the population most interested in the Peace Corps and most available to serve was there. As a group they also had some of the most important qualifications by Peace Corps standards: they were single (or if married, usually without children), reasonably well educated, bright enough or persevering enough to have acquired a degree, interested in the world, young, healthy.

Very early in its existence, the Peace Corps concentrated its recruiting efforts on college seniors. Those who responded in by far the greatest numbers were the seniors in liberal arts programs: the English, history, political science, humanities majors; the foreign language, music, geography, psychology majors. Of course seniors with majors in engineering, architecture, mathematics, chemistry, agriculture, and animal husbandry volunteered also, but their numbers were always small. By a ratio of five to one and more it was the liberal arts student who was attracted to the Peace Corps.

Washington did try to recruit technically trained and experienced people. The National Advertising Council adopted the Peace Corps as one of its public service projects, and Young and Rubicam, a major advertising firm, planned and executed the agency's entire media campaign. Special radio and television appeals were frequently made for people with farming, engineering, nursing, and other technical backgrounds; farm journals and other trade magazines were used. In some cases the Peace Corps entered into contracts with organizations such as the 4-H Foundation and the United Auto Workers for special recruiting services. These associations for recruiting purposes were singularly unfruitful. A fifteen-thousand-dollar contract with the UAW netted the Peace Corps not more than half a dozen volunteers. The 4-H contract produced a few; but many of the candidates were just out of high school, and the Peace Corps' selection division did not find them sufficiently mature for overseas service. Dependent children, financial obligations, and health problems made Peace Corps service impossible for many older, professionally experienced Americans who would have liked to volunteer. Some did become volunteers, of course, but over the years they were a trickle of a few hundred rather than the thousands that poured into the Peace Corps with their fresh BA degrees.

By early 1963 the Peace Corps was firmly, though always unofficially, committed to a policy of building the overwhelming number of its programs around the liberal arts graduate. In one of its rather infrequent lapses into jargon, the Peace Corps coined a name for this kind of volunteer: He was a "BA generalist." By definition a BA generalist was a college graduate with a bachelor of arts degree and no practical skill, training, or experience. Not by definition but by watching him perform overseas in 1962, the Peace Corps knew that the BA generalist brought with him some important assets for living and working overseas. He was long on problem-solving ability. He had language aptitude and a keen interest in his new environment. He could be imaginative, enthusiastic, adaptable, and patient. Not every BA generalist would have all of those qualities; but if he made it through the Peace Corps' rigorous selection process, he would have a reasonable number of them.

Along with these excellent qualities, however, the BA generalist also brought a problem to the Peace Corps, a simple but most perplexing problem: He did not really know how to do anything. He could not show farmers how to introduce new crops and take care of them properly. He could not teach young men in a trade school how to operate a lathe. He could not build a bridge or repair a tractor. A female BA generalist could not teach sewing, train student nurses, or supervise a chemistry laboratory.

Yet here was the Peace Corps' manpower pool. When the hard-working appraisers in the selection division had winnowed out the thousands of applications and letters of inquiries from persons with little formal education and no identifiable skills or other evidence of maturity or success in life; when they had regretfully declined some (though not many) well-qualified applicants because they had dependent children or health or legal problems; when they had eagerly invited the skilled and experienced applicants who were eligible and of course those recent college graduates with degrees in fields such as engineering and agriculture; when all of these things had been done, eight out of every ten potential Peace Corps volunteers were BA generalists.[2]

The BA generalist was clearly going to make up the

[2] The term BA generalist came to include persons with advanced degrees, master's or even doctor's, if such degrees were also in the liberal arts. The term also encompassed persons from such disciplines as divinity and law (unless the volunteer was actually doing legal work). The "BA generalist" tag was also loosely applied to persons who had had two or three years of liberal arts study in college but had stopped short of a degree.

bulk of the Peace Corps. The problem for the Peace Corps staff was to determine how he could be used effectively in developing countries.

Size and the Generalist

The BA generalist made a big Peace Corps possible. While most Peace Corps officials, myself included, bought the Shriver-Wiggins concept of bigness, we learned in time that we bought it at a high price in volunteer frustration and bitterness and in disappointment of the countries in which they served. The big, dramatic start of 1961–62 achieved its purpose of focusing American and world attention on the Peace Corps; and the volunteers, partly by simply surviving overseas, partly by the novelty of their presence, and very much through their individual effort and commitment, gave the new organization a good reputation and an excellent press.

By 1963, however, the Peace Corps was getting clear signals from volunteers and from its own evaluation division that all was not as bright as the public information office releases indicated. The message was that large numbers of volunteers were underemployed and some totally unemployed, that jobs were often fuzzy or nonexistent, that volunteers were frequently not properly skilled or trained to do the jobs for which they had been recruited, that host country officials had been led to expect one kind of volunteer and had received another. Unmistakable in their clarity, evaluation reports and volunteer comments told the Peace Corps to slow up—not stop growing but slow up—to program, select, and train more carefully, and to take time to apply what was being learned from early volunteer experiences.

The evaluation division of the Peace Corps was remarkable in a number of ways. Put together and run by Charles Peters, a West Virginia lawyer and former state legislator, the division employed both on its full-time staff and on spot assignments a group of experienced and able newspapermen, lawyers, and journalists who had no qualms in reporting exactly what they saw and heard when they visited Peace Corps programs. Reporters of the caliber of Timothy Adams of the San Francisco *Examiner* and Kevan Delaney of the Columbia Broadcasting Company joined the division. Richard Rovere, author of many books on American politics and foreign policy, did a number of evaluations. Lewis H. Butler, a lawyer and later Assistant Secretary of Health, Education, and Welfare, served at different times as an evaluator. The evaluators' method was to visit a country for several weeks, talk in great depth with as many volunteers, country officials, and Peace Corps staff members as possible, and then record their findings—and their opinions—in a well-written document.

Peters impressed upon his evaluators that their job was to report exactly what they saw, heard, and felt to Shriver. He was their only audience, though he shared the reports with Wiggins, the regional directors, the concerned country rep, and a few others on a "need to know" basis. Peters tirelessly blocked every effort to encroach on the evaluators' freedom to write the truth exactly as they saw it. He also skillfully sidetracked efforts of the State Department, members of Congress, and the General Accounting Office to get their hands on the evaluation reports. They were for Shriver and whomever he wanted to show them to in the Peace Corps; they would be seen by no one who might use them to embarrass the Peace Corps or people named in the reports. Peters knew that in order to get the kind of totally honest evaluations he wanted from his staff, he had to build that wall of protection for them.

I doubt that any federal agency has ever taken such a completely honest look at itself as the Peace Corps did through its evaluation division. Shriver read the reports and acted on emergency problems that might lead to public blow-ups or scandal. But in their larger and more profound criticisms of sloppy programming, volunteers out of their depth, and host country unhappiness, they were largely ignored in the single-minded determination to create a bigger and bigger Peace Corps. In time the accumulation of the evaluation reports had their effect, but it took years.

The almost manic drive to put volunteers in new countries and to build up their numbers in existing country programs was centered in the four regional offices in Washington. The regional directors were among the very most powerful staff members; they were intensely ambitious for their regions, and the competition among them for available volunteers was fierce. They kept an unceasing pressure on their country reps for new programs, and most reps—equally ambitious for their individual programs—were eager to respond.

The method of allotting volunteers to regions amounted to a kind of numerical Procrustean Bed. The recruiting and selection divisions would estimate the number of qualified volunteer applicants likely to be available for the three yearly cycles (summer, fall, spring), and the regional directors would submit their proposed programs. The total of these proposals would invariably be much greater than the projected supply of volunteers.

The means of adjusting the demand to the supply was through a series of "murder boards" in which the program submissions of all the regions were evaluated and compared and those considered to be weakest eliminated. The machinations of the regional directors to get their programs on the approved "matrix" for a cycle knew few bounds. Sometimes programs submitted by a rep were rewritten in a regional office to improve their chances of being approved. The rewrite might involve changes in the kinds of volunteers requested and the purposes of their proposed work in the country. In some cases the programs were approved and the reps did not learn about the changes until months later. In other cases the regions submitted a program that had not been requested by a country—in the hopes that if it was approved, it would be requested. The result could lead to unpleasant pressure on a rep to get a program requested.

Regional directors were ever on the alert for a block of volunteers who might be available because a projected program in some other region had been scratched from the matrix. When I was rep in New Delhi, I once received a call from my regional director. He told me that he had inside information that a program of thirty trainees for an African program was going to be scratched. He asked me if there was some project proposal that I could get in immediately; if so, there was a good chance that we could get the defaulted Africa trainees.

My Indian colleagues and I did have a program in the early stages of development which would sound very good on paper. We decided to submit it on the theory that we might not get the volunteers later. The program was approved. It turned out to have many problems and resulted in a large number of unhappy and unproductive volunteers for whom new assignments had to be found. I was thoroughly ashamed of my role in that fiasco and I resolved never to play the numbers game again.

"The numbers game" was the apt phrase that volunteers bitterly used to describe the too frequent tendency of the Peace Corps to concentrate on program size rather than quality.

I should at this point say a word in defense of the Washington and overseas staff in this era of the big build-up. The motives in the pursuit of rapid growth were by no means all bad. Without doubt personal ambition and empire building, either conscious or unconscious, were often involved. But, as Professor Ricardo Zuniga, a good Chilean friend of the Peace Corps, has said, "The Peace Corps started as a group of enthusiasts rather than an 'agency.'" We believed in the Peace Corps idea, and we knew that some of the volunteers were doing splendidly. We desperately wanted the Peace Corps to be taken seriously, to have a major impact, and the answer—in part, at least—seemed to lie in numbers. And I think, in part, we were right; but our speed made us miss many important caution and direction signs along the road.

A number of big programs began to emerge after 1962.

India grew very slowly in 1963 and 1964 but by the end of 1966 it was the largest Peace Corps country with more than one thousand volunteers. The Nigerian program grew to over seven hundred volunteers and Brazil passed the six hundred mark. Ethiopia, Colombia, Malaysia, Tanzania, the Philippines, and the Trust Territory of Micronesia at various times had more than five hundred. A number of countries had programs in the three- and four-hundred range: Liberia, Sierra Leone, Turkey, Thailand, Chile, Peru, Venezuela, Bolivia.

Such numbers did not approach the early visions of several thousand volunteers in a single country. They did, however, represent the realistic outer limits of Peace Corps program size for a number of reasons: competition among the four regions for the limited numbers of qualified volunteers, political sensitivity among government officials to excessive numbers of foreigners, the difficulty of finding plausible employment for BA generalists.

In the beginning there had really been no concept of "developing" programs for volunteers to work in overseas. The thought had simply been that a country would request a certain number of volunteers to teach in schools or fill jobs in government departments or programs and that the Peace Corps would find qualified persons and send them over to work at those jobs. That, at least, was the receiving countries' view. For most volunteer teachers the system did in fact work that way: They filled vacancies or made up teacher shortages in schools. But the Peace Corps could fill few of the many vacancies in departments of agriculture, animal husbandry, public works, health, small industries. With the best of intentions, the

Peace Corps wanted to help in these fields, but it was clear that special roles would have to be built for the BA generalists outside the straight government department line structures. Nothing was wrong with this idea in theory. Substantial numbers of volunteers working in special programs might give an important additional thrust to a department's work. The Peace Corps actually favored this concept over what it called, with a tone of disapproval, "slot filling" assignments.

Community Development: Bottomless Pit for BA Generalists

"You know what a BA generalist is?" the young man said to me. "He is the parasite of the Peace Corps."

The young man was himself a BA generalist, but he was no longer in the Peace Corps. He had quit his work as a community development volunteer in a Latin American country after about a year and returned to the United States. He was in Washington for an "exit interview." I was getting ready to return to New Delhi after visiting one of our India training programs and had bumped into the unhappy generalist at the coffee emporium next door to the Peace Corps office.

His story was one that was already becoming familiar to me, even in mid-1963. He had majored in American history at the University of Illinois, had been accepted for Peace Corps training immediately upon graduation, and had gone through community development training for Latin America.

"It was unbelievable," he said. "The language training

was okay, maybe good. At least I could speak a little Spanish when I got there. But we had a ton of lectures on how to do community development—how to discover felt needs and get people interested in helping themselves and helping them organize to get what they wanted. Every expert that lectured to us had a different way of doing it, and a couple of them almost got in a fight one day about what CD is."

"Did you get any technical training besides CD theory?" I asked him.

The young man laughed. "We were going to be rural CD workers," he said. "In ten days they taught us all about growing corn, potatoes, beans, and a couple of other things I can't remember. They taught us about raising chickens and threw in some stuff on taking care of cattle. I believe we got how to fertilize, too. They took us around to fields and barns, but it was still just lectures. I couldn't tell potato plants from bean plants when I got to my village and I still can't."

This was already an old story, too. A rep wasn't sure what his volunteers were going to be doing, so he suggested that the generalists get a smattering of everything in training. The result was that they learned nothing practical about anything.

The volunteer was assigned to a village about seventy-five miles from the district capital. He had no specific job or duties; he was officially assigned to a private organization concerned with agrarian reform, but after some orientation lectures in the capital when his group first arrived, he had seen no one connected with the organization and it was doing no work in the area so far as he could learn.

"The people were very curious about me," the young man said, "because I was the first North American who had ever been in their village, let alone lived there. They were friendly, too; there weren't any Communists in my village like there were in some of the places the volunteers in my bunch were. But mainly the people wanted to know what I was doing there. I couldn't say, 'I'm trying to find out what your felt needs are!' Hell, all you had to do was look around and see they needed everything: more food, houses instead of shacks, medical care, decent clothes, roads that weren't mud bogs. I figured if they didn't feel the need of those things, I'd better not get them stirred up, because I sure didn't see how I could help them get those things.

"Some of the men had heard about farm extension workers and figured I was one of those. They came around and asked me about hybrid corn and soya beans. I couldn't tell them a thing, of course, and that really hurt, because they had had the interest to come and ask. I went into the district capital and tried to get someone from the ag extension department to come out. I got a lot of promises, but no one ever came.

"It would have been great if I could have got the men interested in building better roads or building an aqueduct from the river so they could have water for their fields. But what do I know about building roads or aqueducts? I know the CD theory is to get them organized so they will go out and demand help from the government to get things like that done. I tried to get them interested

in organizing a junta for village improvement. The most
I ever got together at one time was three people, and
one of them was deaf.

"I sort of gave up after that. I play the guitar and sing
pretty good, and I was kind of a star at fiestas and wed-
dings. My rep told me to keep trying; he said I was making progress; but when I asked him how, he didn't say."

The former volunteer gazed off into space for a moment. "You know what finally got me?" he asked. "I realized one day they had a name for me. It was *vago*. In
case you don't know Spanish that means vagabond. They
weren't being mean or anything; but I didn't have a job
or even a government title, so that's just what I was—a
vagabond. I decided I'd better come home."

The young man shook out a cigarette and lighted it.
"I liked those people," he said. He blew out some smoke.
"But I was a lousy community developer."

I suppose he was, but he was far from being alone. In
the years 1963–66 the Peace Corps sent 7,596 volunteers
into Latin America, and one out of every seven gave up
and returned to the United States before his or her two-
year assignment was over. Although there were some
health and compassionate early terminations, the majority of these early returnees came home because they were
unhappy with their work, or frustrated at the lack of it.
There is no way to know how many hundreds or thousands stayed for their full two-year tour feeling, either
correctly or incorrectly, that they had accomplished
nothing. Bitter comments by volunteers at many end-of-
service conferences make me think the percentage was
high.

"You know what I accomplished in two years?" one volunteer said. "I learned to dance the *frevo*. I dance it real well now."

The volunteer was probably not fair to himself in his estimate of what he accomplished, but his judgment does indicate the depth of frustration felt by some volunteers who "stuck it out."

Many Latin officials were equally disenchanted. "We wanted skilled agriculturists," said one. "The great need is to raise more food. We were told that few agriculture specialists were available but that volunteers would be trained and fully capable of helping farmers with their crops. We received nothing of the kind. They are nice young men and women, but they know nothing about agriculture."

Officials expressed similar disappointment in community volunteers sent to work in city slums. "They do not understand our people or our problems," the head of an urban self-help housing program said. "And they bring no skills with which to help."

Such blanket negative assessments were no more accurate than the many U.S. newspaper stories that seemed to have Peace Corps volunteers saving Latin America. The facts were that many volunteers were achieving limited success in their work and a few were succeeding brilliantly. A number of the women volunteers were successful in organizing sewing clubs and mothers' clubs where the women learned child care and nutrition—how to get a better diet for their families out of food available on their incomes. Some of the men volunteers started boys' clubs for sports, physical education, and civic improvement projects. Sometimes volunteers were able to help their village or urban barrio build a school or aqueduct or talk them into digging latrines. More often than not the volunteers did the organizing, found the skilled help necessary, and spearheaded the work. Occasionally, however, a volunteer succeeded in motivating the people to form a junta (village or neighborhood council) and the junta itself came up with the self-help ideas. There was discouraging feedback on juntas never meeting again after volunteers left; but as the volunteers were told in training, developing community spirit is a long-time undertaking.

Here and there a volunteer seemed to blaze like a comet. One young man in an Andean village organized a junta that, with the volunteer's help, built a school, a health clinic, and a road. They managed to borrow a tractor from the government for building the road; and while they had it, leveled and built a sports field. The volunteer started a sports club and made a foray to the capital for equipment. He even started a cooking and nutrition class for women and taught the classes himself, using a book he borrowed from a woman volunteer as his guide.

Another volunteer organized short courses in hybrid corn, pig production, and the use of fertilizers. He also started demonstration plots for corn and the use of fertilizer and insecticides. In addition he worked with farmers who were interested in growing soya beans and grain sorghum. He made constant rounds to talk to farmers about their crops and he devoted all the time he could to helping other volunteers get work started. As might be expected, this volunteer was one of the rare ones with a farm background and a college degree in agriculture and animal husbandry. As an added advantage, he spoke fluent Spanish when he came into the Peace Corps. Nevertheless, many volunteers with good technical backgrounds never achieved a record anything like that.

The Peace Corps kept no statistical record of volunteer success or failure and had limited objective means of judging either. But when failure was defined as the inability of a volunteer to get any work started that he thought was worthwhile or provide any helpful service to the people he lived among, the failure rate was high—at least fifty percent and possibly much more. Concrete evidence of this high rate of failure was to be found in the fact that fifty-six percent more Latin America volunteers resigned early because of personal adjustment problems than volunteers elsewhere in the world; personal adjustment problems were usually related to unhappy work situations. More subjective but more graphic evidence of failure came from volunteers' own estimates of their accomplishments and from the observations of Peace Corps evaluators. Some of the latter estimated CD volunteer job frustration in certain countries running as high as seventy-five percent.

There were many reasons for the failure of volunteers in community development work, all of them known to the Peace Corps. A major reason was certainly the fuzzy sociological concepts surrounding the whole subject. They are perhaps best summarized by a Peace Corps recruiting brochure on community development: "Some have called it a political process. Others have stressed its economic elements. Still others have talked about it in terms of sociology and psychology. It has been debated whether CD is a process, a method, a program or a movement. It has been reduced to self-help on a village level and expanded to embrace whole populations as 'nation building.' The definitions of CD are only slightly more abundant than the number of people who consider themselves expert on the subject."

It is safe to assume that Peace Corps CD trainees have been bombarded with every theory and debate extant on the subject and that they have frequently gone to their assignments in Latin America and elsewhere in the world in a high state of confusion about what was expected of them. Of much greater seriousness, however, is the fact that in the majority of cases this fuzziness carried over to the volunteers' specific assignments. Reps and host country officials were not sure what the volunteers would do when they arrived. This led them to name a number of possibilities with the hope that some of them would materialize. The problem was that this kind of uncertainty made focused, relevant job training for the BA generalist impossible. As a result the preponderance of his training was in language, community development theory, and cultural and historical background studies. Training institutions, with little or no information on what specific jobs the volunteers were expected to perform or with a bewildering array of things they might be expected to do, could provide little job preparation. The prospective volunteer certainly needed all the language training he could get, and he did need some community development theory and cultural orientation. But he desperately needed a job skill in his forthcoming assignment, and that he rarely had when he stepped off the plane in the country that had invited him to come and help.

Often a volunteer was simply dropped into a town, village, or urban slum and told that he was to be a catalyst for community cooperation and action. How he did it was up to him, though he did have his CD theory about how to motivate people to form juntas, agree on their common needs, and band together to help themselves or pressure the government into giving them their fair share of goods and services. He had no clearly defined job that the people could understand and no technical skill to apply if he found one. He was sometimes assigned to a government community development department or a private welfare agency, but usually he received no support or direction from these organizatons, which were frequently moribund, without funds, or not well enough organized or staffed to try to make use of the volunteers. The casualty rate among these free lance volunteers was very high compared to the rest of the Peace Corps; it took a remarkable individual to make anything much of such an assignment. Gino Baumann, a Peace Corps staff member in Peru and Bolivia and an old CD hand, once estimated that not over five percent of all volunteers in free lance community development roles could do well.

Twenty-five percent of all volunteers who served during the years 1963–66 were community development workers. The Peace Corps had CD programs in a few African and Asian countries (with much the same results as described above), but the great proportion were in

Latin America. The evidence was abundant that the Peace Corps' community development programs were in trouble. But the agency did not slow down to let its staff program assignments more carefully and to learn from what was happening. Instead, it hurled thousands of BA generalist volunteers, like infantrymen storming a beachhead, into its own murky and ill-defined version of CD.

Reasons for this persistence are again to be found in the Peace Corps desire to be big and in the necessity to use BA generalists; community development was vague enough to absorb unlimited numbers of them. An even more important reason, however, lay in the vaulting ambition that some senior staff members had for the Peace Corps itself. In a number of his speeches and articles, Shriver talked about the power of the "Peace Corps idea" to change the world. He saw the Peace Corps as America's "point of the lance" in practicing a "new kind of politics of peace effectively, and on a world scale." Wiggins in some of his addresses liked to talk about the role of the Peace Corps in "nation building."

The two staff members most directly responsible for the massive community development program in Latin America, however, were Jack Vaughn and Frank Mankiewicz. Vaughn was the first regional director for Latin America and Mankiewicz the second, and both saw the Peace Corps as a means of politically energizing the depressed Indian and Latin peasants of the Central and South American nations.

Jack Vaughn had a deep attachment to Latin America. As a young man he spent a kind of Ernest Hemingway summer in Mexico, drifting around, earning his way as a professional boxer at a few pesos a bout. He took two degrees in Latin American studies at the University of Michigan. He and his family lived for years in Bolivia and Panama, where he worked first for the United States Information Service and then for the International Cooperation Administration. He spoke beautiful, flawless Spanish.

A man of great human compassion, Vaughn knew intimately the desperate plight of the repressed Indian populations of the Andes and the passive fatalism of the peasant farmers; he knew just how bad the fast-growing slums of Latin American cities were. He wanted the Peace Corps to help these poor people, materially, spiritually, and politically. He often spoke about the Peace Corps helping to "bring the Andean Indians into the twentieth century."

At this point in his Peace Corps service Vaughn's approach to putting volunteers into Latin America was more emotional than analytical. Even after he had become Assistant Secretary of State for Inter-American Affairs and Coordinator of the Alliance for Progress, Vaughn's emotionalism toward the volunteers and their role in Latin America remained. As Assistant Secretary, he spoke to the Peace Corps staff in 1965 and said in part:

> "I've been a Latin lover since 1938, and I've seen a lot of strange things. But I've never seen anything like what I saw in Bolivia a few days ago. I was stationed in Bolivia a couple of times and left there last in mid-1958. The last six months I was in Bolivia . . . I reached the point where I was reluctant to go up on the high plains near Lake Titicaca to hunt and

fish because of the menacing hostile attitude of the Indians. They were all armed, they seemed resentful, didn't speak Spanish, and didn't change. That was seven or eight years ago.

"I visited five villages in that very same area in 1965. In all five I was carried into town on the backs of the Indians who wanted to show me that they were in the human race. They had all built a new school, the first school in a thousand years. They all had a clinic for child deliveries, the first clinic in a thousand years. They all had potable water piped in, and they had done it themselves. They had made more physical progress in a couple of years than they had made in the previous thousand. But more important was the attitude, the openness, the willingness to look you in the eye and tell you about who they were and what they had done, and the pride and self-respect of citizenship. This was done by the Peace Corps. What the Spaniards and the Incas and the Western miners and the diplomats and the AID people couldn't do in a thousand years, the Peace Corps had helped to do in about three years. This is real revolution.

"There are many who think that the Alliance won't work, certainly not in ten years. But here in the toughest most backward area maybe in the world, with the resentment built on centuries of domination and abuse, it is disappearing before the Peace Corps. There is hope and it's in your hands. . . .

"The Peace Corps has made the term "community development" a household term. We still can't define it but it's democratic and has to do with the involvement of individuals in their own institutions.

"We have been criticized over the years for not knowing what our foreign policy is. Well, I can tell all of you here this morning exactly what the U.S. Government policy is in Latin America. What we really stand for is the Peace Corps.

"I can give you our Latin American policy in half a minute. We want to have all of our neighbors truly independent. We want to have a broad and increasing friendship between all of the Americas. And we believe in the Charter of Punto del Este which is almost the greatest thing written since the Bible. . . . It's worth reading because it's our policy and we signed it. It's revolutionary and it's right and it's progressive and it's Christian and it's modern and it's tough and it's almost unobtainable.

"That's what our policy in Latin America is. I think that every potential Peace Corps Volunteer in the world would believe in this. It talks about reform of institutions, the modernization of institutions, the democratization of institutions. It talks about integration, in every sense. It talks about health, education, and food production.

"This is also what the Peace Corps Volunteer is and does and lobbies for. He's independent and goes freely from an independent nation to act independently in his village. He's there to make friends. And everything about him, his reason for going there, his performance, his personality, what he's after, what he prays for, is revolution, is change, is democracy.

So the Peace Corps Volunteer in the very realest sense is our foreign policy in Latin America."

I have no doubt that Jack Vaughn saw all those things in the five Bolivian villages that he visited after becoming Assistant Secretary of State. I doubt that he even forgot that ambassadors, as well as Peace Corps reps, invariably take visiting dignitaries to show places rather than problem spots. Vaughn wanted to see success. He did not want to see failure.

Frank Mankiewicz was the first Peace Corps representative in Peru and followed Vaughn as Latin America regional director when President Johnson appointed Vaughn ambassador to Panama. Mankiewicz was not a Latin American specialist like Vaughn. He was a California journalist and lawyer who had a strong interest in politics and civil rights. He ran unsuccessfully for the state assembly from West Los Angeles and for two years was Pacific Southwest civil rights director for the Anti-Defamation League.

Mankiewicz came face to face with the reality of the peasant and slum dwellers' condition in Latin America and quickly developed a theory of Peace Corps participation in their plight that was even more actively political than Vaughn's. Mankiewicz conceived the volunteers' roles as those of community organizers and community action workers. Such volunteers would live in a village or slum, get to know it thoroughly, learn the power structure, win the confidence of the people. The volunteers would then help the people reach a concensus on their needs and show them how to organize in order to achieve those needs, both through self-help activity and through putting group pressure on indifferent, inept, or corrupt politicians.

In a paper entitled "The Peace Corps: A Revolutionary Force" Mankiewicz wrote: ". . . our mission is essentially revolutionary. The ultimate aim of community development is nothing less than a complete change, reversal—or a revolution if you wish—in the social and economic patterns of the countries to which we are accredited. . . . We talk about development—but the pure economic and physical development of countries will be conducted eventually by the countries themselves, with United States assistance or without it. But the political and social development of the country can only come through the infusion of a kind of revolutionary spirit such as the Peace Corps represents. . . ."

The intentions of both Vaughn and Mankiewicz were benign. They were well aware that national development in Latin America today is concentrated exclusively in the hands of the ruling elite. Even when the elite has the interests of the masses in mind, they act in a highly paternalistic manner. They decide on projects and carry them out *for* the peasants and slum dwellers rather than work *with* them in learning to plan, organize, and provide for themselves.

But however benign in intent and however morally right from the standpoint of the peasants' needs, Vaughn and Mankiewicz's theory and practice amounted to a very high-handed meddling in the political processes of sovreign nations. They might even be said to lay the Peace Corps open to charges of a new form of arrogant United

States imperialism. I think the strongest evidence of the basic ineffectiveness of the community development program as a whole during this period is the fact that indignant Latin American political officials did not summarily order the Peace Corps out of their areas. This did happen occasionally, but it was rare. Most responsible officials very much wanted the depressed populations to be encouraged and instructed in self-help, but what they wanted the Peace Corps input to be was practical guidance of the poor in helping them help themselves to raise more food, keep well, learn a skill or trade, plan and put up a school or health clinic. Such activity would certainly often involve learning the techniques of joint planning and group action. But for the Peace Corps to send down political organizers with no technical skills to contribute or teach was another thing.

The real flaw in the Vaughn-Mankiewicz strategy was the pouring of thousands of ill-equipped BA generalists into Latin America as free lance community development workers. In April 1964, the Latin America Peace Corps country representatives met in Guayaquil, Ecuador, together with CD specialists from the United States and South America. Their purpose was to explore their growing concern about the Peace Corps role in CD and about the excessive early resignation rate of Latin American CD volunteers in comparison to other volunteers.

During this conference the country reps estimated that only ten to twenty percent of their community development volunteers were really doing well. Based on their firsthand observations, the reps also provided Washington with a profile of a volunteer likely to be really successful in community development work:

He has a college degree or its equivalent in working experience.

He is skilled in the basic manual arts.

He usually has a rural background.

He has had two to four years of experience in work which requires dealing with people and organizational effort.

He is in the mid- or late twenties rather than younger.

He speaks Spanish fairly fluently by the time he has been in the country a month.

The difference was profound between this profile and the thousands of recent liberal arts college graduates trying to practice community development in Latin America at that time. The Guayaquil conference also focused on the apparent fact that in order to get larger numbers of volunteers into Latin America, the regional office had permitted the selection standards to drop a notch or two, particularly in regard to accepting college dropouts. The really important message of the conference, however, was that the Peace Corps was not being fair to the volunteers or to the receiving countries by sending young BA generalists into hastily conceived, shapeless, unstructured assignments called community development.

During these years, only one senior staff member fought unceasingly and effectively against putting generalist volunteers into these CD programs or into programs of any type for which they were not qualified. That man was John Alexander, who had been moved from his job as Africa regional director to that of program coordinator for the Program Development Office. In his new job, it was Alexander's responsibility, together with a small staff, to examine all programs proposed by the four regions and decide which programs should be dropped and how the available volunteers should be allotted. In essence, he was the hatchet man on the murder boards. His power was sharply limited, however, because murder board decisions could be appealed to Moyers, Wiggins, or Shriver and frequently were.

No one could have presided over the murder boards and remained popular in the Peace Corps, not even the most cautious career diplomat, and that phrase in no way described Alexander. A man with a brilliant, analytical mind, he had, before coming to the Peace Corps, spent his professional life first as a U.S. government economist in Germany and from 1954 to 1961 as a foreign aid program planner in the Philippines, Laos, Korea, and finally Washington, where for four years he concentrated on economic planning for Africa. Alexander had clear and uncompromising ideas about the purposes of the Peace Corps, what it could accomplish, and about the assets and limitations of BA generalists as volunteers. Also a former boxer, nationally ranked while in college, Alexander never avoided a fight if he could help it, and his program battles with the regional directors, particularly Mankiewicz, were monumental.

Alexander believed that before a volunteer was sent overseas there should be a clearly defined, specific job for him to do—a real job that was understood by the volunteer, the Peace Corps, and the host country. For that reason he strongly favored teaching assignments, particularly

for BA generalists, and had pushed teaching programs
vigorously when he was Africa regional director. He continued to push them as over-all program coordinator, but
he was receptive to any kind of program which seemed
to contain bona fide jobs and for which he thought volunteers were qualified or could be trained. He detested the
numbers game and phony programming. He rejected as
emotionalism or hypocrisy the loudly proclaimed views
that Peace Corps volunteers could bring about revolutions or build nations.

"You people are going to ruin it if you keep talking like
that," Alexander once wrote to me in India after I had
sent in a program description with some exalted phrases
about what the volunteers were going to accomplish. He
continued: "What a fine and modest thing the Peace Corps
idea was in the beginning. Volunteers would go out and
work at a job. If it was a real job, it didn't make much
difference what it was. They would live and work with
the people and learn about them, and the people would
learn something about Americans. That's all Kennedy said
the Peace Corps was: a way to give help where it was
needed and increase understanding. Leave it at that and
maybe it will have something to do with changing the
world someday."

After the Guayaquil conference, Alexander recommended to Mankiewicz that a new category of volunteers
called CD leaders be created in line with the qualifications set out in the profile prepared by the reps. He further suggested that selection standards be raised and
training improved for BA generalist volunteers and that
the number of CD volunteers in Latin America be cut in

half in the future. The CD leaders would be spread out to assist and backstop the smaller numbers of generalist volunteers. Nothing came of these suggestions, and the numbers were not reduced.

Alexander, after attending the Guayaquil conference, visited one CD project in Ecuador that made a lasting impression on him. It seems that eighty Andean families had each been given five acres of land by a wealthy hacienda owner who saw certain future tax and land-law advantages in giving away a piece of his holdings. A government housing agency was undertaking to build a five-room house for each of the Indian families. The problem was that the Indians, who lived in one-room huts with walls made of grass or reeds stretched upon a strong wooden frame, preferred the intimacy of their small dwellings to the bigger houses. They were afraid to protest too loudly, however, for fear that the land might be taken away from them.

The Peace Corps had assigned two volunteers to the housing project, and the rep was going to visit them because he had heard that the Indians were showing pronounced signs of unrest. Alexander accompanied the rep, and they found the volunteers in their house, which was the same one-room-type hut that the Indians occupied. Alexander and the rep were sitting on one of the beds, their heads resting against the grass wall, when someone outside suddenly plunged the blade of a machete through the side of the hut, squarely between the two men's heads.

Nobody, Alexander reported later, went outside to investigate. The volunteers produced a bottle of the local brew called aquavit, and they all had a few drinks.

Upon his return to Washington, Alexander prepared a memorandum for Warren Wiggins describing the incident. He concluded by saying, "Maybe everybody should just leave these Indians alone. I believe they will tell us in no uncertain terms when they are ready to enter the twentieth century."

When the chips were down, Alexander frequently did not get the backing he deserved from Shriver, Wiggins, Moyers, or other members of the senior staff. The pressures for bigness and the rhetoric of the Peace Corps as a dramatic world force were too great. But through his tenacity and bureaucratic skill, he was able to kill many unsound program proposals and keep numbers down in others. Without him, there would have been many more free lance CD volunteers scattered around the world.

Because of his position as chairman of the murder board, his unwavering quest for sanity in program development, and his natural proclivity for a fight, Alexander was one of the most intensely disliked men in the Peace Corps. But Shriver knew his value to the agency. And there was a small group that greatly admired his work —men such as William Josephson and Wiggins, who understood what Alexander was trying to do, though he could not always support him. I counted myself in that group.

Volunteers as Teachers: What Else Do You Do?

In the years of 1963–66 about fifty-two percent of all Peace Corps volunteers were classroom teachers. The two groups, community development workers and teachers, made up over seventy-eight percent of the volunteer total during this period. Teaching was at the other end of the spectrum from CD, at least in several important ways. Teachers' jobs were highly structured, highly specific. They had a certain number of courses to teach to a certain number of students. They had lesson plans to make up and papers to grade. In one sense they had had sixteen or more years of training for teaching—the years they had spent in school and watched their teachers practice their trade.

There were other differences from CD. Except for Latin American and French-speaking Africa, fluency in the local language was not essential to a teaching volunteer's success on the job since the language of instruction was almost always English. And in one sense a BA generalist left that category when he became a teacher. Teachers of science, mathematics, and technical subjects were never considered generalists; but liberal arts graduates who had majored in history, music, art, literature, and geography and taught those subjects also had a specialty. Even the BA generalist who taught English—as most did—had the very great advantage of being a native speaker of the language.

It is true that relatively few volunteer teachers had had previous teaching experience or had even taken education courses in college, but Peace Corps training could and did focus on practice teaching and pedagogical theory and techniques. As with all Peace Corps training, the quality varied with the different training institutions, but the trainers always had the advantage of knowing fairly precisely what the volunteers would be doing in their jobs.

Volunteers who liked teaching—and the majority of those I knew personally did—usually gained confidence in the classroom rather quickly. My educationist friends always pointed out with great consistency that confidence did not mean they were *good* teachers. There was no disputing that, but it did mean that they did not drag around with them the great burden of doubt about their fitness for the job that BA generalists did in many other kinds of work such as health, agriculture, and community development. And this confidence did, I think, contribute to their being good teachers and help them to start or encourage other kinds of school activities that were worthwhile for the students.

There certainly were bad assignments in teaching just as there were in community development and every other activity the Peace Corps undertook. As I have previously mentioned, a volunteer might not have enough teaching to keep him well occupied if his headmaster was suspicious of the Peace Corps or foreigners in general. And more than once a volunteer was assigned to a school in some government minister's home town so that the minister could take credit for having secured a foreign teacher for his home community; as often as not the school was well staffed and the volunteer not needed. Some volunteers were assigned to primary schools and—while there were numerous exceptions—language problems made these jobs frustrating for the volunteers and of marginal value for the students.

Without doubt, the worst teaching assignments in the Peace Corps as a group were in the Philippines, where between 1962–66 eleven hundred volunteers served as teachers' aides. Despite the fact that Warren Wiggins' "The Towering Task" had used the Philippines as an example of a country that could use thousands of young American English teachers, Charles Nelson, the first Peace Corps negotiator to go there in 1961, did not find the enthusiastic reception he might have been led to expect. Ministry of Education officials in Manila told him that there was already an oversupply of teachers in the Philippines, at least in the sense that Filipino teacher unemployment was high because of a shortage of education funds. They thought—quite rightly, I have no doubt—that it would create an intolerable situation to bring in foreign teachers to fill vacancies that their own teachers could fill if the country had money—even though the foreign teachers were free.

Further discussions led to the concept of volunteers serving as co-teachers or teachers' aides. They would not actually teach classes, so they would not be taking a job away from a Filipino teacher (who would still remain unemployed because of lack of funds). There were to be both English language and science teachers' aides, but the roles of neither were ever clearly defined. It was suggested that the English aides could serve as models of spoken English, reciting before classes for imitation by the students (a "nine-thousand-dollar-a-year tape recorder" as one teachers' aide called herself). Further suggestions were that both types of teachers' aides could work with individual students on special projects or by giving special tutoring. They could help teachers design new types of projects and activities and perhaps help them plan lessons and grade papers. They might be able to set up school libraries. They might be able to do things in the communities where they lived.

It was a terrible way to use volunteers.

But for the most part teaching led to bona fide assignments for volunteers. And the volunteers—despite their problems with the rigid syllabus, rote memorization, external examinations, and irrelevant courses and textbooks—in general did well in teaching, liked working with students, and thought they were accomplishing something.

But quite early the Peace Corps itself (in the form of many senior staff members) began to develop grave doubts about the appropriateness of teaching as a Peace Corps activity. The doubts were focused most sharply on the value of teaching English, especially in French-speaking Africa, but other uncertainties began to take root and grow. Questions were raised about whether it was worthwhile for volunteers to spend their time teaching English, chemistry, physics, history, art, geography, and similar subjects to secondary and even elementary school students the great majority of whom were going to drop out of school before graduating, go back to their villages, and spend their lives grubbing a living out of the soil. Some staff members flatly asserted that it was wrong for the Peace Corps through its volunteer teachers to support the preservation in Africa and Asia of a curriculum that had been imported under colonialism and was essentially European or Western.

Related to these doubts was the feeling that teaching was not "Peace Corps" in tone. Especially in Africa, volunteer teachers lived in good houses on isolated school compounds. Their closest associates were their fellow teachers, the educated elite, sometimes expatriates like themselves. Since English was the medium of instruction and encouraged at all times, they seldom spoke the local language as well as non-teaching volunteers. In the seclusion of the compound, they did not get to know the "real" Nigeria or Uganda or Tanzania; they did not get to know the "real" people.

Washington and some reps had a solution for these twin fears that teaching was not important and did not provide the volunteer with a Peace Corps experience. They began to urge—and in some cases hound—the volunteer teachers to move out of their houses on the school compounds and find a place to live in some nearby village or town. Although compound housing was provided free by the school, the Peace Corps felt so strongly about getting the volunteer out of that stultifying atmosphere that it would pay for the volunteer to live elsewhere if necessary.

The Peace Corps also began to urge the volunteers to find some activities in addition to teaching, something away from the school. Suggestions ran to community development and food production; getting a village interested in well purification or building a health clinic; encouraging women to start small vegetable plots; promoting chicken or rabbit raising—almost anything in fact to be involved with "the people."

Teacher volunteers had always had a certain sensitivity about their conditions of service. They were well aware that their housing was not in the Peace Corps image, that their command of the local language was bad, and their experiences in the country were sharply circumscribed by the demands of their teaching duties. Most of all they were aware that teaching, no matter how good, did not produce quick, easily observable and photographable results. After some initial protests, volunteer teachers had wearily, but with basic good humor, resigned themselves to the fact that non-teaching volunteers were going to get all the headlines, all the feature stories, all the pictures in the newspapers and magazines back home. They could not compete with the road builders, the wheat raisers, the nurses vaccinating black children, the mechanic putting a tractor back together.

But the teachers did not react with good humor to being pushed off the school compounds and being told to dilute their teaching with something more important. A few did move away and a few did start other projects. Most however stayed at their schools and turned with deep resentment, sometimes almost a fury, on the Peace Corps administration. The fact that the distance between schools and surrounding villages or towns and the lack of transportation made moving out extremely difficult was the lesser cause of their disenchantment. Their real unhappiness lay in the obvious low value that the Peace Corps put on their work as teachers.

In hundreds of bitter letters and scores of angry conferences volunteers made two simple but fundamental points: (1) Their place was with their students and fellow teachers. (2) If the Peace Corps did not think teaching was a worthwhile activity for volunteers, it should stop sending teachers overseas.

Their logic was sound, yet by the end of 1966 the issues involved had in no way been resolved. Certainly nothing

was wrong with the Peace Corps staff questioning the
validity of teaching as a Peace Corps undertaking. At some
time in his service every volunteer must have puzzled
over the same question. In my own judgment teaching
was and is something volunteers should be doing. For
many, their backgrounds equipped them better for teaching than for anything else, and they could be good
teachers.

It is true that much African and Asian education is a
faded carbon copy of Western education and inappropriate in many ways for the students. The top African and
Asian educators are quite aware of this; changes are being
made, but they are difficult and will take time, even when
there is the highest level political support as in the case of
Tanzania. The fact that volunteers were and are troubled
by the problems of rigid curriculum, emphasis on memorization, and the rest and discussed these matters
frequently with their teacher colleagues and with
administrators will in time be a help to those educational
officials who want change and are working for it. And, as
I have said previously, perhaps the volunteer's greatest
contribution could be and often was the example of the
teacher genuinely concerned about the minds and well-
being of his students.

A prime spokesman for the point of view that English
teaching by volunteers, especially in French-speaking
Africa, was largely a waste of everyone's time was David
Hapgood,[3] who did a number of evaluations for the

[3] Hapgood, a writer and specialist on Africa, is co-author with Meridan
Bennett, former Peace Corps rep and evaluator, of a thoughtful book on
the Peace Corps (*Agents of Change: A Close Look at the Peace Corps,*

Peace Corps. His argument essentially was that few African or Asian students would ever learn to speak English or have any real occasion to speak it. The great majority would drop out of school before graduating and return to their village long before they could achieve any mastery of the language. BA generalist volunteers could more profitably work at something else—Hapgood suggested public health and rural development—and the students would be better off studying something more practical.

After one of Hapgood's attacks on teaching English in French-speaking Africa had appeared in *The Volunteer*, the Peace Corps house magazine, Roger Kuhn, principal drafter of the Peace Corps Act, wrote a short rejoinder, which follows. It expresses my own views on the subject.

A lot could be said about David Hapgood's critique of TEFL (Teaching English as a Foreign Language) but let me comment on one aspect: Hapgood's view of education as a strictly utilitarian exercise.

"Only a handful" of the students that volunteers teach "will have any particular need for English," Hapgood says, so it is a waste of their time and ours to teach it. The same, I suppose, could be said of math beyond addition and subtraction, of physics beyond the lever and the wheel, and art, history and other humanistic studies. Who needs them on the farm? Or digging ditches? Or selling stamps at the post office? These were the arguments made 50 years ago for teaching only vocational subjects to American Negroes.

Boston, Little, Brown, 1968). A fuller statement of his objections to English teaching can be found there.

But Hapgood suggests that for those Africans who will become "airline hostesses, diplomats and hotel waiters" we hold separate English classes. This presupposes identifying them while they are still in school—perhaps by aptitude tests? Heaven save Africans (and the rest of us) from an educational system which tags people and offers them the subjects which will fit them for the future life which the system has chosen for them. What Hapgood proposes is essentially a gigantic track system.

The basis for Hapgood's reasoning is his definition of education as "only the organized means by which one generation indoctrinates the next." That was certainly never the Peace Corps definition, nor the definition of any educator worthy of the name. I think that defines the very opposite of education, which to me is the means by which one generation seeks to equip the next to do better than it did. I also think that's what the Peace Corps is trying to do.

About one-third of all volunteers in French-speaking West Africa were teaching English; perhaps that was too heavy a concentration. It is not beside the point, however, to note that the French-speaking African officials were more interested in English teachers than in other kinds of volunteers. Although the officials were not highly explicit on the matter, it was clear that they did not and still do not want their countries to be totally dependent on the French language with all that that implies about dependence on France. They are also aware that in the late twentieth century, English is the most important world language. They want it.

Whether one agrees with Kuhn or with Hapgood, however, the real point is that, having decided on teaching as an activity, the Peace Corps should have encouraged the volunteers to become the very best teachers they could possibly be. Instead, it made them feel guilty by implying that teaching was not very important after all and it harassed them to make them spend time on things other than their work as teachers.

Some country representatives went along with Washington's drive to dilute the volunteers' work in education, but others argued and protected and guided their volunteers in every way they could. Joseph Murphy, the rep in Ethiopia, sent all his teachers a memorandum entitled "OK—So You're a Good Teacher. What Else Have You Done for Us Lately?" Murphy, a former professor at Brandeis University and later a senior planning officer in the Job Corps, tried to put Washington's attitude in a historical and philosophical perspective for the volunteers. He wrote:

Good ideas have an unfortunate tendency to suffer from hardening of the arteries. When Peace Corps first became involved in teaching projects in Africa, its own mystique and ideology more or less forced it to conceive of teaching in a somewhat less parochial and narrow fashion than the conventional professional establishment generally thought about itself. Since teaching, in our own culture, appears to the non-teacher and especially to the taxpayer as part-time work, as indeed it is for many Stateside teachers, the Peace Corps of course tried to make teaching into a full-time job by recognizing that the teacher has a role in the community and that that role entails an involvement in that community that transcends the confines of the schoolroom. Of course the idea in itself, although neither new nor original, was a good one. It still is a good one. Unfortunately no one was ever quite able to say what that extracurricular activity was supposed to be. And as the Peace Corps grew in size and in the degree to which it became involved in the educational system of developing countries, it sought to do what all institutions do, namely to formalize the structure and delimit the extent and magnitude of this extracurricular involvement. It was an easy step therefore to go from the involvement of teachers in the community to the kinds of activities that would be numbered, measured, counted, and weighed.

I recall, for example, while visiting a Peace Corps Director in Africa several years ago, the pride with which he exhibited to me some mimeographed sheets, each one of which was a kind of loyalty oath by a volunteer that he indeed swore to be the producer of so many chicken coops, outhouses, sheep dips and so on. "Our teachers work eleven months a year," he announced proudly, "and we really have them involved in the community." I understood then, of course, that this Director's concern about how to demonstrate to Washington that his teachers were doing something more than merely teaching had reached a point of relative absurdity. It is not difficult to see why and how it reached that point. But it was indeed a good example of how a good idea became rigidified and became an absurd idea, often with absurd results.

. . . the Peace Corps is a white, bourgeois establishment, and most of us do not by simple introjection automatically understand people in underdeveloped countries and the problems that their children have as students. Understanding, which is the key to being effective as a teacher, comes from all those human virtues that are perhaps most difficult for our species. It comes from empathy, from love, from the kind of confidence in oneself that rests on experience and knowledge. The key to a good teacher anywhere in the world is that that teacher knows that he must make a genuine effort and do a lot of hard work to understand who this child is sitting before him, how that child looks at the world, looks at his past, looks at his future, looks at his parents, looks at his Peace Corps teacher, looks at his classroom, looks at his prospects for the future. In other words, the teacher must know whom he is teaching. The answers to all these questions cannot be found in the schoolroom itself. They are to be found in the village the student comes from, in the home he lives in, in the ways in which his culture has dictated that he be brought up, in the attitude and character of the people who brought him up, in the playground in which he plays, or the streets where he spends his time, in the fields where he works. The good teacher has to know something about all these things if he is to understand what teaching such a child entails. It is a pity that this vital function which can also be called "involvement in the community" could have become so institutionally frozen and systematically confused with formalized, weighable, measurable, touchable projects . . . Some people may become involved in a community by raising chickens, others by becoming interested in the folklore, history, songs, customs of the people. A whole variety of different techniques and instruments can be mastered and utilized. But these have little value in the long run in themselves. They must be understood as vehicles for the single principal objective of the Peace Corps teacher and that is to be an excellent teacher.

Joseph Kennedy, the representative in Sierra Leone, strongly asserted that the volunteer teacher's place was on the school compound where he could associate with his fellow teachers and work with his students outside the classroom as well as inside. He did, however, suggest an important community role for the volunteer teachers.

Formal education in nearly all parts of Africa was initiated by foreign missionaries who established schools to teach the ways of a Western God and the way of Western man as well. . . . In learning the ways of Western man—often for the first time in their lives, Africans slept on beds, ate with knives and forks, drank water not just taken from a muddy stream. The creating of a Western religious, secular man could best be achieved by creating a Western cultural island cut off from the "native negative" surroundings. These schools thus by inculcating Western culture purposely disassociated themselves from the surrounding communities and became outposts against the existing society.

When the colonial governments perceived a need to train African civil servants, those schools which had become havens for Western inculcation divorced from the surrounding African society became the natural breeding ground for an "elite" African who identified with the expatriate world and in turn divorced himself from his own African society.

Out of this past, the secondary schools of today, particularly those with school compounds, are out of contact with the communities surrounding them and education itself is out of contact with the realities of struggling developing nations. A revolution in education in Africa could be effected if schools and communities began to interact and education came back into reality and became relevant to the needs of Africa.

In the United States, the interaction between the school and the community is such a common phenomenon that one hardly gives thought to it. There are PTA's, school sports, plays, exhibits, school assemblies, lectures, and visits to town which bring the community into the school lives of the students. But this is not the case in Sierra Leone and other parts of Africa. The teacher—Sierra Leonean or expatriate—and the students do not concern themselves with the surrounding community. The surrounding community contributes little and shares little in the educational development of the students. (The fact that neither students nor teachers come from [the surrounding] villages where they are studying and teaching of course exacerbates the lack of community interest, but does not render it impossible.)

The big challenge which faces volunteer secondary school teachers is to break these schools out of their isolation, to expand the boundaries of these tight little isolated islands, to establish links between these isolated schools and their communities. There is much greater value in attempting this than there is in the volunteer moving into the town or going out of the school each day alone to get something going, for this is an involvement which still leaves the the schools and the community separated.

Once more we find the Peace Corps proclivity for grandiose rhetoric with talk of "a revolution in education in Africa" and the volunteers' "big challenge" to "break these schools out of their isolation." Exaggerations aside, however, Kennedy was right that there was a role for compound-based volunteers to take a lead in stimulating school interest in the community around it; some volunteers had a fair measure of success in doing so.

The receiving countries did not seem to share the Peace Corps' doubts about volunteers as teachers, nor was there any uncertainty on their part about what they wanted the volunteer teachers to do: They wanted volunteers to teach English, mathematics, science, and other subject matter in the classrooms. Educational officials were tolerant of Peace Corps desires to have volunteer teachers do other things but only to the extent that those things did not interfere too markedly with their teaching duties. Some countries came to rely heavily on Peace Corps teachers and figured the annual input of new volunteers into their fiscal and national school growth planning. At the high point there were 550 Peace Corps teachers in Nigeria. In Liberia volunteers made up sixty-five percent of all teachers with a college degree and in Ethiopia, thirty percent. From the beginning of the Peace Corps through 1969, 1,643 Peace Corps teachers had served or were still serving in Nigeria; 1,090 in Liberia, 1,400 in Ethiopia, 805 in Sierra Leone. Thousands more had taught in more than two score other countries in Africa, Asia, and Latin America.

In general, education officials also became increasingly satisfied with the quality of the volunteer teachers' performance. At the height of the Peace Corps build-up in Nigeria in 1966, a ranking officer in the Ministry of Education expressed his feelings quite clearly.

"There is," he said, "not one of the various foreign aid schemes working in this country that can beat the Peace Corps."

India: The Peace Corps World in One Country

During the years 1963–66 the India program was a microcosm of the Peace Corps world. It became the largest program in gross numbers of volunteers, but it was always the smallest when volunteers were considered in relation to country population. With over half a billion people, India holds one-sixth of the world's population—more than all of Africa and South America combined. When the Peace Corps program in India was at its numerical peak, the ratio of volunteers to Indians was about one to half a million.

But India, in Peace Corps terms, was a big program and as it evolved I think we must have duplicated every good and bad experience of the Peace Corps everywhere else in the world. The word "duplicated" accurately describes what happened throughout Peace Corps programs. We were building so rapidly and the turnover of volunteers and staff was so great that the lessons learned in one country rarely were applied in another. Two phrases frequently heard during this period—and coined, I am sure, by exasperated university academicians who tried to train our volunteers—were "Every year the Peace Corps invents the wheel" and "The Peace Corps has no memory." They meant essentially the same thing, and they were more than a little true.

The first two India projects and for the most part the third had been put together under Washington staff direction before Charlie Houston and I arrived on the scene. The second and third projects were of the same shopping list variety as the first only more so. There were agricultural extension and poultry workers, home economists, science and English teachers, nurses, a group of university teachers, youth club workers, physical education specialists, three mechanical engineers, and even a bee keeper, who was devoted to his calling with a singleness of purpose one rarely encounters today. The problem was finding him some bees to keep.

As with India 1, the second and third groups had a high percentage of volunteers with technical backgrounds appropriate to the kind of work they were expected to do in India. This phenomenon became increasingly rare as the Peace Corps expanded into new countries. The initial pool of technically qualified or experienced volunteers was exhausted, and the trickle that continued had to be shared between an ever-increasing number of programs. BA generalists who were put into shopping list projects hardly ever received any helpful skill training. I well remember one history major who came over labeled "agricultural extension worker" because he had sat through a few lectures on Indian agriculture. He came to Delhi after about two weeks in rural Uttar Pradesh and said he would have to find something else to do. The first day he had gone out with his block development officer to look at crops, the volunteer had commented that one field of wheat looked particularly good.

"Yes, it is excellent barley," the BDO had politely responded.

"We both knew then what I'd known all along," the volunteer said to me. "That as an ag extension man I'd make a good history teacher."

The volunteer eventually became the business manager and sales promoter of a blacksmith's cooperative that specialized in making improved Persian wheels.

Shopping list projects had the advantage in the early days of letting us see volunteers in a wide variety of activities, hopefully teaching us which were right for the

Peace Corps and which weren't. But such fragmented projects also had great disadvantages. The volunteers' jobs were so diverse that they could learn very little from each other's experiences and could not reenforce each other. Because such a welter of government departments and officials were involved, Peace Corps staff had a difficult time establishing any contacts and understanding that would help the volunteers in their work. And there was no feeling of unity or program thrust to give volunteers, or the host country, much satisfaction or group feeling of accomplishment.

The first project that Charlie and I put together was for secondary school teachers of English, science, and mathematics. Volunteer teachers in India had all the problems and satisfactions of those who taught in Africa and elsewhere. Over the years, however, teaching did not prove to be the major activity in India that we had first thought it might. Though English is still the binding language of India, the government is beset with grave linguistic political problems dividing the large Hindi-speaking population from the smaller language groups that want full parity for their mother tongue. English is in some ways caught in the middle of this conflict, and government officials quite understandably did not want to exacerbate the problem by importing hundreds of foreign English teachers.

Though we had a group of teachers from time to time, it was quickly apparent that if the India program was going to grow, we had to find some other ways besides teaching to use BA generalists. Community development certainly wasn't the answer. Almost since independence the Indian government had been a world leader in programs of rural community development. They had built a vast national organization with village level workers reaching almost all of the country's half million villages. Like almost everything in India, the conception and planning were better than the execution; but the problems of the Ministry of Community Development were truly staggering, and accomplishments in the face of them were admirable. We didn't see that a few, or a few hundred, liberal arts Americans could make any real contribution. The Indians must have agreed, for they never asked us to try.

As Charlie and I and our Indian colleagues in the Planning Commission who held the Peace Corps portfolio looked at what was working for us reasonably well in India, time after time we focused on poultry. The few volunteers working in this field were finding eager acceptance by farmers and even city dwellers. And it was not only volunteers experienced in poultry work before coming to India who were having success. Those self-taught volunteers such as Bill Donovan, Sean Doherty, and Tom Kessinger were finding business very good. Furthermore, they quickly developed confidence in their ability to do the job.

We discovered that every state in India had a poultry development program and that most state animal husbandry officers were interested in having—or at least willing to have—some volunteers work at the extension level, as the Punjab volunteers were doing. The fifth group of volunteers to come to India were all poultry workers, destined for the states of Rajasthan and Madhya Pradesh, and with very few exceptions, they were classic BA generalists—history, political science, journalism, and psychology majors, even some with art and music backgrounds.

They received their training at the University of California agricultural campus at Davis, and except for language and cultural studies, they spent their time on just one thing: learning the rudiments of starting and taking care of small poultry units in India. They learned about the right kind of mud brick chicken houses by actually building them; they learned the deep litter, close confinement system of raising chickens by spreading the litter and taking care of the chickens. They learned the right feed formulas and how to improvise with ingredients available in India. They learned to vaccinate, debeak, and kill diseased chickens. They were taught to dress and cut up birds for the market.

After three months of sharply focused training at Davis, these volunteers were as ignorant as they had ever been about general farming and animal husbandry—with the single exception of poultry, and even in that their knowledge had great gaps. But they knew one thing reasonably well: how to house, raise, cull, and keep healthy a small flock of chickens in India. That knowledge was to be their means of performing some useful service in the Indian community to which they would be sent. It was to be their protection against being known as a vagabond; it was to be the basis of their own self-respect.

In general the idea worked. Between 1963 and 1966 ten of India's seventeen states asked for and received volunteers to work in poultry development, and all of them asked for additional or replacement groups after receiving the first. At one point in 1965 almost three hundred volunteers were spending all of their time or part of it helping Indians raise chickens. For the most part they worked with farmers, but they found interest in other places. A number of urban government workers and even businessmen wanted to add to their income through selling eggs and managed to squeeze out space in their back yards for a chicken house. In the city of Agra, I visited one chicken house built on top of a three-story building. Some volunteers worked with schools, where the headmaster was interested in giving his students a chance to learn about chicken raising and also in having an extra source of protein for his boarding students.

The volunteers' work in helping to start poultry units frequently led to related work that took the major part of their time. Some helped farmers organize feed buying or mixing cooperatives. Others became immersed in the business of selling the flood of eggs they were helping to generate. In both Bombay and New Delhi volunteers opened egg marketing stores and in addition developed home and restaurant delivery routes. Although they had Indians working with them, they very much did their share of the work—in keeping with the Peace Corps philosophy of *doing*, not *advising*—and it became a familiar sight to see fair-skinned, blond young men pedaling bicycles or driving motor scooters around the streets of Delhi and Bombay delivering the daily egg order to Indian housewives. The boxes and racks they mounted on their bicycles for safely carrying two or three gross of eggs over the bumpy streets rivaled the imagination of Salvador Dali and Rube Goldberg, but they worked.

At the height of their activity in 1965, we estimated that volunteers were working with five thousand poultry raisers, with a total of about two million laying hens, producing approximately half a billion eggs a year. In a country of more than half a billion people that may seem a paltry total; but in the areas where the volunteers worked, it meant a major jump in egg supply. Millions of Indians who can afford to buy eggs do not eat them because of Hindu prohibitions on consuming any form of animal life. And when the hot weather sets in, egg consumption, even among Indians with no religious dietary restrictions, falls off sharply. There is a widely held belief that eggs are a "hot food" which raises the body's temperature—therefore to be avoided in summer. Volunteers, with excellent reason, feared that a sharp fall-off in egg eating in the long hot season would bankrupt their clients' shoe-string enterprises.

Systematic egg marketing in the big cities was one answer to the problem. Another was a vigorous educational campaign by the volunteers to sell the fact that an egg has no life until it is fertilized by a rooster. Laying hens raised under the close confinement system never come in contact with roosters, and their eggs are therefore unfertile or lifeless. Volunteers coined the phrase "vegetarian eggs" for their poultry raisers' products, and some restaurants and stores actually began to advertise them under that name. The eggs produced by the well-fed, carefully culled hens under the close confinement system were almost twice as big as the products of *desai* hens, the name applied to their sisters who ran free and scratched a living from the soil. These big, clean, carefully boxed eggs quickly acquired another name in a number of places in India, a name given to them not by volunteers but by Indians. They were called Peace Corps eggs.

The volunteers also attacked the problem of the "hot food" stigma. They reasoned that this idea must have originated in the ancient past as a means of discouraging people from eating eggs during hot weather, when spoiled eggs were prevalent and could cause sickness or at least be a very bad buy. Whether or not their theory had any historical validity, the volunteers urged their poultry raisers to store their eggs in the coolest places possible, they improvised cold storage rooms in the egg shops, and they made sure that the oldest eggs were sold first. They guaranteed their eggs to be fresh, and they promoted this guarantee as widely as possible.

I have no way to know how many Indians were persuaded by the vegetarian egg idea or by the fresh egg guarantee. I do know that the eggs sold, even in the cruel pre-monsoon heat when the thermometer stood at 110 degrees and more. We all considered the marketing operation in Delhi and other big cities a real long shot but the only hedge we could think of against the near certainty that eggs would go unsold in many more rural areas where the volunteers were working. The Delhi store started with eggs coming from poultry raisers in three or four volunteer locations. To volunteers manning the Delhi store and promoting customers, the eggs that started flooding in by train and bus looked like an awesome white Himalayan peak. But within two weeks the volunteers were not only selling all their stock but had enough additional orders that they were desperately sending telegrams to other poultry volunteers in the Punjab and Rajasthan to ship them all the eggs they could spare.

To be sure, the volunteers in poultry work had their share of problems and troubles. During 1964–65 the monsoon rains were poor in most of India and failed completely in some places. Grain for chicken feed was scarce and expensive, and it took good flock management to make a profit. We had to face the question of whether grain should be fed to chickens under such extreme shortage conditions; but by making maximum use of grain that had been declared unfit for human consumption and—with the help of AID animal husbandry experts— devising feed formulas that substantially reduced the feed grain inputs, the volunteers felt they were able to justify their work in terms of the protein the eggs produced.

Many volunteers were troubled by the fact that they were never able to help the poorest Indians, the landless Harijans. To raise poultry a man had to have at least a few hundred rupees of cash to invest or have the collateral to get a government loan. Here and there a volunteer, with great persistence or ingenuity, was able to promote a rupee grant from some charitable organization and use it to help a few Harijans get a start in poultry, but that was rare. Almost exclusively, volunteers in poultry worked with Indians who had a little land and a little money, and—when the venture was successful—their efforts helped them to have a little more.

I remember visiting a Punjab farmer with a volunteer who had been working with the man for over a year. The farmer had several hundred fine White Leghorns, which he showed me with great pride. He told me that he was now making about a hundred rupees profit a month from his birds.

"I am using some of the money to send my oldest daughter to secondary school," he told me, and added, "She is the first female in my family ever to go beyond the primary grades."

It wasn't just the extra money, I am sure, that made the farmer decide to continue his daughter's education. It was that little additional confidence, the slight ventilating of his outlook, that had come from making a success of his poultry venture. All of us, volunteers and staff, savored those little triumphs when they occurred and gave them prominent standing beside the many failures: the farmers who lost interest in their poultry, who expected the volunteers to do all the work, who had their flocks wiped out through carelessness with sanitary controls or through bad luck with a mongoose.

Of all the activities we tried in India—and there were many—nothing worked better than our poultry efforts, and few things worked as well. Yet even in poultry the volunteers frequently asked themselves—and me—if they weren't just playing games. The poverty they saw around them every day was so oppressive, the needs of India were so overwhelming, that their slow, often fruitless work in helping a few farmers raise small flocks of chickens seemed a pitifully insignificant gesture. While the volunteers lived on about fifty dollars a month, it still cost the U.S. government eight thousand dollars a year to put each one of them in India and keep him there. The five hundred or so volunteers who worked in poultry in India for two years carried a price tag of close to eight million dollars. What had all of those volunteers and all of that money solved?

The answer, of course, was nothing. And the best and most successful poultry program in the world would not of itself have solved any of India's problems. But together the volunteers had worked with at least ten thousand farmers throughout India, and a fair number of them now had successful poultry businesses or side lines. Two large commercial hatcheries promoting high quality hybrid chicks, Arbor Acres and Rani Shaver, had enthusiastically welcomed the work of the volunteers. By their concentrated work on poultry all over India, the volunteers had helped to focus attention on the possibilities in eggs and chickens as a viable agro-industry. Their efforts added a tangible measure of support to the many state poultry programs and to the work that AID was doing in the field.

The Peace Corps was not designed to be the whole answer to any problems of development. The volunteers were supposed to perform useful work, to learn about the people and the country where they served, and to give the people with whom they lived a chance to learn more about Americans. Most of the poultry volunteers did these things. They could not bicycle the dusty roads and paths of rural India for two years, working, talking, living with farmers, merchants, and government officials, without learning a great deal about the real life of the land. And I am sure that Indian farmers who saw Peace

Corps volunteers sleep all night in a chicken house when there was a disease crisis or a mongoose on the prowl had some new thoughts about Americans.

Throughout the Peace Corps' history the best staff members were those who could learn from the successes and failures of the volunteers and build on their experiences. There was no better method of programming than to let a few volunteers try something and increase the numbers or eliminate the activity according to what happened to them. The India volunteers in poultry were a prime example of this method. As simple as this success formula sounds, not many reps around the world employed it. I would find this most puzzling had I not too often failed to do so myself.

Some reps developed their own theories of what the Peace Corps should be doing in a country or what help a country needed, and they were willing to spend volunteers to prove themselves right. Usually—as in the case of unstructured community development everywhere in the world it was tried—they proved just the opposite. Unfortunately, the best reps, those who built carefully on experience, were not always those who were rewarded with bigger countries or high-level jobs in Washington. Such was the agency's preoccupation with size that those jobs frequently went to the men who seemed to have the dash and flair to build big volunteer programs quickly. The movement of staff personnel was so rapid that such men were usually long gone from a badly programmed, or over-programmed, country before the inevitable reaction of unhappy volunteers and host officials set in.

Realistically, I must give myself mixed marks in the programming of volunteers. For the programs in poultry development and teaching I offer no apologies; one program which featured volunteers directing science teachers' workshops was, I think by general Division of Evaluation assessment, one of the best education programs the Peace Corps ever had. It was repeated successfully in several parts of India. We had a good project (though very uneven volunteer performance) in helping set up workshops for the repair of UNICEF health vehicles. We joined forces with CARE for a reasonably effective program in teaching nutrition and health in teacher training schools, though it was hard on the volunteers who had to move in teams among a number of schools. Every month or so they would have to pack their bags and their teaching equipment and travel by bus or any other conveyance they could locate to another teacher training school. They called themselves the Peace Corps gypsies.

But India is one of the biggest countries in the developing world and, except for Red China, by far the most populous, and among its half million villages and hundreds of teeming cities there seemed unlimited promise almost anywhere Peace Corps wanted to cast its net. This proved to be an illusion that led me and my staff into some serious mistakes. We broke our lance badly on health programs. On the surface rural public health in India would seem to be a natural for the Peace Corps: villagers with nutritional deficiencies and a basic lack of understanding about the cause of disease, villages with impure wells, drainage and other sanitary problems, shortages of medical supplies and services.

On paper it was good but in practice it was a fuzzy, amorphous assignment not much better than free lance community development. The volunteer men and women, almost all BA generalists, had no standing as medical people either with the villagers or the state departments of health. They received little or no guidance or material support from weakly staffed and financed health departments. They did not have the language facility or the deep cultural knowledge necessary—or any meaningful forum, really—to talk with the village women about nutrition and to teach and give demonstrations. The same problems prevented the men—whom we called sanitary engineers in our program descriptions—from stirring up any interest in digging latrines, purifying wells, or tackling drainage or garbage disposal projects. When they did get a ripple of interest, supplies and equipment were usually not to be had.

These health programs came under several titles such as rural public health and expanded nutrition, but they were all essentially the same, and they suffered from the same weaknesses: The volunteers did not have a clearly defined job and a clearly developed skill to apply to it; the health departments had little interest in them and scant means to give them support had they had. For the most part they wandered around from village to village trying futilely to get something started; large numbers gave up in despair and disgust and either went home or stopped seriously trying to do anything; others turned to something else—getting themselves a job teaching at a mission school or throwing in with poultry development volunteers.

My error was not in trying to find a spot for volunteers in the health field: It might have worked. The mistake was in not trying a very careful pilot effort with a few generalists before pumping large numbers of volunteers into what proved to be a fantasy program. One reason I did not was that in the vastness of India and in the welter of its problems, people, and villages, it was hard to think in small numbers, ever. Fifty or even a hundred volunteers seemed rather like a pilot project there, but it was not. Scores of volunteers, unhappy and feeling cheated by not having a real job, was a serious, unpleasant business. Another reason for not always employing the pilot program plan in advance of large numbers was to get a block of volunteers earmarked on the Washington program matrix; an opportunity to get volunteers might not arise again for a while. Sometimes the wait could be as long as a year. We took the chance that our program, without proper testing, would be sound. I offer this by way of explanation, not as an excuse.

I made a mistake in trying to use liberal arts majors in small industry work, again without trying it out in advance. India has thousands of small entrepreneurs, doing everything from manufacturing ball bearings to canning pickled mangoes, and we had consistently had requests for volunteers to work with these manufacturers and shoe-string industrialists. What the Indians wanted were volunteers with backgrounds in things like chemical and electrical engineering, sheet metal work, tool and die making, food processing, and business management.

But such skills were hard to come by, and Washington wouldn't think of sending us six or eight volunteers. According to the formula prevailing at that time, a project had to have at least thirty volunteers and preferably more in order to keep training and other logistical costs at reasonable levels. This meant that, to have any chance of approval, a project submitted by the field had to have a ratio of four or five BA generalists to every "skilled type" asked for. Washington's exceptions to this rule were exceedingly infrequent.

We tried to devise a role for generalists in small industries, hoping that they could be helpful in promotion, working on sales, and perhaps learn enough about business management in training so that they could be useful in India. Occasionally it worked but four out of five times it didn't. Mostly they stood around watching people work ("learning the business" we euphemistically called it for their first three months or so) and drinking tea with the owner, who was polite but as puzzled as they were about what they could do. Volunteers—small industry or any other kind—hated this feeling of uselessness more than anything that could befall them, as of course they should have.

A volunteer who was busy at something he believed had a real relevance to the people he was working with could put up with almost any frustrations or problems of homesickness, language, diet, or bad living conditions. He could not only put up with them, he could work his way through them and come out at the end of two years with an experience he genuinely cherished. The volunteers who did not have a real job to do were unhappy, made trouble for others or got into trouble themselves, resigned and went home or had to be sent home. A few, though not many, quit trying and simply sat out their time as disillusioned and cynical young men and women.

A volunteer, totally frustrated with trying to find something to do in rural health, once said to me, "All the Peace Corps owes me is a job I can do, a real job. If I have that I don't need anything else. I don't need your book lockers or a staff member to pat me on the back, or conferences every three months to talk over my troubles. Just give me a job. That's all I want you to do."

I remember, another time, visiting a volunteer who had grown very moody and unhappy after three months of not being able to get anything going. I figured that he was on the verge of resigning, but when I drove into his place that night I found him excited and almost deliriously happy. He greeted me cheerfully, had beer ready, jumped up repeatedly to bring snacks or pace around his tiny living room. The thought crossed my mind that he might have started using pot, but it wasn't anything like that.

"I worked today," he said after a few minutes. "I really worked." He went on to describe how he had helped a small factory owner figure out a safer and more efficient arrangement of his machines and production materials and then had pitched in to help move everything. "You know," he said, "if I could be busy like that every day, I'd be the happiest damned volunteer in India."

With those words the excitement went out of him, and I could tell from the look on his face that he knew tomorrow he would be back trying to find something to do. That was probably the low ebb moment of all of my years in the Peace Corps.

No volunteer's work, even when there was a well-defined job for which he was qualified, was easy. Teachers, mechanics, poultry workers, nurses, all had problems of understanding unfamiliar systems or organizations, winning confidences, learning to communicate, trying to understand philosophies and customs different from their own, often making do without tools or supplies to which they were accustomed. Almost all volunteers suffered low periods when they thought seriously about resigning, but those who had a real job could nearly always work their way out of these depressions. Without one, large numbers of potentially successful volunteers were overwhelmed by the frustrations and came home early.

There were always five to ten percent of the volunteers who could make something—sometimes something very good—out of non-job situations, whether they were health workers in India, urban or rural community developers in Latin America, or teachers' aides in the Philippines. We could never identify these people in advance through our selection and training procedures. It was only when they were in their assignments that they proved themselves to have a combination of qualities necessary to succeed. The combinations were not always the same but they almost always included an ability to understand, sympathize, and communicate. A person with this ability usually had built in a high tolerance for frustration and a realization that what seemed like small gains to them were often big ones to the people with whom they worked. Luck was unquestionably involved in some of these successes—the right volunteer in the right place at the right time.

But five or ten percent success in these non-job projects added up to a net failure of a substantial part of the total Peace Corps program. I have no hesitation in saying that the most serious mistake of the Peace Corps—by which I mean those of us who made and implemented its policies—during the first five years was the programming of large numbers of volunteers into non-jobs.

Volunteer Life: Another View

One of the Peace Corps' most hallowed clichés is "The volunteers are the Peace Corps." I think what I have written about the years 1963–66 makes clear that the volunteer was in fact sometimes the forgotten man of the Peace Corps. But despite all I have said about volunteer failure, frustration, and unhappiness, a startling fact remains: Ninety-four percent of all volunteers who completed their service between the spring of 1963 and the fall of 1965 stated that if they had it all to do over again and knowing all that they knew about two years of service, they would still join the Peace Corps.

This impressive statistic comes from what became known in the Peace Corps as "close of service" conferences. When the time approached for the first volunteers to complete their two years, Shriver and his senior staff decided that they should be brought together for a final conference in which they would assess their experiences as a group and make recommendations to the Peace Corps. Additional motives for the conferences were to prepare the volunteers for "reentry" into American life and also to let them talk out their gripes about Peace Corps service before they returned home. It was on the close of service questionnaire that ninety-four percent of the volunteers said they would do it again. It is true that only eighty percent of the volunteers said they would serve again in the same country—indicating that the idea of the Peace Corps transcends the actual experience of being a volunteer—but the figure is still a solid vote of approval.

If the work frustration and dissatisfaction were as great as I have indicated, how can this ninety-four percent approval figure be explained? In the first place, approximately fifteen percent of the volunteers who served during this period, world wide, resigned early and returned home. They did not attend close of service conferences and therefore did not express an opinion on whether they would repeat the Peace Corps experience. The answer of many no doubt would have been negative.

The essential answer, however, is to be found in the fact that the volunteer who stuck it out and tried to develop a job for himself could take some real satisfaction in the effort he had made. And in making the effort, he almost invariably made some friends and became involved in some way in the problems and life of his community whether rural, urban, or school compound. When the first effects of homesickness wore off, many of the volunteers became absorbed in the strange, fascinating, and often appealing cultures into which they were

plunged, and over their two years in the country a real
affection for the people and an appreciation of the culture
grew up. Certainly, this was a source of satisfaction for
thousands of volunteers.

There were other satisfactions. The camaraderie of
volunteers, particularly those who had gone through
training and selection together, was very strong. They
met once or twice a year at conferences and visited one
another while traveling about the country on holidays or
vacation. They took vacations together in the country and
to neighboring countries. They shared many problems
and hopes, and the friendships that grew up were often
deep and lasting—as were the romances. It was the rare
group of volunteers containing both men and women
that did not produce at least one marriage, and often there
were two or three.

While two-thirds of those who served during this
period felt that they had done only "moderately well" as
volunteers, it is clear that the richness of the total experience was sufficient to produce a positive feeling about
their two years in the Peace Corps.

A Note on Volunteer Health

From the very first the Peace Corps did a good job of
keeping volunteers healthy. Of course we started with
the advantage that most of them were young and healthy
when they volunteered, and those who were not young
were without exception in good health. Nevertheless,
many volunteers lived under conditions in which health
risks were great: dismal urban slums, remote rural areas,

steaming tropics. Pure drinking water was almost always a problem, as was sanitary food storage. A balanced diet was often not easy to achieve, and most men volunteers knew little about cooking and nutrition anyway. Competent medical assistance was often too far away to be of any help in an emergency.

But between 1961 and 1968 only one volunteer died of a tropical disease—amoebic hepatitis—and the death rate of volunteers overseas is almost exactly the same as it is for the same age group in the United States. About half of the forty-five volunteer deaths that occurred between 1961 and 1968 resulted from car and airplane accidents, drownings, and other kinds of accidents.

As might be expected, the most common volunteer ailments have always been dysentery and stomach troubles. Upper respiratory infections and skin diseases are also among the more frequent volunteer complaints. In some countries, particularly India, some men volunteers experience a rather severe weight loss. But most of these problems can be taken care of rather easily, and on the whole serious illness among volunteers has been rare.

Every Peace Corps program has at least one Peace Corps physician and some have several, depending on the size of the country and the number of volunteers. Until 1968 the Peace Corps received all of its doctors from the Public Health Service; almost without exception the doctors were young men just out of their intern programs; frequently they were no more than three or four years older than the volunteers. Most of them were energetic and full of enthusiasm for their work; they traveled as much as possible visiting the volunteers and taking a first-hand view of their living conditions.

The volunteers received health lectures as a part of their training, but the most careful health orientation—and the one the volunteers listened to most closely—was given by the Peace Corps doctor in their country of assignment. The doctors stressed preventive care: boiling of drinking water, thorough cooking of meat, avoidance of fruits and vegetables that could not be peeled or cooked, making every effort to obtain a balanced diet. Every volunteer received an excellent health kit and a manual for maintaining good health in his particular locality.

In eight years, volunteers reported about one thousand animal bites—a rate ten times higher than for the United States. In some areas volunteers receive a vaccine against rabies; in some countries they are issued snake bite kits. Volunteers receive inoculations and vaccinations for small pox, typhoid fever, cholera, yellow fever, and tetanus; and the Peace Corps doctors are always vigilant to see that they are kept up.

Viral hepatitis was a particular problem for the Peace Corps, especially in some countries with problems of waste disposal and impure drinking water. Peace Corps doctors have pioneered in the use of gamma globulin inoculations to prevent or diminish the effects of this disease from which it frequently takes months to recover. The use of gamma globulin has cut the incidence of hepatitis by fifty percent among volunteers.

Until 1968 the young Public Health Service doctors could satisfy their military obligation by serving on a two-year detail to the Peace Corps. In 1968 the Congress changed the law so that Peace Corps service no longer satisfied the National Selective Service requirement. Overnight the Peace Corps lost almost this entire supply of doctors. We were deeply worried about where to turn for replacement, but it proved to be no real problem. To our surprise, an adequate number of older doctors answered our call for help, some interrupting practices in mid-career, others coming out of retirement or deciding to put in two years in the Peace Corps before retiring. The net result for volunteers has been continued good health support.

The Peace Corps Gets a New Leader

Even with his heavy duties at the Office of Economic Opportunity, Sargent Shriver did not want to leave the Peace Corps. He had built it and had a deep affection for it. Also, I am sure he wanted to continue the active association of his name with a success (which certainly continued to be the Peace Corps' image in the United States) instead of solely with that of the poverty program, which was under political attack from its earliest days. But for that very reason, congressional pressures were building on President Johnson to have Shriver or someone devote all his time to OEO. Johnson wanted Shriver on that hot seat, and on January 18, 1966, he made his move. With his usual aversion to news leaks, he acted so quickly that Shriver was called to the White House on half an hour's notice with no inkling of why he was being summoned.

When Shriver arrived, he found one of his old lieutenants there—Jack Vaughn. The President appeared with the two men at a hastily called press conference and announced that Shriver would henceforth devote himself solely to the poverty program and that the new director of the Peace Corps—upon Senate confirmation—would be Jack Hood Vaughn.

Those who saw Shriver when he returned to his office said he appeared stunned, not by his actually being replaced—which he had known was a distinct possibility—but by the President's lack of forewarning. Jack Vaughn had even more reason to be surprised by the unexpected appointment and some reason to wonder if it was a promotion, for he was at that time Assistant Secretary of State for Inter-American Affairs.

Except for Bill Moyers' meteoric rise as President Johnson's special assistant and press secretary, Vaughn's was the most spectacular of many Peace Corps staff success stories (from the very beginning a Peace Corps executive position has been a blue chip credential for advancement both inside and outside of government). He had a modest enough beginning in government, in 1949, as director of a U.S. Information Service bi-national center in La Paz, Bolivia. Two years later he was transferred to San José, Costa Rica, to do the same job. In 1952 Vaughn transferred to the International Cooperation Administration and served for four years as program officer. He then returned to La Paz as ICA program officer where, interestingly, his immediate superior was Warren Wiggins, then deputy director of the aid mission to Bolivia. After a stint in Washington as a program officer for Europe and Africa, Vaughn received an important promotion when he was sent to Dakar in West Africa and named director of the ICA mission which was to establish aid programs in Senegal, Mali, and Mauritania. It was in Dakar that Vaughn first met the future President, when Johnson, then Vice-President, visited West Africa on a good will mission. But after more than a decade in Latin America, Vaughn's heart was there; and when Sargent Shriver offered him the chance to be director of all Latin American Peace Corps programs, he jumped at it.

Vaughn and Moyers became good friends and shared a strong emotional feeling about the Peace Corps and the importance of its mission in the world. In the spring of 1964, when President Johnson was looking for a new ambassador to reestablish diplomatic relations with Panama—following the Canal Zone riots and diplomatic rupture—Moyers suggested Vaughn's name. Although it might have seemed an assignment for a seasoned diplomat, Johnson followed his special assistant's recommendation and never had any cause to regret doing so. Vaughn assumed the post at a time of maximum tension between the two countries, and in a year's time succeeded in markedly reducing the friction. His knowledge of Panama, his obvious affection for the people, his beautiful speech-making in Spanish, the poker-playing relationship he established with President Robles, added up to a demonstration of honest friendliness that was much more needed in that heated atmosphere than correct diplomacy. Because of Vaughn's fondness for traveling throughout the country to talk with the *campesinos* and to review Peace Corps volunteers' work with them,

President Marco Robles called Vaughn *"El Embajador Campesino,"* the peasant ambassador.

President Johnson named Vaughn Assistant Secretary of State for Inter-American Affairs and Coordinator of Alliance for Progress in February 1965. He had hardly been installed in his new job when the Dominican crisis erupted. The New York *Times* commented later, "Mr. Vaughn has loyally defended Administration actions in that crisis but the evidence suggests that he was a bystander, as President Johnson and Under Secretary Mann did most of the policy making." The *Times* also observed that as a non-career diplomat, Vaughn had "been sandwiched between the career Foreign Service officers below him and the dominating personality of Under Secretary Thomas C. Mann above him."

Whether the appointment as Peace Corps director was a promotion (and as head of a semi-autonomous agency it in fact was) Jack Vaughn loved the job and had a total commitment to it. He took up his responsibilities in a way that suggested there would be little change from the Shriver years. The continued emphasis on bigness was stated forcefully in his early speeches and program decisions.[4] In one press conference he commented that he would like to see a Peace Corps volunteer assigned to every village in Africa, Asia, and Latin America. When I read that, I sent Jack a note saying that if he achieved his ambition, there would be over half a million volunteers in India and I might need some more staff. He wrote

[4] The first year of Vaughn's administration saw the development of programs in a number of new countries: Botswana, Chad, Mauritania, South Korea, Trust Territory of Micronesia, Guyana, Libya.

back telling me not to take his press remarks too literally.

But he vigorously supported the ambitious plans of Ross Pritchard, his hard-driving, numbers-conscious director of the East Asia-Pacific region. Pritchard had come to his Washington job from Turkey, where as Peace Corps rep he had quickly built the program to a peak size of 597. Pritchard firmly believed that the Peace Corps could not make an impact in a country without a large volunteer presence which would form a "critical mass" for promoting new ideas.

The Philippines program had drifted downward in size because of the highly unsatisfactory nature of the teachers' aides jobs. Under Pritchard, however, with Vaughn's early support, the figure moved up to an all-time high of 804. The most ambitious new program, however, was for the Trust Territory of Micronesia, the myriad specks of land scattered over three million square miles of the Pacific. These islands were placed in American trust by the United Nations after World War II, and such names as Saipan, Truk, Tinian, and the Marshalls conjured up many ghosts of that war for the parents of volunteers. Over five hundred volunteers were sent to Micronesia in the first wave of what was by far the most dramatic start any Peace Corps program had ever had. A highly successful campus recruiting campaign in the spring of 1966 had brought them in, and both the University of Hawaii and Westinghouse Learning Corporation were hired to train them; over ninety Micronesians were flown from the islands to Hawaii and Florida to help teach nine different dialects to the volunteers.

The Micronesian program had a great deal of appeal for

the new college graduates. The recruiting brochures announced, "The Peace Corps goes to Paradise," and a color photograph of a beautiful South Sea Island scene conjured up the traditional romantic visions. But, inside, the pamphlet talked about the woes of the islands: the lagging state of education, the depressed economic conditions, the health problems. There was trouble in paradise, the brochure stated solemnly. Most important, however, the recruiting literature spoke of American responsibility to help these islanders who had been so helplessly thrust into the savage fighting between Japan and the United States and for whom the American government had accepted a UN trusteeship. The recruiters hinted or sometimes said flatly that the Trust Territory Administration of the Interior Department—officially charged with administering the trusteeship—had not been doing much of a job but was more interested in its own quasi-colonial well-being. The Peace Corps would work for the people and would put a burr under the tail of the Interior's sterile and sluggish administration. For young men and women becoming increasingly bitter about Vietnam and unhappy generally over American foreign policy and an establishment-oriented society, both prospects seemed immensely satisfying.

In reality, the Micronesian program suffered the familiar problems of too much speed and too many volunteers. At the numerical peak, almost seven hundred volunteers were serving in the islands, which have a combined population of only ninety thousand—a ratio of one volunteer to about every one hundred and twenty Micronesians—

incomparably the richest volunteer-population mix of any
Peace Corps program.

Most of the volunteers were English teachers. English—
or some international language—is undeniably important
for Micronesians as a steppingstone to education, as a
means of doing business with the outside world, and as a
bridge between different island tongues. But there were
so many volunteers and they were spewed out so haphazardly that many of them ended up teaching in tiny
primary schools with not more than fifteen or twenty
children—not a very demanding assignment and a questionable investment of manpower and public funds.

Another group of volunteers worked in health. Their
major effort was to take an elaborate health census of the
islands under the supervision of the University of Hawaii's
School of Public Health. Their work was to be the spring-
board for other groups of health volunteers who would
carry out programs based on the census findings. What
the census revealed, however, was that general health
conditions were such that other volunteer programs were
not needed. While this of itself was good news, it did
raise a question as to whether some more careful investi-
gation at the outset would have revealed that the first
group of health workers was not really needed.

The Peace Corps program in India also had its most
dramatic growth during the early months of Jack Vaughn's
administration. Vaughn's first trip overseas in his new
capacity as director was to India, and his visit coincided
with a trip to the United States by India's prime minister,
Mrs. Indira Gandhi. Mrs. Gandhi made her trip in late
March, 1966, less than three months after assuming office,

and its principal purpose was to bring India's plight more forcefully to the attention of the American people, most especially the President and Congress.

After two years of poor rains, the Indian monsoons failed almost completely in 1965, leaving the country desperately short of food grains. The annual harvest of wheat, rice, and other grains fell from a level of eighty-eight million metric tons to seventy-four million in the 1965–66 season. The most severe famine was in the rice-eating states of Kerala, Mysore, Madhya Pradesh, and West Bengal; food riots broke out in Kerala and other parts of the country. Grain rationing was instituted in cities.

India's need for imported grains in 1966 was estimated at between eleven and fourteen million tons. Clearly, the largest portion would have to come from the United States, and President Johnson had been slow in giving his support to the massive transfer of grain and other needed foodstuffs such as milk powder and vegetable oil. He wanted some assurance that India would not squander its precious resources on further conflict with Pakistan such as that of 1965, which cost the two nations an estimated six billion dollars; but most of all he wanted evidence that India was going to give top priority to increasing its agricultural production, if necessary at the expense of its industrial development. If such conditions amounted to interference in India's internal affairs, at least the President's motives were no more sinister than to see that U.S. aid was not wasted.

The prime minister came armed with the blueprint for a vigorous new Indian emphasis on agriculture, but the

President seemed to be even more impressed by the personal qualities of graciousness, quiet strength, and political wisdom that Mrs. Gandhi brought with her. On March 30, 1966, President Johnson sent a message to Congress in which he restated his interest in the world food supply and his especial concern for the grave problem in India.

"I am asking the endorsement of the Congress for a program that is small neither in its magnitude or concept," the message said, and went on to propose the supplying to India of six to seven million tons of food grains as well as one hundred fifty million pounds of vegetable oil and one hundred twenty-five million pounds of milk powder. In a part of the message that was to become extremely significant to the Peace Corps, the President said:

> India's Government has adopted a far-reaching program to increase fertilizer production, improve water and soil management, provide rural credit, improve plant protection, and control food loss. These essentials must be accompanied by a strong training and education program.
>
> If they can be used, I feel certain that American agricultural experts would respond to an appeal to serve in India as a part of an Agricultural Training Corps or through an expanded Peace Corps.

On the following day, March 31, a cable from Warren Wiggins to Jack Vaughn arrived in New Delhi. Citing the presidential message, Wiggins said it seemed to him like a direct challenge to the Peace Corps to increase dramatically the number of volunteers in India in the field of food production. He conjectured that by priority recruiting, the Peace Corps could send one thousand new volunteers to India by the end of 1966, some of them agricultural specialists to backstop the BA generalists who would receive special training in food production.

We had about seven hundred volunteers in India at that time, and my staff and I had projected another four hundred to be phased in during the year. To have that figure increased by one hundred fifty percent seemed to me to be courting disaster, especially with the increase to be made up mainly of generalists in agricultural work. I objected to Washington, but my protests were those of a lame duck rep because I had already received my orders to report to Washington and become director of training. Plans for the dramatic response to the President's challenge went forward.

The results were entirely predictable. A campaign to recruit substantial numbers of volunteers with farm backgrounds or agricultural degrees failed completely. The new groups were made up almost entirely of BA generalists, and their training was for the most part inferior because of the haste and size of the operation. The programs in which the new volunteers were to work were hastily contrived and their individual locations inadequately scouted. Because of other desperate staff needs around the world, my two very able deputies, Francis Macy and Glen Fishbach, were taken from India at this time and made country representatives in Tunisia and Iran. At this time of unparalleled growth, the Peace Corps in India had a completely new change of top staff. To make matters worse, if possible, the supply of male volunteers ran low and a fairly large number of women

volunteers were recruited for these rural agricultural assignments—over the strong but unheeded protests of Macy
before he went to Tunisia.

The experiences of the volunteers who went to India
during this big build-up were equally predictable. As had
been the case with badly conceived programs from the
beginning of the Peace Corps, a minority overcame their
handicaps of background, training, and fuzzy assignments
and developed useful work for themselves; the staff was
able to find suitable new jobs for some others. But the
majority either resigned and came back to the United
States or spent their two years in India with the frustration
of knowing that they had not really been a help to the
Indians.

An embittered woman volunteer from this period in
India wrote to *The Volunteer,* the Peace Corps' in-house
magazine, that she and her husband had been in India
for one year without work. She said in part:

> The problem now seems to us—Peace Corps didn't
> find us a job. They said they did, but we don't have
> one, and I think a fairly good case can be made that
> they could have suspected as much before we came.
> . . . I am told to "branch out," to be "creative."
> Frankly, we've tried and been unsuccessful—we're
> failures then. And to make matters worse, since we
> haven't produced anything, or come up with some-
> thing clever, our pleas are not quite listened to—we
> are dismissed as cranks.
>   . . . We would like to ask: How many other Vol-
> unteers are stuck without jobs, were sent into "un-

structured" programs and told to be "creative" and found only emptiness? . . . It seems to us that the Peace Corps has not fulfilled the responsibility it had to us, of finding us a job for two years. It has played a big game with us, gotten us to India, given us a "site," put us on a list, and is not taking responsibility for the consequences of that action.

In March 1967, I returned to India briefly and had occasion to talk to an Indian agricultural officer who had received one of the volunteers from the big build-up of the previous year. This was the first volunteer he had ever been assigned.

"He knew nothing of agriculture," the Indian said, "and I realized immediately that the Peace Corps is not a program of technical assistance but rather one of cultural exchange. I am not opposed to cultural exchange, but we should not receive it under the false label of agricultural help. Our problem is too serious for that."

I wish I could have told him that his case was the exception; but at that particular moment in the Peace Corps' history, I knew the opposite was true.

CHAPTER FOUR

A Step Toward Maturity: 1967–69

Jack Vaughn was a traveling director. He spent fully a third of his time flying around the world to talk to volunteers, trainees, and staff. He visited all but a few of the countries with Peace Corps programs, and the number reached sixty during his years as director.[1] He was also a listening director. Every overseas staff member returning to Washington on business was automatically booked for a leisurely talk with Jack, and he saw as many former volunteers passing through the Washington office as he possibly could. By the time a year had passed, he had a thoroughly detailed knowledge of the total Peace Corps program, its strengths and weaknesses, its promise and problems.

Vaughn also had a very different administrative style from Shriver's. Shriver put men and ideas in conflict and frequently achieved brilliant results by carefully controlling the tensions that developed. Vaughn was quiet, low-

[1] The additional countries to receive Peace Corps programs during the years 1967–69 were Paraguay, Gambia, Tonga, Western Samoa, Upper Volta, Lesotho, Fiji, Dahomey, and also Ceylon, which terminated its association with the Peace Corps in 1964, invited a new group of volunteers in 1968.

keyed, sought to reduce staff conflict. He did away with an upper crust layer of associate directors and made himself much more available than Shriver had been to his four regional directors and to the directors of the offices of recruiting, selection, training, and management: the operational arms of the Peace Corps in Washington. This group, together with Vaughn and his deputy, formed the "operations committee" of the Peace Corps; and, while conflict never died out in the Peace Corps, a real spirit of teamwork, respect, and even affection grew up among these men.

As quickly as he could, Vaughn filled these key jobs with men who had had long and successful staff experience with the Peace Corps overseas; and he did not necessarily equate success with a person's having built or run a big program. As his director for Africa, for example, he chose C. Payne Lucas, a young Negro who had been on the staff of a small Togo program and then had served as rep in Niger. The Niger program had had less than fifty volunteers when Lucas was rep, but the dedication and industry of the group in that bleak desert country had become almost a Peace Corps legend; and Lucas had established a rapport with Niger President Hamani Diori that is unmatched in Peace Corps annals. During a state visit to the United States, President Diori stated, "I consider the Peace Corps the best gift that the United States has made to Niger."

For his North Africa-Near East-South Asia director Vaughn named Robert Steiner. Steiner started the Peace Corps program in Afghanistan, and in the beginning the volunteers—like all foreigners in the country—were confined to the capital city of Kabul by government order. When Steiner left after four years, the volunteers had so won the government's confidence that they were working in the most remote parts of the country. The director of selection became Joseph Farrell, who had been executive officer of an atomic submarine, the *Woodrow Wilson*, before resigning from the Navy to join the Peace Corps. Farrell had served on the staff as rep in Honduras and had built a reputation as the man who got things done. Selection, with over one hundred and forty staff members plus a number of psychologists on part-time duty, had always been the division of the Peace Corps with the greatest coordination problems. Farrell's job was to keep up or improve the professional quality of selection while making the whole operation run more efficiently.

Seymour Greben, the rep in Malaysia and a man who had a magic touch with volunteers, became director of recruiting at a time when—because of the war in Vietnam —magic was needed in the job. Douglas Stafford, a refugee from the business world and IBM, who did much to straighten out a demoralized Peace Corps program in Liberia, was chosen as director of management. Paul Sack, who ran the sensitive and politically troubled Tanzania program for two years, became director of program planning and review. While Sack's division was not strictly operational, his shop—which replaced the old murder boards—was so vital to everything we did that he was a member of the operations committee. William Moffett, director of the program in Chile and a man with years of Latin American experience, received Vaughn's nod as director for that region. I was his director of training.

In only one instance did Vaughn deviate from his principle of bringing in men with maximum Peace Corps field experience to fill these key positions. For a long time he had tried to get Russell Davis, Professor of Education and Development at Harvard, to join his staff, but Davis's many commitments made such a move impossible for him. In 1968 Vaughn was determined to get the strongest man possible to take over the seriously inflated East Asia-Pacific region with its huge Micronesia and Philippine programs. He sent me to Cambridge with instructions not to come back until I had persuaded Davis to take the job.

Fortunately, Russ Davis is one of my closest friends, and I know well his questing and restless spirit, which has taken him to years of development work in places like Nicaragua and Ethiopia, a visiting professorship in Korea, and short-term consultation jobs in a dozen other countries in Asia, Africa, and Latin America. In a couple of evenings talking with him at his home I was able to get him deeply interested in what we were trying to do to make the Peace Corps a more effective organization. He applied for a leave of absence from the Center for Studies in Education and Development, which his dean reluctantly approved. In Davis, Jack Vaughn had acquired an experienced administrator, a man with a vast knowledge of the problems of education in developing countries, and one of the world's few real experts in planning human resource development.

I have the greatest admiration for Vaughn's performance after his early shakedown months as director. As his experience and knowledge grew, he knew that some basic changes had to take place in the Peace Corps if it was to

survive. He began to support positions and policies some
of which were diametrically opposed to his old days of
cramming volunteers into unstructured CD programs.
The men he brought onto his senior Washington team
showed his determination to put the overseas experience
of staff and their volunteers to work in reshaping the
Peace Corps.

Though it is no doubt an overgeneralization, it has always seemed to me that Shriver was most preoccupied
with the image of the Peace Corps—as I think in those
formative years he should have been—and that Jack
Vaughn became most concerned with the substance of the
Peace Corps: how to be sure that there was a real piece
of work for volunteers who were sent overseas, how to
see that they were best prepared for that work, how to
give them the best support possible.

I think Jack expressed it best one night when he and I
sat late in his office talking about what the press and congressional reactions would be to a significantly smaller
Peace Corps. "They'll say we're losing our charisma and
that the fire is gone," Jack said. He lighted his pipe carefully and then added, "But what I'd like to do is make the
Peace Corps as good as Sarge said it was."

Wiggins Resigns

Warren Wiggins resigned as deputy director on February 1, 1967. No one but Sargent Shriver had at that time
remotely influenced the development of the Peace Corps
to the extent Wiggins had, but in his year as Vaughn's
deputy he withdrew increasingly from decision making

and from active participation in the agency's policy debates. He and Vaughn were friends, but the fact that on
two earlier occasions in their careers Wiggins had been
Vaughn's immediate superior probably created an awk-
wardness between them in their new relationship. In any
case, Wiggins wanted to move on, and he was eager to
try out some of his Peace Corps theories in a private firm
for which he had received financial backing.

No one who worked with "Wig" will forget his idea-a-
minute mind, his bureaucratic savvy, his administrative
firmness. His two major contributions to the Peace Corps
as it evolved in the early years were the concept of bigness, the dramatic start with large numbers, and the
emergence of a directly administered Peace Corps rather
than one that reviewed and financed volunteer programs
of other organizations. Direct administration was the
means by which the big, dramatic, fast start was possible.
The emphasis on numbers and the neglect of other institutions and organizations that wanted a more vital association with the Peace Corps caused great problems for
the agency. The fact remains, however, that a Peace
Corps with exciting numbers working in dozens of countries in the first eighteen months and a Peace Corps that
quickly developed its own image and style were responsible for the national acclaim and world attention the
young agency achieved. They were the ideas that were
right for that moment in the Peace Corps' history, and they
belonged to Wiggins more than to anyone else.

Warren Wiggins probably weighs one hundred forty
pounds after a good meal. But when President Johnson
nominated me to follow him as deputy director of the

Peace Corps—a nomination recommended by Jack Vaughn, of course—I stepped into a pair of giant shoes.

BA Generalists for Specialist Jobs

Our experience in India with liberal arts volunteers working in poultry was by no means an isolated phenomenon in the Peace Corps world. In Chile scores of generalist volunteers worked effectively in the country's forestry program. Their jobs were in reforestation, working with villages in planting and caring for new trees on the barren Andean slopes. They have been responsible for the planting of over five million trees, and the Chilean forestry department consistently asked for new groups of these volunteers.

In Malawi volunteers with no medical background were trained to give and read tuberculosis skin tests, collect sputum specimens, and learn to look for symptoms such as coughing, chest pain, night sweats, and loss of weight. Initial studies showed that there might be as many as fifty thousand cases of tuberculosis in Malawi and a much higher infection rate than in other countries. Since there are only about eight hundred hospital beds in the entire country, the volunteers were taught to administer medicine to infected persons in their villages and to monitor their progress by keeping checks on their symptoms, temperature, and weight and by arranging for periodic X-ray and sputum examinations. In one year the volunteers tested thirty-three thousand Malawians and diagnosed and began treatment of over one thousand cases of tuberculosis. A similar project in Bolivia was

equally effective. In Togo generalist volunteers were
trained to help start and run an inland fisheries project,
and in Thailand and the Philippines BA generalists
worked with real success in malaria control programs.

These Peace Corps projects, and a few others like them,
stood out as oases of success in a sea of unstructured community development, vaguely defined rural public health
activity, and equally vague rural community action and
urban community action projects—all of which produced
a few outstanding volunteer successes and much confusion, inactivity, and failure. In late 1966 and 1967, as
Vaughn pulled his experienced field men in to form
his Washington team, we began to see the oases more
clearly. Perhaps, as reps working individually, we had
always seen the one or two in our own countries but
had not realized their significance in the years when numbers dominated the Peace Corps. Charlie Peters's evaluation reports had certainly spotted these projects as
winners; but Charlie's evaluation shop was not involved
in operations, and his reports tended to cause a stir of excitement or resentment and then somehow get filed away.

But now those of us who had worked with scores of
projects and hundreds or even thousands of volunteers
were together on the same team, and we knew that the
dominant patterns of the past had to be changed. In the
field there were now experienced reps—in many cases our
deputies or other staff who had moved up[2]—who spoke
our language, sometimes better than we did. The message

[2] For example, four members of the staff in India when I was in charge
there went on to become able and successful reps: Glen Fishbach in Iran,
Felix Knauth in Somalia, Francis Macy in both Tunisia and Nigeria,
Kellogg Smith in Tunisia.

that began to be heard and understood was that numbers were no longer the important thing. What was important· were clearly defined projects with clearly defined volunteer responsibilities for which persons with liberal arts backgrounds could be clearly trained.

There was more to it than that, of course. Experience had taught us that if there was to be much chance of project success the project had to be in a field that was important to the host government, an activity on which it put a true priority. More than anything else this meant education and agriculture. In education we, for the most part, did all right, as I have tried to make clear earlier in this book. But how to do anything in agriculture with English and history majors?

Shortly before I left India I called together the agricultural representatives of the Ford and Rockefeller foundations, AID, the UN Food and Agriculture Organization, and a couple of senior Indian government agriculturalists and asked them that same question: Could BA generalists do anything useful in agriculture in India? They were fascinated with the problem and spent the whole afternoon throwing out ideas and talking them over.

They had all known volunteers, and they agreed that some of their most important assets were dedication, industry, patience: all important qualities in extension work. And everyone agreed that if you took a narrow enough, a sharply enough defined, slice of agriculture, you could teach such a person all he needed to know to be technically competent in that one thing. They suggested such things as Mexican wheat in Madras and the new "miracle" rice in West Bengal and talked about how a person could learn enough about them in three or four months to be sure of what he was doing. If the person were then put in an area where the state department of agriculture was pushing the development of such a crop, he might really help promote a priority program.

What these men were talking about, of course, was what we had already done, somewhat by accident, in poultry and what the Peace Corps had done elsewhere in forestry, tuberculosis and malaria control, fisheries, and a few other things. They were saying it could be done with food crops.

So we decided to try it, though I was back in Washington before the staff—and mainly Kellogg Smith, the director in south India—got it underway. They picked a program that the state government of Mysore was intensely interested in: the promoting of the new hybrids—maize, wheat, sorghum, millet—in a recently irrigated part of the state. The volunteers' job training concentrated exclusively on what they would need to know in order to talk about and demonstrate the growing of these hybrids—particularly maize and wheat—in that part of south India. All generalities, peripheral information about agriculture, extraneous subjects were rigorously weeded out. Most important: the hybrid grain training took place at a village level training center in Mysore, near where the volunteers were going to work. The other intensive part of their training was in Telegu, the language of that part of India.

The staff worked carefully and long in deciding where to place the volunteers. Something new was tried: Volunteers were assigned alone in villages but only in villages where a "sponsor" could be found, a progressive farmer who would offer the volunteer hospitality, free housing, and at least a small piece of land where the volunteer could plant demonstration crops. The hosts were selected on the basis of interest they showed in growing hybrid grains and of course on their willingness to receive a volunteer. Their only payment was any help the volunteer might give them with their crops.

The project produced no miracles, but by a number of measures it could be counted a success. And miracles hadn't been expected. The volunteers had been seen by the Mysore government, by the Peace Corps staff, and by themselves as simply an additional work force, a supplement to the regular Indian extension agents, or village level workers, of whom there weren't nearly enough. The host idea did work, and the volunteers, in this environment with no other native English speaker close by, made much faster progress in getting a working command of the language than volunteers assigned in pairs. Almost all said they preferred this single assignment after they got used to it and did not want to be teamed up with other volunteers.

The volunteers did not keep any precise records for some time, but a survey of fifteen of them working in one district revealed that in that planting season they had assisted farmers in planting twenty-one acres of hybrid millet, twenty-eight acres of hybrid sorghum, ninety-six acres of hybrid maize, and almost two hundred acres of Mexican wheat. The volunteers were working with about five farmers each, which meant that their contribution to grain production but much more importantly to spreading the message of the high yielding hybrids—and providing visual evidence for thousands of other farmers—was not inconsiderable.

Speaking of the volunteers' contribution, the Deputy Director of Agriculture in Raichur District, who had twenty-four volunteers working with him, said: "In Raichur District, where irrigation has come very recently, farmers have to learn a lot about irrigation. And demonstrations under irrigation were our main item of work through which we wanted to put it across to the farmers that a certain 'package' of practices was necessary to ensure a good crop. These boys have done very well in taking up the demonstrations. They were ready to go into farmers' fields from morning until evening—work with the farmers, take up the sowing, show them how to use fertilizers, how to spray their crops with pesticides, how to level their lands, and how to irrigate. They would do all this, and keep continuously following it up 'til harvest."

Strong evidence that the agricultural authorities of Mysore were and are satisfied is that they have continued to ask for additional "batches" (as the Indians say) of volunteers to carry on this kind of work. For me, however, the most convincing evidence is the volunteers themselves, who are invariably the sternest judges of what they have accomplished. I have met several volunteers from that experimental Mysore group, and every one I have talked with felt that his achievement coincided reasonably with his expectations.

"I've heard a lot of questions about whether volunteers produce as much food as they eat," one said. "I know damned well I did, and a lot more will be produced because I was there."

As I have said, this concept of sharp, highly specific job definition coupled with careful site selection had been developing in a number of Peace Corps programs around the world, but beginning in 1967 it slowly grew into a dominant Peace Corps programming philosophy. In the field of food production in the Peace Corps, wheat became the focus in Afghanistan, Nepal, and Morocco; rice in the Philippines with some activity in Ceylon and India; sugar beets in Iran; potatoes in Bolivia; in Ecuador and a number of other countries, cattle and sheep production.

Together with this approach to using BA generalists in food production grew the practice of placing the few trained or experienced agriculturists who did join the Peace Corps so that they could play a backstopping role for the generalists. Out of a group of forty volunteers, four or five might have ag degrees or real farm experience. If they were carefully located they could carry on their own work as volunteers and still be a real help to the BA generalists in their area. We also tried to recruit more specialists and fewer generalists as staff members and had some success at this. But, even with these aids, the generalist was still ninety-five percent on his own and he made it that way.

In the Latin America region under Bill Moffett, and with Jack Vaughn's complete blessing, the old unstructured community development approach slowly—but not without a good deal of anguish—gave way to the new concepts of programming and training. More and more projects with a clear and sharp focus for volunteer activity began to show up in that region:[3] raising the size and quality of potatoes and introducing improved sheep shearing methods on the Altiplano of Bolivia, improving swine production in Chile, providing a credit program and extension help for potato growers in Peru.

Not that the Latin American volunteers or staff gave up on the concept of community development. If anything, they became even more committed to it as the years passed, but not to the unstructured, free lance variety that had caused such frustration and disappointment. Now strong host country structures or programs for the volunteers to work within began to be sought. And so that volunteers could have a meaningful place in such programs, a specific job was identified for them, and they were given sharply focused skill training for it. The idea was the same as that now growing steadily in the other Peace Corps programs. In the Latin American region, however, the switch to specific job responsibilities within government programs was a more traumatic change from the free-wheeling patterns of earlier years in Latin America.

The community development interest was retained, however, and all volunteers who went into these programs were given training in CD philosophy and techniques. The job and the job skill were seen merely as the entry into the community, the means by which the volunteer established his credibility. He might be helping the Boliv-

[3] Such projects had been present here and there for years in Latin America in specialized, non-CD, fields. I have mentioned the Bolivia tuberculosis project. In Colombia a major project in television education was a distinct success. In Ecuador volunteers had been working at rural electrification since 1963.

ian Indians grow better potatoes or get much more wool from their sheep and process it better, but his major purpose in being there was to try to help them see that by working together they could do more for themselves and get a fairer share of government services to which they were entitled. It is true that the best volunteers everywhere in the world brought this extra, and perhaps most important, dimension to their work; but in Latin America it was always heavily stressed. Many volunteers never saw beyond the potatoes and the sheep, of course, but—unlike the old days when it was succeed as a community organizer or fail completely—they could now feel that they had done something to justify their two years in a country.

When the Latin America country reps assembled for their annual conference in the summer of 1968, there was not one dissenting voice from a special CD committee's clearly enunciated view that the only sensible way for the Peace Corps to proceed in community development was for the volunteer to have a clear-cut job and the skill to do it and that the job be within the framework or program of a strong host country agency.

"Gentlemen," Bill Moffett said, as he listened to the unanimous agreement with this position, "we have come to the end of an era."

The Emergence of Training

From the early days of 1961 Shriver had assured the American public in general and the Congress specifically that Peace Corps volunteers would be well prepared for their demanding work and life before they were sent overseas. Being well prepared called for an almost frightening combination of skills, knowledge, and attitudes: The volunteer would have to possess the technical skills to do the job for which he had been recruited. He would have to have a reasonable facility with the local language. He would need a knowledge of the country to which he was going, an understanding of its people, and a respect for and appreciation of their culture. He would need a knowledge and understanding of America sufficient to talk intelligently to interested and perhaps suspicious foreigners. He would have to be physically, mentally, and emotionally, ready to live in a culture radically different from his own.

How was this to be done? How could it be done without a training period that would be longer than the volunteer's service? And, clearly, a few months—three or four at the most—were all that could be taken out of the prospective volunteer's two-year commitment for training; nor would the Peace Corps' budget permit more.

The first director of Peace Corps training was Dr. Joseph Kauffman, who had earlier in his career served as dean of students at Brandeis University.[4] Dr. Kauffman quite logically turned to America's colleges and universities for help. If the expertise for the Herculean training task ahead was to be found anywhere, it was surely there. The response from higher education was extremely gratifying. Professors, research specialists, deans, and presidents converged on Washington from all over the nation, responding on a moment's notice and breaking

[4] Dr. Kauffman is now president of the University of Rhode Island.

long-standing engagements if necessary to do their bit for the new Peace Corps. Sessions lasting into the early morning hours were held on how to train volunteers in languages, foreign cultures, American studies, staying healthy, international affairs, physical conditioning, community development, teaching English as a foreign language, and a number of other technical skills. In some cases detailed training plans were prepared.

Scores of schools offered their facilities and staffs to help the volunteers get ready. Just a few of the colleges and universities to answer the early call for help were the University of Michigan, the University of California at Berkeley, Michigan State University, Antioch, Northern Illinois University, Texas Western College, UCLA, Georgetown University, Harvard, Notre Dame. Great or small, famous or little known, they wanted to be a part of the Peace Corps idea.

And yet, with all the attention and cooperation it received from American academia, training almost immediately became the whipping boy for all Peace Corps disappointments and failures, and the whipping boy it remained for years. The volunteers themselves were most vociferous in expressing their unhappiness with training. In the first place, when they volunteered for the Peace Corps they had expected to step into a new and exciting world. Instead, usually just a month or two after graduating from college, they found themselves right back on campus, sitting in the same classrooms from which they had just escaped. They were hearing the same professors lecture on American history and government, on the geography and culture of the countries to which they were going, on international communism in the world today.

They were attending language classes and laboratories, but most of them knew they were not getting nearly as much language training as they needed. Except for those who were going to be teachers, their job training was usually an assortment of general lectures or superficial demonstrations on a variety of things they might be doing when they reached their assigned country. Whether his trainers or the Peace Corps knew it or not, the volunteer knew—with a feeling of frustration and fear in his guts—that he had not been trained to do anything.

One of the worst things about the three-month period had nothing directly to do with the content of training but rather with the constant concern of who would finally be selected to be volunteers and who would be "deselected." Throughout the training period, the trainees were observed and rated by a pair of psychologists, the training staff, and sometimes a psychiatrist. "Mid-boards" and "final boards" were convened at which these persons gathered to discuss every trainee in meticulous detail and to decide which of them were qualified to become volunteers and which were not. Trainees detested this feeling of being constantly under a microscope and on trial, and much of their creative energy went into trying to figure out the responses and actions that would win the approbation of the training staff and "assessment" officers. In some of the more unenlightened programs assessment and the fear of deselection were actually used to intensify the pressure on the trainees and heighten the tension they were naturally under. This was done apparently on the theory that it would reveal something about the trainee's stability and ability to stand up under pressure. In the early days I saw a group of new volunteers arrive in their country of assignment almost in a state of shock from the selection strain they had been under and coldly furious about the ordeal they had been put through.

The Peace Corps reps who received the volunteers were equally dissatisfied with training, chiefly for one reason: The volunteers were too often not able to do the things the reps had told the host government officials they were going to do. The reps grumbled about other things: The volunteers' language level was too low, they seemed tense and unsure of themselves, they didn't have the "Peace Corps spirit." But the reps' major indictment of training was that it did not get their volunteers ready to do a job. The reps made their opinion of training loudly known to Shriver and to their regional directors. As a result, the various directors of training and their training officers were among the most harassed individuals in the Washington Peace Corps headquarters.

There were good training programs, of course, even from the beginning. The first group of volunteers to go to Ghana received their training at the University of California at Berkeley. The training program was directed by David Apter, a distinguished young Africanist whose specialty is Ghana. From his vast personal knowledge he could make the country and its problems come alive. He could tell the volunteers specifically and in detail what they would encounter as teachers in Ghana and how they could best get ready to succeed. I talked to many of the

Ghana 1 volunteers when they vacationed in Nigeria, and they all had high praise for their training—a rare thing indeed. The training of the early Tanganyika volunteer surveyors, first at Texas Western and later in Tanganyika, was considered successful. The first volunteer teachers for India who received their training at the University of Wisconsin, Milwaukee campus, were very satisfied with their program, as was I.

But these were infrequent exceptions. Inevitably, perhaps, the Peace Corps vented much of its frustration over training failures on the colleges and universities that had volunteered to help them. Peace Corps staff charged with training liaison nagged the university contractors about spending too much time and placing too much emphasis on the academic part of training: cultural, historical, and geographic area studies; American history and government; world affairs and communism. They complained that the universities weren't using their best people in Peace Corps training. They complained that their language teaching methods were old-fashioned, better suited to getting Ph.D. candidates ready to pass reading tests than volunteers to speak to farmers in the African bush.

Most of all the Peace Corps complained that the universities weren't putting enough time in on job skill training and weren't being effective in the time they did devote to it. There was less criticism of the preparation of volunteers for teaching assignments, but even in that category, the Peace Corps felt the universities weren't providing for enough practice teaching. In general broadsides of criticism about the quality of training, the

Peace Corps accused higher education of being rigid, timid, unimaginative, and slow.

In the early 1960s American academia was in no mood to take that kind of criticism from such an upstart organization as the Peace Corps. They in turn accused the Peace Corps of being chaotic, fickle, impertinent, shallow, and faddish. A dean at a prominent Eastern university, announcing to the press a rupture with the Peace Corps, stated that "no university worth its salt" would let a government agency tell it how to do its job. In a number of cases powerful university presidents brought senatorial and even White House pressure to bear on the Peace Corps to try to keep it from breaking off a training contract it was unhappy with.

The facts are that most of the criticism of both the Peace Corps and the universities of each other were basically accurate. Universities did overemphasize the academic parts of training because they were best equipped to offer lectures on geography, history, anthropology, and so forth. Most of the schools did not have language professors with the backgrounds necessary to organize high intensity programs focused on speaking facility; and even if they had, where were the teaching materials for such languages as Quechua, Twi, Fang, Kapingamarangi, and Kissi? In general they did prefer to keep training in a familiar classroom format and on campus. Without a doubt, their job training—except for preparing teachers—was weak, often very weak.

Yet most of the universities' shortcomings in training could be traced to the Peace Corps. The Peace Corps grew at such a pace that its actions did at times border

on chaos. To mount any kind of decent program a training institution needed four or five months to put its
staff together, get a detailed picture of what the volunteers needed to learn, and pull their course materials
together. Instead, a school was lucky to get two months'
notice, and many a training program was put together in
two weeks. University of Hawaii officials insist that a
planeload of trainees arrived at Honolulu airport one day
with absolutely no advance notice from the Peace Corps
that they were coming. Frequently the Peace Corps kept
a university dangling for months over the possibility of
training a group of volunteers; usually the training contract was signed, but sometimes it did fall through, and
the university could not give a firm commitment to any of
its faculty members about Peace Corps summer employment (when seventy-five percent of all training took
place). Under these conditions it is little wonder that
the best faculty people were often not available to the
Peace Corps.

The basic problem was that the Peace Corps overseas
staffs simply could not put projects together fast enough
to take care of the large numbers of May and June graduates interested in becoming volunteers. The projects were
frequently so hastily and sloppily devised that a rep
would sometimes cable in many changes in what the
volunteers were going to do after the training program
was half finished. No institution could manage good training under such conditions. Training program directors
often built their programs with the scantiest kind of
information about what the volunteers' jobs were to be.

The Peace Corps sought panaceas for its training woes

in new theories, ideas, and sometimes gimmicks. At various times it urged its training contractors to concentrate on sensitivity training, high intensity language sessions, physical training (throwing volunteers into a pool of water with their hands and feet tied to make them confident and self-reliant), training in slums and on Indian reservations, and hiring former volunteers to do much of the training. The training institutions always went along with these new directions, sometimes agreeably, sometimes with ill grace, but increasingly with weary observations about the Peace Corps' latest fad to save training.

It is rather astonishing that, despite the conditions under which training was done for so many years, so many good university people and so many good universities stayed with us. Such schools as the University of California (UCLA, Berkeley, and Davis campuses), Dartmouth, Antioch, and the Universities of Wisconsin and Hawaii never gave up on the Peace Corps, and through their patience training did get better and selection more humane as time went on. Some of the training devices the Peace Corps wanted to push—such as training off-campus and saturation language learning—were sound, and when they were the universities successfully developed them. In many cases the ideas actually came from the university people who were deeply interested in the Peace Corps.

There were pay-offs for the schools that stuck with the Peace Corps training. Dean R. Freeman Butts of Columbia Teachers College—which trained hundreds of volunteer teachers and trained them well—once told me that many faculty members considered the Peace Corps a source of many of their most capable and most interesting graduate students. They had first come to Teachers College as Peace Corps trainees, liked the school and the faculty they met, and returned after their Peace Corps service. The dean of another Eastern school told me that the presence of Peace Corps training programs on its campus over the years had revolutionized language teaching in the school itself. And of course the opportunity for faculty members to travel in Africa, Asia, and Latin America in connection with training programs was attractive to both the schools and the faculty persons involved.

But even though there were some evolutionary, incremental improvements in training over the years, there was no way that the really fundamental advances necessary could be made until the Peace Corps itself changed some of its ways and shed some of its myths. In 1966 training was still as much maligned as it had been in 1962. The regional staffs and the Division of Training in Washington had for years carried on a demoralizing, internecine warfare, each accusing the other of responsibility for training disasters. The Division of Training maintained that the regions failed to supply project information vital to building training programs and that they made capricious and fatally late changes in training requirements. The regions complained that training officers didn't keep them informed and chose training institutions without consultation with the region concerned. The training institutions complained that they received instructions, often flatly contradictory, from both the Division of Training and the regions.

When Jack Vaughn offered me the job as Director of Training, John Alexander, who knew the Washington situation as well as any man, advised me not to take it. His reasons were two: Training could never do all of the things expected of it and hence would always be marked with failure. Secondly, the regional directors had always had and would always have the ear of the Peace Corps Director. Their recitation of the reasons for training failures would always be heard more clearly than the background voice of the training director. It was a loser's job.

I realized that Alexander was probably right. I knew that the regions dominated the Peace Corps. I was aware of the exaggerated public claims made about training and of the angry frustration in the agency when the Division of Training and training institutions could not produce the Public Information Office's image of the ideally trained volunteer. I certainly knew that the basis of all good training had to be sound program development by the field staffs, for I had seen my own faulty programming lead inevitably to weak training. There was no reason to believe that I, like every training director before me, would not be at the mercy of the regions and the reps.

I took the job, however, because Jack Vaughn wanted me to, and I never regretted the decision. In fact the nine months I spent in training, before becoming deputy director, were among the most interesting of all my time in the Peace Corps. I had the good fortune to take over that heretofore hangdog division at just the right time.

Jack's style of stressing cooperation made it easy for me to carry that message to the training staff and to promote it in the regions. More basic, as I have indicated earlier, the men that Jack was bringing into Washington in key staff spots had had many of the same experiences overseas and had learned the same lessons. We spoke the same Peace Corps language. When Frank Mankiewicz left, taking with him his driving determination to pack as many volunteers as possible into Latin America for revolutionary purposes, no matter what their training or experience, my task became much easier. Bill Moffett believed in community development, but he also believed that a volunteer should have a job and know how to do it.

In this climate it was easy to stress the fundamental point that we could not have good training unless we had a clear and detailed picture of what the volunteers were going to do overseas. It is a source of amazement to me now that it took us six years to learn that decent training was impossible unless the trainers knew what the volunteers were supposed to do overseas. But we were always running in those early years, and emotion was always valued over analysis in the Peace Corps. If we did not invent the phrase "gut feeling," we raised its use to a high art as a means of winning arguments.

A second fundamental point that found growing acceptance was that if you tried to train a volunteer to do too many things, he would end up unable to do anything. Of course Alfred North Whitehead and other educators had made that discovery long before we did in the Peace Corps, but somehow we had not got the message. To stress this point about training of course put the burden where it had to be—on the field staff who had to identify jobs specific and limited enough that training for them was possible.

I do not mean to suggest that these changes, so crucially different from the Peace Corps' earlier programming practices, took place overnight or with great ease. They were still evolving in 1969 when Jack and I and most of Jack's senior Washington team left the Peace Corps.

Another aspect of training in which Jack was most interested was to increase the emphasis on language training. As a fluent speaker of Spanish and a good speaker of French, he knew that no single tool would be as valuable to a volunteer as a reasonable command of the language of the country to which he was going. The Peace Corps had always paid lip service to the importance of language and had made extravagant claims about volunteers speaking African and Asian languages. The facts are that from the beginning fairly good Spanish and French training took place because volunteers going to Latin America and French-speaking Africa were utterly helpless unless they had a decent base in those languages on which to build. But with few exceptions volunteers outside those language areas went to their assignments with totally inadequate language preparation. They might have a small vocabulary, be able to utter some amenities and ask simple questions, but they could not carry on a sensible conversation. Always a few of the most linguistically accomplished and most determined volunteers acquired a good speaking command of the language during their two years abroad, but most did not.

Great variation had always existed in the number of hours spent on language learning in training programs. Some early programs budgeted fewer than one hundred hours for language and three hundred was about the maximum that the most enthusiastic language supporters in training could manage. Clear guidelines did not exist. How much language learning went into a training program depended upon how a number of people felt about its importance: the rep, the training project director, the Washington training officer, the desk officer, the regional director. They rarely agreed.

Charlie Peters had for years hammered the importance of maximum language training in his evaluation reports and had finally prevailed upon Shriver to decree that all training programs must have three hundred hours of language. This was a major breakthrough, but the policy was probably ignored as many times as it was observed, as I learned from a survey I made in 1966. But Jack's unrelenting determination to get more language into training was a powerful help to me as was a 1966 research report by Dr. John Carroll, an outstanding linguist who has been of great help to the Peace Corps. Dr. Carroll's report, entitled *A Parametric Study of Language Learning in the Peace Corps,* put forth convincing evidence that a volunteer with no previous knowledge of the target language would need four hundred contact hours of training to achieve the level of "two" on the foreign service language scale, and the FS-2 means nothing more than that the speaker can carry on limited social and work-related conversations. The scale goes on up to FS-5, which means the speaker is bilingual.

The Carroll report made the additional point that volunteers who arrived in a country below the FS-2 level frequently did not achieve that level for from five to six months. Furthermore, Dr. Carroll's study concerned Spanish, an "easy" language compared to Korean, Telegu, Bicol, or many African languages for which only the most meager learning materials existed.

Neither budgetary nor time considerations would permit the stretching of training programs much beyond the traditional twelve weeks, though in exceptional cases we slipped the limit up to as much as sixteen weeks. But clearly if time was going to be made for giving a volunteer a job skill and for language learning, some of the Peace Corps' sacred training cows had to be jettisoned.

We started with physical education or physical fitness training. From sixty to ninety hours out of every training program were devoted to swimming, calisthenics, track, soccer, and other sports. We dropped the whole PE track and kept a variety of sports equipment available in case trainees wanted to work out in their free time. There were of course some outraged cries about this move, particularly from PE instructors, but we saved from sixty to ninety hours; and I was never able to see any noticeable difference in the physical condition of volunteers who followed this change from those who preceded it.

Health education had always taken about thirty hours of training time. Much of this time was spent in lectures about tropical medicine and in the showing of films of grotesque tropical diseases. Volunteers I talked with were almost unanimous in feeling that it was largely a waste of time. We decided to substitute one session in which trainees were given a good briefing about the specific health conditions of the country to which they were going, because such conditions might be a factor in their deciding whether they wanted to go or not. A booklet was then passed out to them telling them how to stay healthy in that country. That was it for health education. When they reached the country, one of the first things they received was a careful, detailed talk from the Peace Corps doctor about how to take care of themselves in the country; at that point they were ready, even eager to listen. We saved twenty-five or more hours with this change.

Our training program directors became masters at handling with lightning speed the congressional requirements of instructing the trainees in the "history and menace of communism." American history, government, and cultural studies were shortened. Also, I had come to believe that you could over-teach a trainee about the country he was going to, thus taking away some of the fun of finding out for himself. And, too, almost the best way for a trainee to learn about a country was through his language instructor, who was always from that country. The more time spent with the instructor, the more the trainee would learn about the customs and culture and in a way he was likely to remember.

The time saved by these changes went into increased skill training and increased language learning. I am not suggesting that cuts in such programs as physical training and cultural studies were of themselves good, but I think they were sound in terms of how we were able to invest the time saved.

Two other major changes took place in training throughout 1967–69. One was the move to private companies as trainers. David Lilienthal's Development and Resources became our main trainer for India and produced some outstanding agricultural training of BA generalists. Westinghouse Learning Corporation became our main trainer for Brazil. General Dynamics and Educational Services, Incorporated, were among several other private, non-academic organizations that trained for the Peace Corps during those years.[5] These organizations probably did less well than the colleges on academic studies, were about on a par in language learning, but did much better in job skill training.

The other major change that occurred after 1966 was a strong shift to conducting a part or all of volunteer training in the country where they would serve. There was nothing new about in-country training. The first volunteers to go overseas in 1961 had part of their training in Tanganyika; the first Nigeria group, described in Chapter One, had most of its training at the University College of Ibadan. But in the early years only a few such programs were tried, and for the most part they were not considered very successful. The problem was that in too many cases the trainees were taken to a country, placed in some col-

[5] The private organization that holds the record for Peace Corps training, however, must be the Experiment in International Living at Putney, Vermont. Gordon Boyce, the president of the Experiment, was one of Shriver's earliest advisers and then volunteered his organization's facilities and personnel for training. The Experiment has trained forty Peace Corps projects.

lege, and put through the same kind of academically oriented program they would have received in the United States. While the trainees were bursting to get out and see the country they had come to work in, they were confined in classrooms for weeks listening to lectures about the country.

Such mistakes continued to be made even in 1967 and later but with much less frequency. With programming and training increasingly focused on a specific job and job skill, it quickly became clear that the best place to get ready for that job was in the country where it was to be done. There was no better place to learn about raising beets in Iran than in Iran. Learning to work with Indian farmers could best be accomplished in Indian villages. And what better place and way to become familiar with the culture of the country? But positive results did not come automatically simply because the training was done outside the United States. Careful planning had to be done and good people found to guide the training; otherwise, the natural benefits of the in-country setting would inevitably be lost.

By mid-1969 more training was taking place in the country of assignment than in the United States. A common pattern was for the trainees to receive several weeks of concentrated language instruction in the U.S. and then take their job training in the country where they would serve. It was important for them to have a start on the language when they arrived, and the concentrated drill necessary, with its monotony and stress, could best be done in classrooms in America rather than in similar classrooms in Venezuela or Thailand—with the trainee looking longingly out the window at the country he wanted to explore.

Finally, major changes took place in the selection process in training. The concept of selection as a means of deliberately putting pressure on trainees was effectively done away with. And through the leadership of such competent professional psychologists as Abraham Carp, Robert Voas, Robert Dorn, and Thomas Graham—to name but a few of many—the emphasis came to be on helping a trainee analyze his motives for volunteering for the Peace Corps and helping him to try to decide, as training progressed and he learned more about what his life as a volunteer would be, whether this was what he really wanted. The process came to be called "self-selection." The final responsibility for selection did continue to be vested in the same kind of panel I have earlier described, and I would not pretend that trainees lost all their hostility to selection; but the process was certainly more humane and more helpful to the individual in 1969 than it was in 1961.

The Peace Corps' Color Problem

Not all Peace Corps' problems, by any means, were solved in the 1967–69 period, and one of the most serious was the problem of color.

Most briefly put, the Peace Corps' color problem is that it is almost all white. The agency of course does not keep any statistics by race (nor by religion or creed), but simple observation over the years has made it quite clear to anyone interested in the subject that few black, brown, red, or yellow Americans become Peace Corps volunteers. While blacks now make up about eleven percent of the total U.S. population, some staff members have estimated that they constitute five percent or less of the Peace Corps.

Five percent might have been a fairly accurate guess for the first three or four years of the Peace Corps' life; but the number of blacks has dwindled sharply since 1965, and I would guess the percentage at closer to two percent today. In the last six months before leaving the Peace Corps in late 1969, I visited many training programs that had not a single black trainee. That same year a group of training officers did an informal color survey of their programs. Out of fourteen hundred trainees, twelve were black. Mexican-Americans and Indians are too infrequently seen in the Peace Corps even to hazard a guess at numbers or percentages.

Peace Corps officials have always expressed great concern over the paucity of minority group representation in the organization. Always sensitive about image, they have become increasingly aware of the picture quite accurately forming in the public eye of the Peace Corps as an outfit for white middle class college graduates (ninety-seven percent of all volunteers have been to college, eighty-eight percent of them acquiring one or more degrees in the process). The college grad label has pained the Peace Corps egalitarians but not nearly so much as their agency's pigmentation, and the latter has been cause for caustic editorial comment overseas, particularly in black Africa.

The cost to the Peace Corps has been more than a tarnished image, however. My own reading, and that which

I have taken from my fellow reps and staff members, is that black and other minority volunteers have at least as good a record of service overseas as whites, can make some contributions to understanding that whites can't, and have tremendous opportunities for personal growth. They also have staying power. I suppose I had about two dozen black volunteers in my programs in Nigeria and India. Not one failed to serve out his full tour, a remarkable record when compared against the over-all average for that large a group.

There are several reasons why minority volunteers tend to do well overseas. In the first place they have had plenty of experience with cultural confrontations in the United States; they have learned plenty about adapting to an alien society, and they didn't learn it from lectures by an anthropologist. A large percentage of the minority volunteers, particularly Indians and Mexican-Americans, have grown up in rural areas and have much practical knowledge of farming. Most Mexican-American volunteers, who usually opt for service in Latin America, start with a tremendous language advantage. And perhaps they all try harder because they have learned they must.

One of the half dozen best volunteers I ever had in India was Harold Crow, a Cherokee Indian born in rural Oklahoma. Assigned alone in a very isolated part of West Bengal, he introduced hybrid chickens into a wide area, started a feed cooperative, succeeded in getting farmers to grow their own feed grain, and—as a sideline—took the lead in building up local interest in family planning services. This same volunteer later became a staff member and then, while still under thirty, was made rep of a small but tough program in Uruguay. He was later placed in charge of the larger program in Panama. To be sure, Hal Crow was no ordinary young man, no matter what his race and color. He took degrees in art history and theater arts from West Coast colleges, did some acting on television, and became an expert on Tibetan *t'hankas* (religious cloth and oil paintings) while in India. So much for stereotypes.

Minority volunteers often find that they are in particular demand to discuss life in America because the people they live among know that they can get information from another point of view, and they are intensely interested in doing so. One of the black volunteers in India was so much sought after for talks to school groups and civic organizations in a wide area around where he lived that he finally had to limit his engagements to two a week in order to get his work done.

"The questions always get around to race prejudice in America," the volunteer once told me, "and I try to tell the truth like I've seen it. I tell them what a Chicago ghetto is like, but I tell them how I came out of one and got my college degree. It's funny. I never thought I would hear myself defending America. But when some guy gets up and starts crowding me to tell how bad prejudice is in America, I can't help thinking about the villages I've seen around here where the untouchables can't even use the wells the other people use. I always try to tell the good with the bad, and I turn the questions around so they can look at themselves and see how race or religious prejudice is with them."

One of the big surprises that many minority volunteers

have is to discover how much prejudice, often focused on color, exists in Africa, Asia, and Latin America and how it often affects them personally. A volunteer of Japanese descent working in Colombia found that he was subjected to a great deal of rude attention and harassment. His answer to how he felt about it was this:

"You may respond that I should ignore such people and foster friendships with individuals, counterparts, etc. I agree one hundred percent with this theory. However, when I can't play billiards without being harassed by bystanders; when I can't enter a restaurant without hearing *Chino* jokes directed at my presence; when I can't enter a bus without having people whisper, '*Mire* [look at] *el Chino*' (like maybe I have four heads); when I can't attend a movie without having a lit cigarette thrown challengingly at my back; then I say to myself, is this the people I am indirectly trying to help? . . .

"As a Peace Corps volunteer, I would not have stayed here if I didn't think I could have changed part of this social malaise. How do I feel about my relationship with the Colombians now? Well, the few Colombian friends I have know that I am a sensitive human being with feelings and emotions just like they do and above all that I am Glenn Tamanaha, posing not as a Japanese, an American, or a Peace Corps volunteer, but as an individual asking and demanding respect as an individual."

Dolores Trevino, a Mexican-American volunteer from Texas, also encountered a surprising kind of prejudice in Colombia. Here is her description of it:

"The inhabitants of Pitalito in southern Huila have grown accustomed to the volunteers with light hair, blue eyes, and hard-to-understand Spanish. To Colombians, all people from the U.S. are *monos* [light]. So when I arrived, looking as Colombians do and speaking Spanish with ease, they just couldn't take me for a Peace Corps volunteer.

"I thought everything was fine, but by the end of the week [which later turned into a month], I was quite tired of hearing 'When will a *gringo* Peace Corps volunteer come?' or 'You're a Mexican and Mexicans don't know as much as *gringos.*' I didn't mind the Mexican part, but I did mind the 'you don't know.'

"I grew quite angry when the mayor's daughter, who had met me as the new Peace Corps volunteer, asked another volunteer who was visiting when a volunteer was coming to Pitalito. I told the mayor's daughter I was the Peace Corps volunteer and planned to stay for two years, and that if she didn't already know it, it was time she found out. I also told her I hadn't come to meet their nice *gringa* stereotype. She looked quite shocked and left without another word. It must have gotten around, because I wasn't asked or told anything about *gringos* any more. And I was consulted more often and included in noticeably more work.

"The *campesinos* and urban people began to respond better than ever. Their disapproval turned to curiosity, and I was given a chance to show my abilities as a volunteer. Now they often tell me how glad they are to have a *gringa-Mexicana*. My ability to communicate well is the core of this."

One of our black volunteers in India, shortly after taking up his residence in a large Punjab village, was riding his bicycle down the street one day when a merchant stand-

ing outside his store pointed to the volunteer and said
something about *bundar* (monkey). As the episode was
later described to me, the volunteer—who was six feet
three and weighed well over two hundred pounds—got off
of his bicycle and walked over to the merchant, who was
a short, fat five feet four. The volunteer towered over the
man, smiled down at him, and said politely, "Would you
repeat what you said. I didn't hear you."

The merchant vanished into his store; the volunteer
got on his bike and rode on. He never again heard a dis-
paraging remark. He stayed in the village for two years,
made friends, and became an effective agricultural
worker.

Most black volunteers prefer to serve in Africa. While
nearly all I have known have had positive feelings about
their experience, they have also discovered that going to
Africa was in no sense returning home. Instead, their years
in Africa have given them a sense of their "Americanness"
that they had never known before—an understanding that
there is a black Americanness that, though different in
many ways, is just as fundamental as a white one.

Peace Corps service as a means of becoming better prepared to work on America's domestic development problems is a subject that David Riesman has addressed
succinctly and lucidly. Riesman, a distinguished sociolo-
gist and a former member of the Peace Corps' National
Advisory Council, says:

"Without an understanding of the problems of the underdeveloped world, what is often called the Third World,
it is very difficult to get a perspective about and leverage
on American domestic problems. The sense of urgency in

many young people is very great, and this sometimes leads to a certain mindless throwing of themselves into the problems of the ghetto in frantic activism from which the outcome is frequently disillusionment because of the inability to make substantial changes or even to know what changes are possible and desirable.

"The idealists find themselves exploited by ghetto factions seeking their own advantage, and especially if they have come from middle class Negro backgrounds, they may be as little prepared for this as idealistic whites from a wealthy suburb. The Peace Corps is a fine antidote against an over-impetuous, over-romantic view of change and what it takes—and an excellent antidote to over-pessimistic appraisals of contemporary America. That is why I encourage young people who will have many years to live and to devote to this country's problems to take what looks like a detour into the Peace Corps or into a like program in order better to prepare themselves for work here at home.

"When I say this, it often sounds as if I am perfectly prepared to exploit the residents of a barrio in Bogotá or the secondary school students in a Northern Nigerian school for the further education of young American activists. And these activists frequently worry that, because America seems to them in such dreadful shape, they have no business going overseas and imposing what they regard as defunct values on anyone else.

"In fact they are often useful overseas and rarely do harm, and they discover that the values they are rejecting are often those which are desired by the radical elites of the Third World. . . ."

If there are so many good reasons for having a large minority group representation in the Peace Corps, why has the agency been so unsuccessful in getting any substantial number into service? On the surface it would seem to have tried. A good deal of national advertising has long been directed at stirring up minority group interest. A 1970 ad on the subject is headlined: "If the Peace Corps is lily-white, it's your fault!" Special recruiters have scoured the campuses of all-black or mostly-black colleges, and the agency has spent a good deal of money on research into the attitudes of black college students toward the Peace Corps.

The research did little more than confirm what the Peace Corps had already learned from experience about why more black college seniors do not apply for service. The first and most important reason is economic. A great many black college students are under financial pressure, sometimes severe. Many come from low income families, and there is the need to start making money as soon as possible to pay back money borrowed for school, to add to family income, to help finance the next brother or sister in line to go to college.

Most black seniors feel they should get a job and get started on a career. The Peace Corps looks like a costly detour, no matter how much they might personally like to take it. And rapidly increasing job opportunities for graduating blacks assure that they do not opt for the Peace Corps because there is no other alternative. An official at Morgan State College, a black college in Maryland, told me that in 1965 only three industrial recruiters came on campus to interview graduating seniors; in 1968 the figure jumped to *three hundred*. Officials on other black campuses told me the same story. The search for black talent by business and industry has suddenly become a big and competitive business, and it is perfectly understandable that the black graduate with his new diploma wants to take advantage of it. The Peace Corps, offering a subsistence income overseas and seventy-five dollars a month readjustment allowance at the end of service, does not compete well.

The Peace Corps has always taken great pride in the fact that its volunteers do not profit financially from their two years of service, no matter how much they may benefit from travel, living in a foreign culture, and new work experiences. It is clear, however, that another view of this is possible, and it has often been expressed by blacks: The Peace Corps is for the affluent, for those who can afford to delay the money-making process, for those who can afford to wait two years to start a career. The Peace Corps has from time to time talked about giving extra money to well-qualified but economically disadvantaged applicants, but the talk has never resulted in action. The concepts of not benefiting materially from service and of treating all volunteers exactly the same are apparently too sacred parts of the Peace Corps mythology to tamper with.

The second reason holding back many black college seniors from applying for the Peace Corps is the feeling that the place for them today is not overseas but in America, to take their stand with their black brothers in the struggle for justice. This is a powerful motivation and one which tends to ride roughshod over the logically

sound arguments, like Riesman's, that service in the Peace
Corps would make many of these people more effective
in the future in the very difficult task of changing the
ways that white Americans think about black Americans.
Here the Peace Corps can do very little but be as persuasive as possible and try to get the black volunteers who
have served overseas to speak out on what they think the
experience did for them.

Everything that has been said above about the reluc-
tance of black college seniors to join the Peace Corps
probably also applies to Mexican-Americans and to American Indians. But thus far I have been talking only about
why the application rate of black Americans in college is
much smaller than that of white Americans. Of course,
those without college degrees or without two or three
years of college stand almost no chance of being invited
to Peace Corps training. Several times, at moments when
the Peace Corps has been particularly concerned about
its color problem it has conducted special recruiting and
training programs for minority persons. One such experiment was carefully to choose a small number of black
Job Corps graduates and give them several weeks of
special training before putting them into a training group
preparing to teach in vocational schools in Malaysia; in
another case they were to work as members of water well
drilling teams in India. Although the number of dropouts
and deselections from training were high, those who did
make it through the training process had successful tours
of duty overseas; in one or two cases the performance
was brilliant. This kind of recruiting and training is very
expensive, however, probably costing about five thousand

dollars per trainee; it also consumes a great deal of staff time. As a result, very few of these special programs have taken place.

Two special recruiting and training programs for American Indians were disastrous failures. With the help of an organization called Oklahomans for Indian Opportunity, the Peace Corps tried to recruit Indians with a farm or rural background or with some practical job training or experience. Recruiters sought them out for personal interviews wherever possible. The backgrounds of practical work experience and job training of many of those invited looked rather promising.

About thirty Indians were invited to the first training program, which was held in the summer of 1967; but only ten appeared when training began at the University of Oklahoma. Like the earlier Job Corps experiment, the training for the Indians was arranged in two parts. In the first part at Oklahoma, the little group was by itself, and the emphasis was on improving their verbal skills, beginning Spanish language training, and simply getting them to talk about themselves and their reasons for volunteering. There is no reason to believe that this part of the training was not a good idea, and all ten of the Indian trainees said that they found it helpful. They were then transferred to a "regular" training program at the Peace Corps training center in Puerto Rico, a program made up as usual almost entirely of BA generalists. During this program Indian trainees received no special attention and no thought was given to special training needs that might be required by their backgrounds. The theory seemed to be that if they were to succeed as volunteers in Latin America, they would have to be like BA generalists. And the best way to see if they were like them or could learn to be like them was to let them take the same program as "regular" trainees.

It should be said that those who planned and ran the training program no doubt did not want the Indians to feel segregated or that they had to receive special attention. But the fact is that they did need special attention and training. Special emphasis should have continued on the development of their communicative abilities. Particular effort should have gone into getting them ready to make the most of their rural backgrounds and job skills. Careful counseling about their specific assignment in Latin America would have added to their confidence as well as their ability to perform well. These things could have been done without segregating them. They were not done.

Only two of the ten Indians became volunteers, and one of those was the only college graduate in the group. The eight others resigned before the end of training.

A year later a second Indian group was recruited with very much the same kinds of persons as the first group. Recruitment was much more successful, with thirty-three reporting to training, but the training was carried out along exactly the same lines and with the same philosophy that had obtained with the 1967 group. The results were even worse. Of the thirty-three only six survived training and two of those resigned after only a short time as volunteers. It was clear that the Peace Corps learned absolutely nothing from the first training experience, and it did not try a third.

Lawrence O'Brien, who succeeded Charles Peters as director of the Division of Evaluation, personally investigated these training fiascos and, in a report classified more highly than the usual evaluation document, blistered the Peace Corps for its cultural insensitivity. And he later remarked to me, "It is frightening that such a thing could happen twice in an organization whose very life depends on understanding other cultures."

If the Peace Corps is going to increase the number of blacks, Indians, and Mexican-Americans in its programs, it will have to find new ways of attracting them, quite possibly by making it economically feasible for them to join. It will have to find more relevant selection standards, and it will have to give up treating them like the annual crop of BA generalists; it will have to create more appropriate and no doubt more costly training. There is no evidence yet that the Peace Corps is seriously enough concerned about its color problem to do these things.

A Smaller Peace Corps

In late 1968 we bit the bullet on Peace Corps size. The agency reached its greatest volunteer strength overseas —15,556 in 1966—during Jack Vaughn's administration; but it was Vaughn, with solid backing from his senior officers, who near the end of his appointment made the decision that the Peace Corps should reduce its numbers. The relevant figures are those showing the total number of persons registering for Peace Corps training:

Year	Number Registering for Training
1962	4,431
1963	4,947
1964	8,079
1965	8,719
1966	11,210
1967	8,627
1968	7,821
1969	5,650

Except for 1966, the Peace Corps input of new trainees leveled out from 1964 through 1968. The big jump in 1966 is accounted for entirely by the dramatic increase in the India program and the starting of the big program in Micronesia. Except for those programs, 1966 would have looked very much like the year on either side of it. My point is this: But for the atypical year of 1966, the volunteer trainee inputs over a five-year period were very similar. The drop in 1969 of more than two thousand signaled a major turning point in the Peace Corps' philosophy.

The press, as always, saw in this sharp drop evidence that the bloom was off the Peace Corps, that Vietnam was hurting the Peace Corps, that American youth in 1969 would have no part of the establishment, even the Peace Corps. The fact is that we had the qualified applicants—including five hundred college graduate married couples —the money in our budget, and the overseas program requests for twenty-five hundred more trainees than we invited in 1969.

But the time had come to face a fundamental reality: Many of the requests for volunteers could not stand up under the careful program exploration and specific job definition that we were now asking of our field staffs. If we developed some jobs carefully—which took a great deal of staff time—and then accepted all of the fuzzy requests too, just to keep the numbers up, we would still be playing the old numbers game.

We also knew that, even in late 1968, some of our country programs were badly inflated with volunteers with poor jobs or no jobs. India, Micronesia, the Philippines, and Colombia were among the countries most seriously oversupplied with volunteers in weak assignments. By deciding not to put new volunteers into similar assignments as the volunteers already there finished their tours, we reduced the numbers in those countries by more than one thousand. By applying the same standards to our other programs, we lowered the total by another thousand.

This reduction was by no means a unilateral exercise on our part. The state governments of India had made it very clear to us that they wanted fewer volunteers with more clearly defined responsibilities and higher skills or better training. Education officials in the Philippines said quite plainly that they would rather have thirty volunteer teachers with classroom experience and master's degrees in education than three hundred of old BA generalist teachers' aides.

We doubtless could have kept our total volunteer strength at a level with that of previous years by increasing the number of community development volunteers in Latin America and by padding programs in a number of countries that seemed less concerned about volunteer program quality. And we were certainly under no pressure

from the Micronesian and Colombian governments to reduce the program size.

But we had to make these reductions to be consistent
with our own program philosophy that had developed
under Vaughn, and we had to be responsive to countries
such as India and the Philippines, who wanted quality
instead of quantity. Perhaps the numbers game was not
completely dead as 1968 ended, but it was mortally
wounded.

The Shadow of Vietnam

The Peace Corps improved steadily in its work overseas
after 1966, but its publicity and image steadily worsened
in the United States. The chief reason for this was the
growing fury of college students, as well as liberal writers
and commentators, over President Johnson's escalation
of the war in Vietnam. The Peace Corps was inevitably
identified by many with a rigid and unresponsive government establishment. Frequently expressed was the view
that serving in a government-financed Peace Corps, in
the face of U.S. actions in Southeast Asia, was an intolerable hypocrisy and provided Johnson with a peace token
to which he was not entitled.

As early as 1965, Gerald Berreman, a University of
California professor, was advising students to stay out of
the Peace Corps as a protest against the war in Vietnam.
"The government," he said, "wants the Peace Corps to be
a play pen for activist students to keep them out of the
kitchen when the adults are cooking up the war in Vietnam." In *The Nation* of February 26, 1968, Professor Ber-

reman returned to his theme with a vengeance in an article entitled "The Peace Corps: A Dream Betrayed." His main point was that the war in Vietnam had badly, perhaps fatally, damaged the credibility of the Peace Corps both at home and abroad. Professor Berreman stated, "The American dream which generated the Peace Corps has been betrayed in the past seven years by the drift of the nation ever more deeply into a war which is antithetic to everything for which the Peace Corps would have to stand if it were to have a chance for success. The betrayal of the idea of the Peace Corps in this period is, therefore, the betrayal of the American people who voted for Johnson and Humphrey in 1964 as peace candidates."

A number of other writers and commentators sounded the same cry. Some threw in for good measure that the Peace Corps was a form of cultural imperialism which should be stopped because the United States had no culture or values worth exporting. Others professed to believe that the Peace Corps was now deliberately recruiting "bland" volunteers who would quietly do their work and not question U.S. foreign policy.

In almost all cases these attacks came from persons who had in earlier years strongly endorsed the Peace Corps, and they show more than anything else the depth of despair over their inability in any way to alter the course of the Vietnam conflict. They were simply lashing out blindly at anything connected with Johnson and his Administration. Occasionally their blows were both bitterly personal and quite irrational. Paul Goodman, who should at least have been ashamed of his McCarthy era tactics, called Jack Vaughn a "CIA type." Goodman knew better than to say that Vaughn was or had been in the CIA, a statement that would have been grounds for libel; his phrase "CIA type" applied the damning brand without really meaning anything.

Marshall Windmiller, a West Coast radio commentator, said in a late 1967 broadcast: "Vaughn is a vigorous anti-Communist and cold warrior who had helped to develop American counter-insurgency policy in Latin America. He had been taken out of an earlier Peace Corps job to be sent to Panama as ambassador by President Johnson after rioting in 1964 had precipitated a rupture of relations with that country. Panama is important to the United States not only because of the canal but because we have one of our largest camps there for training counter-insurgency forces." Jack told me he was astonished to learn that he was a specialist in counter-insurgency and that President Johnson had picked him for Panama to look after counter-insurgency training.

But it was the beginning of a grim, humorless period for the Peace Corps that continues to this day. Internally, the agency, like the nation itself, was bleeding over Vietnam. More and more volunteers overseas felt compelled to speak out publicly against the war. The overwhelming percentage of both men and women volunteers were bitterly opposed to what the U.S. was doing in Vietnam, and on the part of many of the men a strong motive in joining the Peace Corps had been to delay their military service by two years. They wanted their protests to be heard and they wanted the countries in which they served—which were usually critical of the U.S. about Vietnam—to know how they felt.

Our problem was that volunteers' protest about Vietnam was news simply because of their Peace Corps label. U.S. newspapers would print letters from volunteers, regardless of their quality, simply because the designation Peace Corps Volunteer followed the writer's name. And newsmen overseas hearing about volunteer protest actions or plans could be counted on to file a story that would get wide circulation. As a result we were under continuing pressure from some congressmen, the White House, and the State Department to curb the volunteers' protest activities. Many newspapers of conservative persuasion editorialized against the protests and called for the volunteers to be sent home.

Only one volunteer was in fact terminated for war protest activity during Jack Vaughn's administration, but that one expulsion received immense newspaper attention because of a resulting court action and created much negative publicity on college campuses across the nation. The volunteer involved was a teacher in Chile named Bruce Murray; and for Peace Corps volunteers, former volunteers, and staff everywhere, his termination and the subsequent events have become known as "the Bruce Murray Case." *The Volunteer* magazine of March 1970 contains the following summary of the case.

The events leading to Murray's termination began in May, 1967.

A group of Volunteers in Santiago circulated a petition calling for the cessation of American bombing of North Vietnam and immediate negotiations to end the war. Names of signers were to appear in local newspapers.

Murray received a copy of the petition by mail at his post in Concepción, where he taught music, and signed it.

Then-Ambassador Ralph Dungan learned of the petition and told Chile Volunteers that publication of their names in any Chilean paper would result in their expulsion.

Jack Vaughn, then Peace Corps Director, also wrote the Volunteers to say that publication of their petition with their names would be a breach of the Peace Corps' apolitical role in Chile, and he warned them they were in danger of "administrative discipline," including expulsion.

Murray did not agree.

He was angered by Vaughn's letter and subsequently wrote a reply in which he agreed that Volunteers "should not meddle in the politics of the host country," but insisted that this restriction should not include "international policies of the United States which may be of interest to the host country."

Murray sent copies of his letter to Vaughn, Chile regional director Kirk Breed, country director Paul Bell, and the New York *Times*.

The *Times* did not publish his letter.

But a few days later, United Press International wrote a story describing the Peace Corps clampdown on Volunteer signing of anti-war petitions which was carried by *El Sur*, a Concepción paper, on June 16.

Murray read that story and, thinking it incomplete, translated his *Times* letter into Spanish and sent it to *El Sur*.

El Sur published the letter on June 17, and this led to Murray's expulsion.

On June 20, country director Bell recommended Murray be sent home. He called Bruce to Santiago and, after a short discussion, put him on a plane to Washington. Bell told him he was being returned for "consultations," but not for termination.

Murray arrived at 806 Connecticut Avenue on June 21, where he learned otherwise.

He called home as soon as he checked in and learned also that he had been reclassified 1-A by his draft board two weeks earlier, and that his notice was on its way to him in Chile.

Murray remained in Washington for a week of "exit interviews," including a short session with Vaughn. He was officially terminated on June 28.

But his problems had only begun.

Murray asked his board for an occupational deferment so that he could return to Concepción to continue his music teaching.

The board said no and ordered him to report for induction.

At that point, with the help of Civil Liberties Union lawyers, Murray filed suit against his local draft board, the Rhode Island Selective Service, the Peace Corps and the U.S. Attorney General. His contention: that Peace Corps had violated both due process and his constitutional rights in terminating him; that a conspiracy existed between Peace Corps and the Selective Service to expedite his reclassification, and that the Selective Service had violated its own required procedures in refusing to grant him a new deferment.

This was the "Bruce Murray case," the first legal test of Peace Corps policy governing Volunteer freedom of expression overseas.

Trial was held in the U.S. District Court in Rhode Island, and on Christmas Eve, 1969, Judge Raymond Pettine found in favor of Murray, though rejecting the allegation that a conspiracy existed between Peace Corps and the Selective Service.

Pettine ordered Peace Corps to "expunge" documents in Murray's file concerning his termination, and to reimburse him for his plane trip home. He told the draft board to return to Murray the 2-A classification he held as a Volunteer, making it valid through his originally scheduled completion of service date, when he would have been 26 years old. And, most important for Murray, the judge quashed the criminal indictment standing against him.

Much of Judge Pettine's decision dealt with his ruling that the selective service acted improperly in its handling of Murray's appeals. The judge also criticized the Peace Corps for not properly adhering to its own regulations in the steps that must be followed when a volunteer is terminated. He did state that the Peace Corps had violated Murray's First Amendment constitutional rights in terminating him. The judge said: "Murray spoke about matters of vital interest to him as a human being, a United States citizen, and a Peace Corps volunteer. Any inhibition on speech so far removed from the government interest alleged to support it must fall."

But in an earlier ruling, Judge Pettine also said: "There can be no question that the interest which the government seeks to protect is a valid one . . . it can be conceded that in some circumstances the Corps' interest in remaining apolitical with respect to host country politics can reasonably be protected by termination or transfer policies narrowly applied so as to forbid the feared intrusion."

The two statements really threw the whole issue back to the Peace Corps, where it remains a serious point of tension and a matter of fierce debate to this day. In the long months before Murray ever decided to take his case to the courts, the Peace Corps staff agonized over what the agency could or should do about volunteer protests over Vietnam. There was probably as much deep disenchantment over the war among the staff as there was on the part of the volunteers, but the staff had to consider many factors and had to try to make the volunteers consider them.

Because of their Peace Corps label and their locations abroad, volunteers attracted unusual attention with their protests. Yet they were supported abroad by U.S. taxpayers' money, and many millions of those taxpayers did not share their views about Vietnam. To what extent did their protests provide useful propaganda for North Vietnam, China, and Russia? To what extent did they affect the morale of American forces in Vietnam? There was no doubt that the volunteers' actions were bringing about

the disaffection of many Americans who had previously
supported the Peace Corps, and this included some in-
fluential members of Congress. Officials of some of the
host countries, particularly those with highly authoritarian
governments, frowned on protests that could serve as
examples for their own youth (this fact of course could
be used as an argument for the protests, as well as
against).

Our chief concern always was that protests by volunteers overseas would increase to such a level or take such
a form that we would receive an ultimatum from the
White House or the State Department that protests by
volunteers overseas must cease. Vaughn and his senior
staff knew that such an ultimatum would be unenforce-
able and that any attempt at rigid prohibition of protest
would destroy the Peace Corps. That we never received
such an order is testimony to several things: Vaughn's
efforts to make the White House and State understand
the realities of the situation, a level of understanding at
the White House and in State for which they are often
not given credit, unceasing work on the part of Peace
Corps overseas staff in discussing the implications of protest with the volunteers, and basic good sense on the
part of volunteers in deciding what forms their protest
would take.

In our discussions with and instructions to volunteers
we began by saying that they were free to write their
congressmen and the President—identifying themselves as
Peace Corps volunteers if they wished—expressing their
views of Vietnam. If they wrote letters to American newspapers or magazines, we asked them not to identify

themselves as Peace Corps because of the implication that
their views might have agency sanction. If they circulated
and sent petitions, we asked the same thing for the same
reason. We asked that they refrain from protest activities
in their country of assignment. One by one the volunteers
tested us on all of these conditions, and one by one we
retreated. We knew that any large-scale terminations over
Vietnam protests would kill the Peace Corps on American
college campuses. By the end of 1968 there were really no
formal Peace Corps administration limits on volunteer
protest over Vietnam. We simply appealed for the exercise of good judgment and made it known to the volunteers that they were adults responsible for their actions.
It was the only position we could take and preserve the
Peace Corps, and it was of course the correct position.
With hardly any exceptions, volunteer protests over Vietnam have been thoughtful and low-key. They have continued to infuriate many Americans, including some
congressmen and newspaper editors, and the Peace Corps
administration simply had to learn to live with that
problem.

During 1967–68 there was also continuing pressure from
volunteers and many staff members for the Peace Corps
to take a formal position against the American government's participation in the war in Vietnam. There was no
way that the Peace Corps, a government agency in the
Executive branch, could take an official position against
the rest of the Executive branch. The director of the
Peace Corps could denounce the war in Vietnam and
submit his resignation to the President, but that would
still be a personal action. Many people, both inside and

outside the Peace Corps, were prepared for Jack Vaughn to take that action. For a number of good reasons, he was not.

It was also during these years that the first serious and persistent questions were raised as to whether an organization with the objectives of those of the Peace Corps should or really could be a part of government. The right-to-protest issue had pointed up the fact that, whether they were very visible or not, the Peace Corps did have ties to the White House and the State Department. At a time of intense unpopularity of the American Government in many parts of the developing world, the Peace Corps' tag as an agency of that government brought down on it a degree of suspicion that made the volunteers' work much more difficult. And there were charges that the Peace Corps, as a government agency, could not be free to pursue the kinds of programs that might be best for a country but would have to conform to whatever official view the U.S. government might have as to what was good for a country.

A great deal was written and talked about internationalizing the Peace Corps under the United Nations, which would accept qualified volunteers from any member nations interested in sending them. Such prominent figures as Senators Fulbright and Hatfield expressed great interest in an international volunteer program as a substitute for the Peace Corps. In 1969 the UN undertook a feasibility study of such a program and announced in mid-1970 that a start with about twelve hundred volunteers would be made in 1971. Regardless of the future of such a UN program, I certainly think the United States should participate fully in the experiment.

I can record my own views quite succinctly on whether
the Peace Corps can or should survive as a government
agency. I think it would be better if it could be privately
financed; I see no possibility of any private organizations
putting up the money necessary to bring this about. If
money could be appropriated by the Congress and given
without strings to an especially created public foundation charged with running the Peace Corps, I would
favor such a plan. The foundation would have a board
of trustees made up of distinguished Americans and
possibly citizens of other countries. This board would set
policy for all Peace Corps undertakings and would be
completely free of congressional and other governmental
controls, except those of audit. While at first glance such
a proposal might seem like fantasy, I am not at all certain that properly worked out and presented, the Congress might not be very interested in such an idea.

Meanwhile, I think that a Peace Corps as a part of
government is much better than no Peace Corps at all.
I believe that over-all the problems arising from the Peace
Corps' being a government agency have been handled
well and that they have been exaggerated by strident
elements of the press and general anguish over Vietnam.

Fortunately, and for many of the reasons described
earlier in this chapter, the work of the volunteers overseas during this period has been of generally high quality.
Had it not been, our troubles would be greatly compounded. During 1970 I traveled extensively in Africa

and Asia as a private citizen. What I saw of the Peace Corps in many countries compared very favorably with—in a number of cases was superior to—the work of volunteers during the earlier, more tranquil years.

CHAPTER FIVE

Mr. Nixon's Peace Corps: 1969–70

With the election of Richard Nixon in November 1968, speculation began about what he would do with the Peace Corps. He had said almost nothing about the agency during the campaign, but now his negative comments during his 1960 campaign against Kennedy were recalled. One congressman actually wrote some of his volunteer constituents overseas that they would be coming home soon because Nixon was certain to kill the Peace Corps.

Peace Corps headquarters went through a tense three months between the election and inauguration, during which time we heard not one official word from the incoming Administration and hardly any unofficial ones. We did learn that a task force was meeting in New York to talk about volunteer programs of all kinds, but no one from the Peace Corps was invited to attend. That in itself seemed a bit ominous. How "political" were the Republicans going to make the Peace Corps?

They could make it very political, indeed. The "plum book," a document listing all government jobs unprotected by civil service status, contained practically the whole Peace Corps staff, overseas and in Washington, above the grade of secretary. The Peace Corps has but two presidential appointments—those of director and deputy director—positions where a new Administration might reasonably be expected to want its own people. But in theory at least hundreds of Peace Corps staff members were vulnerable.

Jack Vaughn in 1969 was as much enamoured of the Peace Corps as he had been in 1961, and he desperately wanted to stay on as director. As a registered Republican there was even a chance that he might be retained, especially if Nixon wanted to give a strong early signal that he considered the Peace Corps "non-political." There was a great deal of speculation about who would become the new director if Jack were not retained, but the rumors lacked credibility even in a Washington ready to believe almost anything.

Finally, just two days before the inauguration, Secretary of State Designate William Rogers visited Peace Corps headquarters and talked to Jack. I was in California at the time, but within an hour of the meeting I received a phone call. I could tell from the background noise that a celebration was in progress, and the word that came over the line was that Jack had been asked to stay on.

When I returned to Washington, however, I found a subdued Jack Vaughn. Jack told me that in response to his direct question about what he should say to the staff about his future, Rogers had said to tell them he was staying on. But, Jack said, Rogers had made it quite clear that what he meant by "staying on" was until the new Administration had selected its own man to head the Peace Corps.

And, Jack said, the Secretary Designate had implied that the selection would not be too long in coming.

It wasn't. In early March an inadvertent White House news leak suggested that a new Peace Corps director had been chosen, and within two days the official announcement came that President Nixon intended to nominate Joseph H. Blatchford to replace Jack Vaughn as director of the Peace Corps.

The shock throughout the Peace Corps was profound because the staff had accepted at face value Jack's words that he had been asked to stay on. Great bitterness was expressed at the new Administration's "betrayal," and the new director designate certainly came in under a cloud of hostility.[1]

After all of the famous names that had been bandied about as possibilities for Peace Corps director, the selection of Joe Blatchford came as a distinct surprise. He certainly was not a big name: not half a dozen people in the Peace Corps building had ever heard of him. But if one closely examined his credentials, he did not come off too badly. He had a deep and sincere interest in developmental problems of Latin America and a concern for relationships between the two American continents. While a law student at UCLA he had organized his own good will tour to South America, a jazz band in which he played saxophone. A member of UCLA's national collegiate championship tennis team, he also took on the best players in the cities they visited.

[1] President Nixon quickly named Vaughn ambassador to Colombia, an action which only slightly lessened the disenchantment of the Peace Corps staff.

After his trip Blatchford got the idea of forming a private volunteer organization that would send volunteers to work in community development projects in Latin America. He went to work on the idea actively in 1960 and succeeded in collecting $160,000 from forty American and Venezuelan corporations to support the work of a community development organization he called ACCION. The first forty American ACCION volunteers went to Venezuela in September 1961, making Joe Blatchford's private volunteer organization exactly contemporary with the Peace Corps of President John Kennedy. ACCION of course never reached the magnitude of the Peace Corps, but through its first eight years—all of which time it was under Blatchford's direction—it sent more than one thousand field workers and staff members to Latin America for work in civic development, job training, construction, and education. More than three thousand companies contributed nearly nine million dollars in cash and services to ACCION during that time. Two of Blatchford's supporters were Nelson Rockefeller and Donald M. Kendall, president of Pepsi-Cola and a long-time ally of Richard Nixon.

In 1968 Robert Finch encouraged Blatchford to take leave from ACCION and run for Congress in the Seventeenth Congressional District of California (the Los Angeles harbor district). Blatchford made the race and lost a close contest to a former lieutenant governor of the state. But the effort brought him to the attention of the Republican party, and when a search for the new Administration's director of the Peace Corps began in earnest, Blatchford quickly amassed an overwhelming number of points: He was young, thirty-four. As a jazz musician and

star tennis player, he was something of a swinger. His
private enterprise version of the Peace Corps was sweet
to Republican ears. He knew about living and working
overseas and he spoke good Spanish. The support of
Kendall, Rockefeller, and Finch was the absolute
clincher.

At his confirmation hearings before the Senate Foreign
Relations Committee, the only serious reservation about
the appointment was raised by Senator Fulbright, who
asked Blatchford point blank whether he intended to use
the position of Peace Corps director as a steppingstone to
future elective political office. Blatchford replied that he
had no plans to run for elective office. Republican members of the committee protested that it was unfair to ask
him to speculate about his possible future in politics.
Blatchford was confirmed with no negative votes.

The new deputy director of the Peace Corps was
Thomas Houser, a Chicago lawyer who had been Senator
Percy's campaign manager and naturally had the strong
endorsement of the senator. I had accepted an appointment as research associate at Harvard to begin in the fall
and agreed to stay on in the Peace Corps for three months
to help in the transition. These months gave me an excellent view of the changeover.

It was not an easy time for Joe Blatchford. There was
strong pressure on him to open the doors for a whole
stream of Republican patronage candidates. One of the
wisest moves Blatchford made was to bring onto his staff
Mrs. Elizabeth Williams, who had been Robert Finch's
administrative assistant in California before coming with
him to Washington in his new post as Secretary of HEW.

Blatchford gave Betty Williams the job of screening all job referrals from the White House and the Republican National Committee and bouncing all of those who did not seem to have genuine qualifications for Peace Corps work. Betty had the connections throughout the new Administration's structure to carry out this thankless task without bringing down the wrath of the Republican powers on Blatchford's head. His good judgment in getting this woman and her courage and skill are responsible for preventing the Peace Corps from becoming riddled with hack political appointees.

Actually, Blatchford was very careful, even cautious, with the appointments that he made during the months I was there. He brought experienced Peace Corps field staff into a number of key appointments in Washington. He put new staff candidates through an interview process that was even more exhaustive than Shriver's and Vaughn's had been. He wanted to be sure that his initial appointments—especially for overseas positions—were as above reproach as they could be.

For the key Washington jobs—the regional directors' positions—Blatchford retained the most experienced, successful Peace Corps veterans available. Fortunately, at a time when there was a mass exodus of Peace Corps staff out of the agency, Blatchford was able to attract top quality men to these jobs: Walter Carrington, an eight-year staff man in two countries and former rep in Sierra Leone, as director for Africa; Robert White, former Latin American deputy and a veteran of years of service overseas, as Latin America boss; Joseph Kennedy, former evaluation staff member and brilliantly successful rep in

Africa, as East Asia Pacific director; William Dyal, ac-
knowledged as one of the most successful reps in Peace
Corps history, as North Africa-Near East-South Asia director. The regional directors were able to keep experienced men and women on their staffs, and the work of
the agency was therefore able to go forward without the
disruption that might otherwise have occurred.

Not that it was a happy time in Peace Corps Washington. Blatchford did not prove to have the colorful
qualities of Shriver or the quiet warmth of Vaughn. He
sensed the hostility of much of the old regime staff but
did not seem to know how to overcome it. He made a few
appointments to his personal staff which were immensely
unpopular. Some efforts too quickly to change recruiting
and selection procedures resulted in a nearly disastrous
breakdown of the whole machinery.

Blatchford announced a set of new directions for the
Peace Corps that seemed to all who knew the past like
old directions revisited. He called for the recruiting of
more experienced, mid-career people, more skilled workers—electricians, plumbers, mechanics, farmers. He
wanted more minority group representation in the Peace
Corps. In a move that was touted as a really new departure he announced that the Peace Corps would recruit
two hundred families for Peace Corps service in the first
year of his administration.

In fact, not even this latter move was new. In 1965
Shriver had become excited by the possibility of recruiting five hundred medical doctors as volunteers. Since
most of them would have families, it was decided that
they would be sent overseas in the volunteer leader

category, which permitted the taking along of families. Instead of five hundred doctors, the Peace Corps finally got together about fifteen with families in a first pilot project. It was so costly and complicated that nothing further was done with the idea.

Blatchford's scheme seemed to be running into the same fate. After a year only ten families had been recruited and put through training for service overseas. The Peace Corps, by its legislation and by its overseas support facilities—or lack of them—is simply not equipped to place and maintain families abroad. Blatchford's other new directions were all paths that had been trod by both Shriver and Vaughn without much success. There was no evidence in late 1970 that Blatchford would be any more successful. It was clear that the BA generalist was still the backbone of the Peace Corps and was going to continue to be. Indications were that persistent effort might change the ratio of generalists to skilled workers from 95–5 to 90–10 but certainly not more.

I think it is quite clear that Joe Blatchford knows this, but he has two good reasons for continuing to talk publicly about a new type volunteer: older, more mature, more highly skilled. One reason is that it still makes good copy as a new direction for the Peace Corps. The other reason is dissent over the war in Vietnam. Volunteer protests continued into 1969 and 1970; some incidents, such as a few volunteers in Tunisia turning their backs on Secretary of State Rogers during a speech, received wide publicity. Over two hundred volunteers overseas participated in various ways in the November 1969 anti-war moratorium.

Blatchford's Republican support is much more conservative than that that Jack Vaughn and I had to deal
with and his White House and congressional pressures
much more severe. Even so, a memorandum that he sent
to the seventeen Republican members of the House Foreign Affairs Committee on April 14, 1970, is an astonishing
document. Its original version is the one which follows:[2]

SPECIFIC STEPS TAKEN TO DEAL WITH PROTESTS AND TO RECRUIT NEW TYPES OF VOLUNTEERS

A. *Dealing with Protests*

1) Upon my appointment as Director, the Secretary of State sent a telegram to U.S. diplomatic Posts
which contained a statement that ". . . Volunteers
will be expected to refrain from all political activities
in the countries in which they are stationed."

2) I called all Country Directors together in Washington last September and emphasized the need for
closer cooperation with Embassies and other U.S.
agencies. I also made clear Peace Corps policy pro-
hibiting public political activities by Volunteers.

3) On October 30, 1969, I issued guidelines to
overseas staff on the issue of free speech which contained the statement: "We simply cannot have it
both ways; we cannot both claim to be apolitical

[2] The version above was recalled a few hours after it was sent to the
committee. A second version was then submitted; the new memorandum
omitted the last sentence of item B5 and the section entitled IN
SUMMARY.

and insert American foreign policy issues into the host country scene."

4) The Secretary of State and I remained in close touch during the moratorium and the Vice President's trip to Asia to forestall any possible incidents. As a result, less than 200 Volunteers participated in moratorium activities. The Secretary and I permitted letters or petitions to be sent to Ambassadors or to the Vice President and meetings were permitted with the Ambassadors or their staff at which U.S. foreign policy was explained.

5) We found it necessary to terminate 12 Volunteers and one staff member in four countries who insisted in abusing the right of expression and to publicly demonstrate.

6) Unfortunately, newspaper accounts have exaggerated or erroneously reported incidents, thus creating a false impression of widespread Peace Corps protests. We have initiated a campaign to work on a personal basis with Washington newsmen to keep them accurately informed and thus prevent this kind of reporting in future.

B. *Actions Being Taken*

1) Adoption of higher standards for Volunteers recently graduating from college and personal screening of all applicants invited to training.

2) Better utilization of background investigations to weed out undesirable applicants. A letter to me dated March 8 from Chairman Robert Hampton of the Civil Service Commission stated, "In the opinion of

our security appraisal officers an excellent job is being done by the Peace Corps."

3) Emphasis throughout training on the obligation of Volunteers to serve the host country and to refrain from taking part in any protest activities.

4) Initiation of staff training programs so that staff is fully prepared to inform Volunteers of Peace Corps policy and to enforce that policy.

5) Reorganization of the agency, resulting in an 18 percent reduction of Washington staff which will be increased to 22 percent by June 30 and a 10 percent reduction of overseas staff. Implementation of an aggressive staff recruitment program to hire staff members who understand and support the new directions of the Administration.

6) Initiation of a policy of recruiting different types of Volunteers—people with more maturity, greater experience and training such as skilled technicians from the ranks of labor, farmers, professional people in the fields of engineering, architecture, etc.

I have traveled to over 20 U.S. cities making speeches and TV appearances telling about the new directions of this Administration. Neil Armstrong has been making speeches before engineering and scientific groups. George Meany is giving his personal support and the AFL-CIO national convention in Miami issued a proclamation supporting the new Peace Corps recruitment program. Henry Ford and other businessmen are actively recruiting from business.

For the first time in Peace Corps history married

couples with families can serve. During 1970 we are attempting to attract 200 families with dependents on a pilot project basis. If successful and if we receive our requested Congressional authority, we hope to increase substantially the number of families in the Peace Corps.

We have held meetings with Secretary Laird, Secretary Hardin, and Secretary Shultz to secure broad cooperation in moving the Peace Corps forward to a more prominent role in technical assistance for underdeveloped countries.

RESULTS. Although total applications from the college campuses are down this year, applications from those over 30 years of age are up 110 percent over last year. Those with agricultural degrees are up 27 percent and those with skill backgrounds are up 50 percent. We have received inquiries from 2200 families interested in the Peace Corps, almost all with skill backgrounds. Last week alone we had 1200 inquiries from farmers. Five families are currently in training for Bolivia. They are skilled tradesmen, very idealistic, and support the Administration's policies. Some have sons in Vietnam.

IN SUMMARY

We inherited a very difficult situation resulting from Volunteers just out of college with strong liberal views. We have also had to weed out many members of a hostile staff hired during the past eight years of Democratic administration and unwilling to accept the new Administration. There were no clear policies or guidelines on dissent and political protests overseas. There was no personal screening of Volunteers prior to training. There was no adequate staff training. Some members of the press were anxious to embarrass the Administration by exploiting a few Volunteers' protests against U.S. foreign policy.

In spite of this, the Peace Corps offers the Administration great potential if the correct steps are taken. I believe we are well on the way toward eliminating public protests and changing the type of Volunteers who go overseas. This Administration can have a real and lasting impact only on the new people going overseas. Some 4,000 Volunteers will be sent this summer and in little more than a year from now, all Volunteers overseas will have been selected during this Administration. They will have better screening, training, and guidance. Most important, they will be people with more experience, skills and maturity—the best kinds of Volunteers to represent America abroad while meeting the needs of developing countries.

Evidence indicates that the firings of protesters Blatchford refers to never occurred, that they were in fact resignations. But the fiction has helped to give Blatchford an image of toughness on protest with certain elements where the image is important to him. Much of the memorandum is in fact fiction, but the fact that Blatchford found it necessary to send it indicates the pressure that was on him in early 1970.

Despite these pressures and the shockingly low morale among the Washington staff, I have already indicated that the Peace Corps programs I visited in Africa and Asia in 1970 seemed solid with the volunteers doing good work. They seemed to be little affected by the unhappiness and tensions of headquarters. Whether that kind of immunity can continue is questionable, but it does make clear what anyone long in the Peace Corps has always known: The very heart and being of the Peace Corps is overseas in the individual work of the volunteers, and Washington is very remote to this reality, whether it is a Washington of Democrats or Republicans.

Part II

The Peace Corps in a World at War

CHAPTER SIX

The Peace Corps and Global Politics

For an organization dedicated to peace, the Peace Corps
has known but small measure of that precious commodity.
It was born in the chill of a cold war that produced such
noxious flowers as the Bay of Pigs and the Cuba missile
crisis. It has grown up in the shadow of an Asian war
that divided the American people and made Americans
overseas as unpopular as they have ever been. It has done
its work in parts of the world most buffeted by the rising
currents of nationalism, xenophobia, and racial pride.

Because of these currents, entire Peace Corps programs
have been summarily thrown out of several countries—
Guinea, Mauritania, Gabon, Libya, Somalia—for purely
political, nationalistic, or xenophobic reasons. Programs
have been terminated in three other countries—Indonesia,
Ceylon, Pakistan—less dramatically but just as firmly, because of foreign policy or ideological differences with the
United States. Individual volunteers have been picketed,
shouted at, assaulted, and spat on by Africans, Asians,
and Latins who resented their presence. Moscow, Peking,
and the radical press of dozens of developing nations have
heaped unending abuse on the Peace Corps and its volunteers.

Yet the men who built the Peace Corps in Washington and those who have run it overseas have steadfastly maintained from the beginning that the organization is non-political and in no way an instrument of American foreign policy. This position has been assailed as either naïve or hypocritical by enemies, critics, and persons who have wanted to use the Peace Corps in a foreign policy fight. The philosophical soundness of the position has been questioned by many volunteers and a few staff members, most notably Frank Mankiewicz.

The truth, of course, lies somewhere between the concept of aseptic apoliticality and the charge of being a callous tool of the State Department. But on a straight line it lies infinitely closer to the former than the latter. Philosophically, the Peace Corps is committed to a belief that change is possible, and in many places around the world volunteers have come into conflict with forces that do not want change. This, admittedly, is a political situation in an abstract sense. Similarly, it has been argued that, by working in countries run by corrupt oligarchies or dictators, the Peace Corps supports their evil regimes. I would dispute this charge even while admitting that the allegation is not implausible.

But on a concrete level those who enforce Peace Corps policy have done everything possible to maintain a doctrine that the Peace Corps works with people, with individuals, in the countries where it serves and not with governments or political regimes. And this very definitely includes staying clear of the United States foreign policy apparatus maintained within those countries. Holding to this position has taxed the ingenuity and integrity and tested the maturity of thousands of staff and volunteers over the years. It has also more than once called for a display of quiet courage.

In the 1969 House hearings on the Peace Corps bill before the Subcommittee on Appropriations, Chairman Otto E. Passman, congressman from Louisiana, long a Peace Corps foe and personal enemy of Jack Vaughn, then Peace Corps director, made a savage attack on the volunteers' rights of free expression overseas and strongly asserted that they should unwaveringly support official U.S. foreign policy, whatever it might be. Passman had just come from a junket to Asia and had talked with a group of volunteers in Bangkok, who had expressed to him privately their unhappiness with America's Vietnam policy. Jack's replies to Passman were quiet but unequivocal. Though in the following exchange I have abridged the congressman's bombast, I have in no way distorted his point of view.

MR. PASSMAN. . . . I was shocked to hear them expressing themselves vocally in opposition to our Vietnam policy. I would not do that any more than I would shoot my brains out. The Peace Corps volunteers do not have to comply with the same rules and regulations that our Foreign Service officers do, do they?

MR. VAUGHN. No.

MR. PASSMAN. . . . When I get on a plane to go on one of these trips, I brag on our foreign policy. You would think I made it. I never say one word detrimental to my country or its policies. . . . No American, to my way of thinking, should be permitted to go abroad until he takes that same oath of allegiance to this great country that the people down at the State Department take. . . .

MR. VAUGHN. Dean Rusk has said repeatedly that Peace Corps volunteers are not a part of U.S. foreign policy, not to be considered as such, and if they were—

MR. PASSMAN. Why do you not take the initiative as an American, and recommend that we amend the legislation or policy so these kids—a lot of them spoiled, disappointed in love, or something—will go out and take the same position as the State Department people? What would you do, my dear friend, with our military personnel if they got out there and started spouting off like these Peace Corpsmen? They would be given a general court-martial, would they not?

MR. VAUGHN. I would like to have some indication that they have been spouting off. . . . Don't you talk to Americans in a different way than you talk—

MR. PASSMAN. I talked to them as a group. This was not individual Peace Corpsmen. This was the whole group. If I had a chartered plane at my disposal and had had the authority, I would have pulled them all in by the nape of the neck and put them aboard that plane and flown them back to the United States. I thought this year you would have come around to saying we want the Peace Corpsmen to support the same foreign policy that our troops in Vietnam, who would be given a general court-martial if they took the same position as these people in the Peace Corps. Why don't you give some thought to it, Mr. Vaughn? These people are supposed to impart our correct image in foreign countries. If they spout off to me, they are going to spout off to others.

MR. VAUGHN. I do not think that is the case at all.

MR. PASSMAN. You use the word "I do not think." I can tell you that is the case. You know very well we have had a lot of trouble with them even in this country after they have returned from their tours of duty overseas.

MR. VAUGHN. I think the purpose of the Foreign Service officers and the military is so totally different. Peace Corps volunteers go out, not to carry out U.S. foreign policy, but to serve a foreign country and its people.

MR. PASSMAN. What is the Peace Corps supposed to do if it is not to impart the friendly image that we want the foreign countries to have about Americans? If these youths go overseas and are hostile to our foreign policy and so express themselves, as has been reported in the press, are they helping America? Why shouldn't they support the same policy as these boys over in Vietnam, some of whom have died since we started these hearings? Why shouldn't your people support the same policy, Mr. Vaughn?

MR. VAUGHN. Because they go out as free individuals from a pluralistic society.

MR. PASSMAN. The military people who go overseas, aren't they free? Aren't they free Americans?

They are serving their country with pride and are glad to serve it.

MR. VAUGHN. They are at war.

MR. PASSMAN. I know that, but how about the Embassies? They are not at war. They support our foreign policy, do they not? Do you think Mr. Johnson would send a single Ambassador to a foreign country if he did not support our country's foreign policy?

MR. VAUGHN. We are talking about two completely different concepts.

MR. PASSMAN. They are not different. They are also Americans trying to impart a correct American image.

MR. VAUGHN. It indicates to me how totally you misunderstand the concept of the Peace Corps and what it is setting out to do.

MR. PASSMAN. . . . Your concept of our foreign policy is such that I do not think you should be in the position you hold. If you do not advocate that all Americans who go out of this country to represent the United States, support our foreign policy, then I am thoroughly disappointed in you.

Minor comic relief occurred at this point when Congresswoman Julia Hansen of Washington broke in to say, "Good Lord, Mr. Chairman, how can you say that? Nixon has been padding around the world advocating a different foreign policy." Passman reminded Mrs. Hansen that Mr. Nixon was traveling as a private citizen, and Mrs. Hansen reminded the chairman that that particular private citizen wanted to be President of the United States.

It takes but a modicum of insight to understand that the kind of young men and women capable of being successful volunteers would not join the Peace Corps if they were forced to parrot an official U.S. foreign policy line, no matter what it might be. It should be equally obvious that most countries would not receive volunteers if they were foreign policy propagandists. Quite possibly Mr. Passman was aware of both these facts and saw his position as a quick method of doing away with the Peace Corps.

The kind of pressure exerted by Passman to make volunteers adhere to a particular U.S. foreign policy line is an extreme example; but with the escalation of the Vietnam war it was a constant problem that took many forms, as I will explain later. While I am on the subject of pressure and courage in defending the Peace Corps' apoliticality, however, I would like to tell one more story about Jack Vaughn.

Jack came into my office one morning in early October 1969. "I had a call at home last night," he said.

The call had come from a member of President Johnson's cabinet. What the gentleman wanted was the name and address of every person who had served as a Peace Corps volunteer. The Humphrey campaign people wanted to put out a special mailing pleading for the active support of former volunteers in his bid for the presidency. The Vice-President's name had always been closely associated with the Peace Corps, and young people had seemed to do all right for Eugene McCarthy.

"What did you tell him?" I asked.

Jack puffed on his pipe. "I told him no."

No is a hard answer for some men to take. The cabinet member called Jack again a few nights later and repeated his request. Jack told me about it the next morning. The gentleman had been a good deal more blunt this time. He reminded Jack that he had received all of his big breaks under a Democratic administration. He reminded him that as a presidential appointee he was not subject to the Hatch Act and now was the time to do something helpful. Jack had tried to explain his belief that to take the Peace Corps into politics this way could be fatal to it. The cabinet member was not sympathetic.

"What now?" I asked.

Jack thought for a long time. "I'm going to call Humphrey," he said.

He got the Vice-President on the line immediately and explained to him why he thought the idea could have very serious consequences for the Peace Corps. I could not hear Mr. Humphrey's replies, but it was clear that he agreed with Jack.

"Thank you very much, Mr. Vice-President," Jack said, and that was the end of the matter. The lists of names were never touched.

I am happy to say that I know of no other attempt—and I am sure there has been none—to use the Peace Corps in partisan U.S. politics.

The Peace Corps' hardest line has always been taken in regard to the partisan politics of the countries in which it serves. Neither volunteers nor staff are ever to engage by word or deed in the partisan political affairs, at any level from village to national, of their host country. With the debatable but important exception of the Pacific Trust Territory of Micronesia[1] this policy has always been un-

[1] Volunteers serving in Micronesia have maintained that the effective government of the islands is the United States Trust Territory Administration of the Interior Department. Therefore they reason that volunteers, as Americans, have the right and duty to comment on the policies and performance of the governing agency. Many volunteers have felt that the TTA has been sluggish and unresponsive to the Micronesians' needs and that too many TTA employees have a "colonist mentality" and are overly interested in their own prerogatives and comforts. Even more serious, large numbers of volunteers have felt—and with considerable evidence to support their feelings—the TTA has purposely neglected the political education of the islanders. The United States, the volunteers believe, clearly intends to maintain some kind of permanent relationship with Micronesia, even though a plebescite on self-determination may be held some day. These points of view by the volunteers have led to some tense moments between the Peace Corps, the Trust Territory Administration, and the American military, with its large interest in Micronesia.

The most highly publicized encounter concerned a volunteer named Todd Jenkins, who was serving as a teacher on the island of Kili in the Marshall District. When Jenkins and his wife were there in 1968, Kili had for twenty years been the "temporary" home of the people of Bikini, who had been moved to Kili when the U.S. wanted their atoll for atomic testing. Jenkins became aware of the deep desire of the Bikinians to return to their ancestral atoll. Life had not been easy for them on Kili, a single island surrounded by treacherous waves; fishing was very poor and trading conditions hazardous much of the year. They longed for their atoll with its sheltered lagoon, the staff of life for all Marshallese.

Jenkins drew up a persuasive, fact-filled petition calling for the return of the Bikinians to their atoll and sent it to the president of the United Nations Trusteeship Council. The petition made clear the hardships of the Bikinians on Kili, emphasized that at least as early as 1966 Atomic Energy Commission scientists had pronounced Bikini safe for human habitation, and drew attention to a letter dated September 1966, from the TTA high commissioner to the Kili magistrate saying . . . "it may be possible to resettle Bikini in the not-too-distant future." Jenkins asked in his petition, written in February 1968, "When is the not-too-distant future?"

The petition received a good deal of press attention, including a story in the New York *Times,* and of course caused more than a little unhappiness in the Interior and State departments. At Peace Corps headquarters we took the position that the petition was a well-researched, well-presented, temperate document submitted by a volunteer in the best interests of the people with whom he was working. The Trust Territory Administration stated rather stuffily that they had been considering the

derstood, agreed with, and observed by Peace Corps people. Significant violations since the Peace Corps began in 1961 can be counted on one hand, a remarkable record when one considers how deeply engrossed volunteers and staff become in the lives and problems of the people with whom they live and work.

A volunteer in an East African country developed strong sympathies for a group of political exiles from the country and entered into fairly extensive communication with them. The security police discovered this liaison and asked that the volunteer be removed from the country. Although there was no evidence that the volunteer planned to assist the political refugees in any way that would be detrimental to the country, indications were that the refugees planned to call on him for help. The Peace Corps and the volunteer himself recognized his bad judgment and he was withdrawn. In every other way he had been an outstanding volunteer: he went to another part of Africa and continued to work as a private citizen.

A volunteer in a West African country was terminated after he tried to smuggle a friend in political trouble out of the country.

In a Latin country in 1969 government army troops began rounding up, at gun point, the poor people of several city *barrios* and transporting them to nearby sugar cane fields for forced labor. A Peace Corps volunteer

return to Bikini for some time, a fact made obvious by the high commissioner's letter of 1966.

The Bikinians were still on Kili in August 1970. An Interior Department official informed the author that they would be moved to Bikini "as soon as housing was ready." The official did not speculate on when that might be.

working in the *barrios* became so incensed at this abuse of police power that he wrote, printed, and distributed a stinging condemnation of the government for its actions. Though government officials were furious, they were also red-faced at the publicizing of their use of troops to get labor for big landowners' plantations. They called off the troops immediately, and the volunteer was allowed to remain in the country, through the deft diplomacy of the country rep.

The latter example is more difficult to judge than the first two. The volunteer was outraged at what was being done to his poverty-stricken friends, and he was the only one who could take action without fear of perhaps lethal reprisal. But what he did could easily have led to the Peace Corps' being expelled from the country, and ending the work of a hundred other volunteers. Some might argue that the risk was worth taking. Those responsible for the Peace Corps as an organization would not agree but, as actually happened, would intercede for the volunteer if they could.

No doubt understanding high-level country officials and effective staff work have defused other political bombs involving Peace Corps volunteers. Nevertheless, the volunteers' restraint and good judgment in not involving themselves in other people's partisan politics has been a distinguishing feature of the Peace Corps' first decade.

CHAPTER SEVEN

The Cold War

Senator John F. Kennedy, formulating his ideas for a Peace Corps as he conducted his presidential campaign in the fall of 1960, clearly believed that such an organization could help the United States in its cold war struggles with Russia and Red China. With some of his first statements about a Peace Corps, he thrust it squarely into the cold war. Speaking in Chicago on November 4, he said:

> . . . as a counter to the flood of well-trained and accomplished tacticians now helping nations with their problems that the Communists are sending out, I believe an American Peace Corps as a supplement to our selective service that now draws only a fraction of our young men, could be trained to help these people live a life of freedom in agriculture, in handiwork, in road building, in government and other skills, young Americans who will represent the cause of freedom around the globe.

In a television show on the eve of the election, Kennedy answered a question from the audience about how he would stop the Communists. He gave some standard proposals such as maintaining our military vigor, properly exploiting our natural resources, and stepped-up education in science. Then he added:

> I have suggested having a Peace Corps of young men and women who will be willing to spend two or three years of their lives as teachers and nurses, working in different countries which are backward and which are just beginning to develop, spreading the cause of freedom. Maintain our strength here, maintain our military defenses, speak quietly, associate ourselves with peace, try to distribute our food and other benefits we have to less fortunate people so that they know we are interested in them, and I believe if we do these things communism can be checked, but more important, freedom can begin to grow back of the Communist curtain.

Other leading political figures saw the Peace Corps as a weapon in America's fight against world communism. In 1961 Hubert Humphrey said that the Peace Corps was "to be a part of the total foreign policy of the United States . . . to combat the virus of Communist totalitarianism." Other members of Congress talked about the Peace Corps as a vehicle for "exporting our American values."

Members of the congressional committees that worked on the first Peace Corps bill were determined that young Americans going abroad should be equipped to deal with communism in whatever ways they might find necessary. In the general provision of the Peace Corps Act that authorizes training for volunteers before they are sent overseas, only one subject is specifically required: "Training hereinabove provided for shall include instruction in the philosophy, strategy, tactics, and menace of communism."

I think there is no doubt that Kennedy and Humphrey's statements about the Peace Corps as a weapon against communism were intended entirely for domestic consumption. They felt that this justification would be the most persuasive with certain elements of the American public and the Congress. Their major emphasis always in talking about the Peace Corps was that it would provide needed help to developing nations, foster communication and understanding between Americans and people of other nations, and serve as an outlet for American idealism.

Still, their words had set the Peace Corps firmly in the context of the cold war; and in any case it is impossible to believe that the Russians, Red Chinese, and other Communists everywhere would not have seen it that way. The presence of hundreds and then thousands of young Americans working away at jobs all over the developing world was an immediate and persistent challenge to their propaganda machines.

Radio Moscow attacks began almost as soon as the Peace Corps was given life by President Kennedy's executive order and have continued unabated ever since. Peking and Havana broadcasts have taken up the attack occasionally but have left most of the work to the Russians. While radio has been the main instrument of propaganda, anti-Peace Corps pamphlets have sometimes appeared in countries, and articles have been planted in sympathetic or subsidized newspapers and magazines. The similarity and often identical nature of these pamph-

lets and articles leave little doubt as to the central production source.

The first Radio Moscow attack of which I am aware
occurred on March 16, 1961, and established one of the
main themes of all subsequent propaganda when it announced that the Peace Corps had been set up for the
purpose of gathering espionage information "for Allen
Dulles' agency." Allen Dulles was then head of the Central
Intelligence Agency. Less than two months later Tass, the
official Soviet news agency, made the bold announcement that Sargent Shriver was in fact the number one
CIA agent. Predictably, the two succeeding directors of
the Peace Corps have been labeled CIA employees. The
most familiar line is that the Peace Corps is really a CIA
operation and that Peace Corps volunteers are spies carefully selected by CIA staff.

The propaganda can be wildly ludicrous, as in one
pamphlet which asserted that "Peace Corps candidates
are rejected if they miss a nickel at fifty yards with a Colt
revolver." Even Tass was not above charging that an evil
Peace Corps woman in Somalia tried to teach her students
the "indecent movements" of the twist. The Indian Communist periodical *Blitz* ran a series of lurid stories accusing Peace Corps volunteers of secretly spreading
diseases among the poultry flocks of farmers in Maharashtra State. While we may laugh at such absurdities, they
do not necessarily seem at all absurd in areas of the developing world where newspapers are a rarity and a
village is fortunate to have one radio. There the printed
word and the mechanical voice have a special influence.
In Maharashtra the *Blitz* articles coincided with an out-

break of coccidiosis, a serious chicken disease, and the poultry volunteers were in some cases seriously set back in their work.

A cleverly written and well put together booklet entitled *The Truth About the Peace Corps* appeared in India in 1968. In one interesting passage it attempts to explain the true motivation of volunteers that the Indian reader of the booklet may have seen working hard and with seeming dedication in his country.

> What is the explanation of the zeal and seemingly selfless service of the Americans from the Peace Corps? First of all the volunteers' "selfless labor" is liberally remunerated. During the two years that a volunteer stays abroad he or she has over 200 dollars paid into a savings account every month at a bank in the United States. On returning to the States a volunteer stands to get a bonus of 2,000 dollars and a three-months' paid leave. To top it all, there is a permanent, well paid job waiting at the Corps headquarters or some other government office. In the United States, with its ever-present millions of unemployed, mostly young people, this is a golden opportunity.

The facts are these: A volunteer receives in an escrow account seventy-five dollars for each month of satisfactory service, on which he pays U.S. income tax. He receives no special bonus beyond this amount and he receives no leave, paid or otherwise, after returning to the United States; in fact, he ceases to be a volunteer immediately upon leaving his country of assignment. There is no guarantee of a job with the government or anywhere else.

Perhaps suspecting that some readers will not be convinced that all volunteers are mercenaries, *The Truth About the Peace Corps* continues:

True, a proportion of the young volunteers are not motivated by material advantages. They are eager to serve people. But the admirable zeal of these young Americans is being conveniently utilized by the bosses of the Corps and also (we shall deal with it further on) by the American cloak-and-dagger department—the Central Intelligence Agency.

In most cases by far the honest American lad joining the Peace Corps is completely unaware that, in doing so, he has become a tool in the dirty—and, in the long run, criminal—hands of intelligence agents.

How? Very simple. Every employee of the Corps staying abroad must periodically compile and submit to his superiors detailed reports. These are of a uniform pattern supplying information about the social and property status of the people he meets, their views and sentiments, their innermost desires, habits, etc. The data thus obtained is compiled at the Corps headquarters, analysed and sent on to interested bodies in the United States. Apart from the secret service, which is naturally always eager to obtain the information, the data is simply priceless to big corporations, enabling them to cull local business partners as they see fit. Thus even earnest Americans who join the Corps become enlisted, willy-nilly in the shabby cause.

The usual line of attack is a good deal more heavy-handed than the above passages from *The Truth About the Peace Corps*. The following, from a Radio Moscow broadcast beamed at Korea, is typical:

> . . . the official explanation for the presence of the so-called U.S. Peace Corps units in South Korea is that personnel of the Corps are assigned to the mission of propagating culture among South Koreans and making it easier for South Korean children and young people to receive education. This is the official explanation by the Seoul puppets, who parrot Washington's propaganda.
>
> But facts show things to be quite contradictory to their words. As is known, U.S. imperialism has never done anything merciful and altruistic in its relations with underdeveloped countries in Asia, Africa, and Latin America. Washington, which is well aware of the fact that the time during which it could without restraint plunder colonies has unmistakably passed, now employs effective means to expand its sphere of influence in politics, economy, and ideology. The subversive activities of the Peace Corps, which may appear to do no harm, must be classed among Washington's machinations.
>
> Nearly 170,000 U.S. Peace Corps personnel have gone to fifty foreign countries. The U.S. ruling circles yearly appropriate more than one hundred million dollars for the maintenance of the Corps.

This is a large sum of money, and we know that U.S. capitalists never waste their money. What then is the explanation for the ever-increasing size of the fund for the Peace Corps?

The answer can be found in the words of Shriver, the first director of the Peace Corps. In his book, *Point of the Lance*, he has admitted that the U.S. Peace Corps is in effect an idealogical weapon for infiltrating other countries with a view toward providing effective and necessary conditions to secure U.S. interests. The point is that Washington is trying to keep countries under its control and influence while keeping an eye on possible outbreaks of national liberation flames. It is easy to understand the assignment of Peace Corps units to such missions.

Before leaving for their assignments in foreign countries, Peace Corps volunteers are sent to military camps where they take lessons in handling various weapons and are given portable radio communications equipment and instructions on codes.

I have no idea as to the source of the 170,000 figure. The number of volunteers who had gone overseas at the time of this broadcast would have been more like 35,000.

The able civil servants who handle Peace Corps programs in the receiving countries know that propaganda of the kind I have quoted is nonsense, but millions of the people they serve do not. Also, nationalist groups, leftist politicians, and even opposition party members in some countries make a good deal of use of such material, whether they believe it or not.

With but few exceptions, Communist propaganda is little more than a minor irritant to volunteers once they have established themselves in their community. Its effect on the total program is harder to assess, but again it probably cannot be rated as a very serious problem to date. The reason this is true is to be found in the extraordinary effort the Peace Corps has made from the beginning to disassociate itself from any kind of U.S. intelligence activity. Even the appearance of the Peace Corps' being connected with any intelligence effort is actively guarded against.

Almost all developing nations have a deep and abiding suspicion of the U.S. Central Intelligence Agency. Those of us who have lived with that suspicion know that one proved case of CIA infiltration into the Peace Corps could be fatal to the whole Peace Corps organization. Sargent Shriver was equally well aware of how attractive a cover the Peace Corps, with its thousands of volunteers scattered in hundreds of villages and cities throughout the developing world, could be to the CIA.

One of Shriver's earliest acts therefore was to go to President Kennedy and seek his support in keeping CIA hands off the Peace Corps. The President promised Shriver that there would be no CIA agents in the Peace Corps and issued such instructions to Allen Dulles. Lyndon Johnson and Richard Nixon, when they succeeded to the Presidency, kept that order in force.

Shriver rightly concluded that this agreement at the top, while imperative, was not enough. He knew he could not prevent wild charges of the Peace Corps' being infiltrated with spies. He could, however, do a great deal

bush air operations were CIA covers; the number of times you were wrong would be insignificant. We dropped our negotiations with the airline.

We worked out another important safeguard with all the intelligence agencies. No one who has served in the Peace Corps as volunteer or staff is eligible to be employed by such an agency for at least four years after leaving the Peace Corps. Even former volunteers doing military duty will not be assigned to intelligence work. Should a former Peace Corps person be hired after his period of ineligibility, he will not be assigned to work in the country in which he served as a volunteer. Shriver and his general counsels were pleased at the cooperation they received in working out this regulation.

As any bureaucrat knows, the gap between formulating policy and implementing it can be awesome. What was to prevent an ambitious or hard-pressed CIA agent in the field from trying to use volunteers? Even more likely, what was to keep aggressive and information-hungry political officers in American embassies from visiting volunteers or inviting them into their homes and pumping them about people, conditions, and political attitudes in the area where they lived? It was well known that volunteers got closer to the people and knew more at a grass roots level than almost any other foreigners in a country.

I once had to complain to an ambassador about a consul general who was soliciting local details from volunteers. We had a confrontation in the ambassador's office, and the ambassador told his man in the plainest of terms that it was never to happen again. The consul general accepted the decision but with ill grace. Volunteers were excellent sources of "reportable information," he said bitterly, and it was too damned bad that the Peace Corps could not consider itself a part of the team.

Such a viewpoint has been relatively rare overseas. With only one or two exceptions ambassadors have clearly understood that volunteers must not be used as sources of information and have made this fact very clear to their staff officers. Peace Corps representatives have been hawkishly vigilant on this score. Volunteers are told that if there is ever any infraction of this well-understood rule by embassy people, they are to report it to a Peace Corps staff member immediately.

Most country reps do not require written reports from the volunteers about their work. In some countries where suspicion and xenophobia run especially high, reps ask volunteers not even to write detailed letters about their experiences. These are extreme measures, but time has shown that extremes are necessary in fighting widespread suspicion of America's intelligence apparatus.

Tanzania's President Nyerere once remarked that while he had never seen a shred of evidence of CIA involvement in the Peace Corps, the problem was that members of his government believed otherwise. Nyerere went on to say that it just did not seem to be the nature of an intelligence agency to leave untouched ten thousand of its countrymen scattered about in tempting places overseas. Nyerere said that he believes our denials are made in good faith, but he pointed out that the same denials would have been made by the National Student Association a few years ago.

Disclosure that the CIA had infiltrated student delegations going overseas again challenged the Peace Corps' credibility. Once more it was useful to be able to point to our safeguards against being used as a spy cover and to be able to say that there was no factual evidence on record that it had happened even once. Still, each new revelation of the CIA's ubiquitousness adds to the Peace Corps' problems.

Shortly after the CIA-NSA scandal broke, a Liberian woman in this country spoke to me with some amusement about the shock and indignation expressed on the editorial pages of America's newspapers. "I never realized," she said, "that you people did not know what your Central Intelligence Agency is doing overseas. We have known it for years."

Whether they have "known" it or not, they have believed it; and, as Nyerere observed, either way the Peace Corps has a problem.

Because one of the basic Peace Corps goals is to foster communication and understanding, both Shriver and Vaughn were eager to have Peace Corps programs in Communist countries. Vaughn particularly expressed this desire in a number of public statements. Except for some low level and unproductive discussions with the Yugoslavs, however, not the faintest signal of interest has ever been received from any Communist country.

To the contrary, whenever Communists have taken over a government they have shown quick aversion to any Peace Corps volunteers who might be in their midst. Although public announcements stated that the Peace Corps left Indonesia through mutual agreement in 1965, the fact is that Sukarno, rapidly moving into the Red Chinese sphere, found the Peace Corps an embarrassment and asked for the volunteers to be removed.

When the Communist party of Kerala State in India won the 1967 election, one of the early announcements of the new Communist chief minister was that all Peace Corps volunteers in the state would be asked to leave. The Kerala program consisted of rural health workers as well as groups of volunteers assisting poultry farmers and small industry entrepreneurs. The health volunteers, near the end of their tours, were allowed to finish their work, but a withdrawal request on the poultry and small industry groups was made to the central government in New Delhi.

Although the Peace Corps and the Government of India were unhappy at Kerala's action, the Peace Corps held to its tradition of not in any way putting pressure on any government to take or keep volunteers if they were not wanted. We immediately signified our readiness to withdraw the volunteers and looked around to see if they were wanted and could be useful elsewhere in India. The state of Mysore quickly asked for the entire poultry group; but before we could place the small industry workers, a small assortment of engineers and men with business management and marketing backgrounds, word came from Kerala that that group could finish its work in the state. This about face resulted from the protests of the factory owners and businessmen with whom the volunteers were working.

It is tempting at such time to react with righteous indignation. It would have been satisfying to have said to the Kerala government, "Either they all stay or they all go." But the Peace Corps exists to serve and work with people, and wherever the opportunity presents itself that consideration must prevail. The decision makers of the Peace Corps have an outstanding record in holding to that basic principle, sometimes in the face of considerable pressure. The small industry volunteers stayed in Kerala and the poultry workers left.

The poultry volunteers were no sooner gone than the farmers made a protest similar to the one that had kept the small industry group in Kerala. The Kerala government inquired about the possibility of their coming back. But the volunteers were already at work in Mysore and a commitment had been made to the Mysore government. Again, it was tempting. To have the volunteers go back to Kerala by popular demand after having been thrown out by a Communist regime would have made a great story for U.S. consumption. But the Peace Corps resisted the story; the volunteers stayed in Mysore.

The Peace Corps' cold war problems with Russia have included two very clumsy attempts on that country's part either to subvert or compromise a volunteer. In the first case, in an Asian country, a Russian tried to bribe a volunteer to give him reports about Peace Corps activities in the country and also provide him with information available to the volunteer in the ministry for which he worked. In a country in North Africa, a member of the Russian Embassy attempted to get a volunteer to "collaborate" on articles, which would be printed in Russian publications. The Russian plied the volunteer with gifts of cigarettes, vodka, and money, all of which the volunteer turned over to the country rep when he reported the incident. In both cases word was got discreetly to an appropriate host country official, and there was no further activity by the Russians. The attempts were so amateurish that they must have been on local initiative.

The Russians have always exhibited a good deal of interest in how the Peace Corps works. The Peace Corps has never been bashful about putting out reports about itself and the work of its volunteers, and these reports are available to anyone. Perhaps the Russians have gathered and digested all of them, but sometimes I wonder if that method would not have been too easy.

In two cases overseas the Peace Corps discovered that the Russian Embassy had rented space in offices immediately above or connected to Peace Corps offices with the obvious intention of eavesdropping. In Iran a volunteer waded across a river, not knowing that at that particular point the river marked the boundary between Iran and Russia. The volunteer, Tom Dawson, was arrested by border guards immediately upon touching the opposite shore. He was taken to the city of Baku and detained for three weeks. When our embassy finally effected his release, he reported that most of his intensive questioning had been about the Peace Corps and its work in Iran.

In an early unclassified Peace Corps file in Washington I once saw a note that the FBI had reported that one of its "black" agents was asked by a member of "the other side" to obtain a copy of the Peace Corps handbook for them. Anyone in Washington is welcome to walk into the Peace Corps building at Connecticut Avenue and H Street and pick up a copy of the handbook. It is also available at Peace Corps recruiting booths on hundreds of college campuses.

But apparently there is a right way and a wrong way to conduct espionage.

Russian and bloc country interest in the Peace Corps has for some time made us think that they would very much like to mount some such effort of their own. A most revealing passage from a Czech political magazine article on the Peace Corps states:

> It must be admitted that the Peace Corps Volunteers have indeed established close contacts with local inhabitants in many countries. The overwhelming majority have succeeded in adjusting to the unfavorable climatic, material and other living conditions of the new surroundings. This has been the basis of their success. Their activities have produced concrete results in education, health services, construction of various installations, etc.
>
> The Peace Corps is an extraordinarily important tool for anti-communism. It achieves its goals not with subversive activities, but . . .—with most effective help in those sections of national economics, culture, education and welfare and in other branches of life where the developing countries feel the acute necessity of help.
>
> The success of the Peace Corps should also provide us with food for thought . . . there is no doubt that the Peace Corps brought a good deal of results, which helped toward the faster development of the countries of Asia, Africa and Latin America. . . . If

the altruism of young Americans has produced positive results in spite of the fact that the Peace Corps' intrinsic nature is to serve the policy of American imperialism, think of the results the altruism of our own young people could produce if their efforts were allied with the humanistic goals of our own foreign policy.

Anyone who has seen the isolation and closed community atmosphere of the compounds in which Soviet technicians live while working on foreign aid projects abroad cannot quite imagine ten thousand young Russians scattered throughout Asia and Africa working, living, traveling with almost no supervision except that provided by the host government. It could greatly further the exchange of information and ideas. I think they could do a good job, and I imagine they would remain loyal Russian citizens. But I do not believe that the Soviet ideological bureaucrats who make such decisions will find the courage to make that one in our time.

Meanwhile they continue to chop tirelessly at the American Peace Corps with their verbal meat axes in a little noted battlefield of the cold war that has now lasted a decade.

CHAPTER EIGHT

Nationalism and Xenophobia

The Peace Corps was somewhat astonished when in early 1966 it received a cautious inquiry about the availability of English teachers from the North African country of Libya. Except for the former French colonies of Morocco and Tunisia, Arab nations had shown little or no interest in the Peace Corps, and Libya was generally considered one of the most conservative and xenophobic of the Moslem countries—for excellent reasons. Its strategic location on the Mediterranean Sea and its thin but verdant and productive coastal belt have been coveted by alien people since the days of Homer. Its Tripolitanian coast had been successively fought over and occupied by the Phoenicians, Carthaginians, Romans, Vandals, Byzantines, Normans, Spaniards, and Turks. Very early the Greeks had colonized the eastern part of the country and named it Cyrenaica. The Arabs had come, too, in A.D. 643, and had stayed, not in the great coastal cities but in the hills, plains, and deserts of the vast hinterland. They had fought constantly with the indigenous Berbers and eventually replaced them as the dominant stock.

The last occupier was Italy, taking Libya from Turkey in 1912 and holding it in a harsh and repressive grip for thirty years; the Senussi tribe of Cyrenaica for two decades carried out a bitter but ultimately futile guerrilla war against the Italians. During the early 1930s Mussolini, dreaming of a new Roman empire, sent large numbers of settlers to the country.

The last chapter in a history of invasion took place during World War II when the desert forces of Rommel and Montgomery rolled back and forth across the country, leaving the British in control. French forces moved into the deep desert areas and occupied the Libyan province of Fezzan. After the war dozens of proposals were studied as to what the fate of this geographical pawn of the centuries should be. Agreement could not be reached, however, and in November 1949, the United Nations decreed that Libya should become a fully sovereign country not later than January 1, 1952.

It is doubtful that a country ever began its life with a greater paucity of assets. Many of its towns lay in ruins as a result of the tank battles that raged up and down the coast. Farms had been abandoned; there was little business activity and no industry. Per capita income was not more than thirty dollars a year. The illiteracy rate was at least ninety percent. A total of sixteen Libyans held university degrees. There was no such thing as a national treasury. There was, however, a national heritage: a deep-rooted knowledge that outsiders meant trouble.

Desperate for money, the new Libyan government negotiated an agreement with the United States for a major U.S. Air Force base to be located near Tripoli.

From the beginning this base has been a source of irritation and one more highly visible sign of foreign occupation. The Libyans also accepted a large U.S. aid program, welcoming the money more enthusiastically than the technicians to help them spend it. Large numbers of educated Arab refugees from Palestine were imported to help run the government and hundreds of Egyptian teachers were brought in, but even these Arab brothers were watched with a wary eye.

The discovery of great pools of high quality oil in 1959 seemed to give the Libyan government confidence. With a population of less than two million, Libya was on the threshold of becoming a rich nation. Many oil companies were operating in the vast desert stretches of the country pouring in men and millions. The government leaders saw that Libya was once again being invaded, but this time, they believed, the invasion could work to their country's benefit.

This would only be true, however, if they could educate their people to take over the jobs from the foreigners as fast as possible. The government adopted a program of maximum investment in education at all levels and increased the numbers of Libyans being sent abroad for university and graduate study. They also decided that they must have a language besides Arabic since so much of their contact was obviously going to be with the oil-consuming nations of the West. The language they decided to emphasize was English.

Contract English teachers from Egypt, Britain, and the United States had been in Libya since independence but in small numbers. The government wanted a bigger and surer supply. These were the reasons behind the first approach to the Peace Corps, and the program negotiation was surely the strangest in the Peace Corps' history.

Libya wanted only fifteen teachers the first year—a trial. The Peace Corps agreed, though such a small number would be expensive to train and staff overseas. Libya wanted the Peace Corps teachers to sign the same contracts that all other expatriate teachers signed; they would also receive the same salary and benefits from the Ministry of Education that other teachers received. The Peace Corps agreed. Peace Corps people were not to be given any special billing as volunteers in the schools to which they were assigned; they were simply to be designated as contract teachers like other foreigners in the schools. The Peace Corps blinked a bit on that one but agreed.

The rub came when the Peace Corps started talking about sending over a Peace Corps representative and opening a Peace Corps office. That would be unnecessary, the Libyans said. Other expatriate teachers did very well without someone from their country to watch over them. Surely people from the Peace Corps could do as well.

The Peace Corps tried to explain that its volunteers were different, more than just classroom teachers. They would help organize community projects, teach adult classes at night, develop extracurricular programs for the school. For these things they might need guidance. The Libyans were puzzled. Perhaps they had not made themselves clear, they said. They wanted classroom teachers, not jumping jacks (though they did not use that term).

Finally a compromise was reached. The Peace Corps would send over one staff person who would maintain liaison with the Ministry of Education. He would not carry the title of Peace Corps director and he would not open a Peace Corps office. If he visited volunteers, he would do so as inspector for the ministry and not for the Peace Corps. To all of these conditions the Peace Corps agreed, but on one point we were adamant: There could be no screening on the basis of religion. If in the luck of the selection process, Jews were invited to the Libya program, if they accepted and succeeded in training, then they must be accepted as teachers in Libya. The Libyans agreed.

The first small group of volunteers made up of single men and women as well as married couples, arrived in Libya in the fall of 1966. Their training at Princeton had been good. They had a good academic knowledge of Libya, its people and problems; they had a satisfactory start on Libyan Arabic; they knew the rudiments of teaching English as a foreign language. They had also got the message very clearly: Even if they were not going to be labeled "Peace Corps Volunteer," the Peace Corps expected them to perform in every way like one.

They did. They became serious teachers, some of them handling English classes in several schools. Whether they were assigned to a remote oasis town in the Fezzan or to a big high school in Benghazi, they showed a special interest in their students and in the community around them. They worked hard to improve their Arabic and in so doing widened their own range of interest in the land and the people.

During their tour Egypt and Israel fought their six-day war. Every Arab nation was caught up in the emotions of hate and religious fervor, exacerbated by the disastrous defeat of the Egyptians. Radio Cairo beamed its accusations against the United States throughout North Africa. Libya did not break diplomatic relations with the United States, as some Arab countries did, but the pressure on Americans and Britons living among the Arabs became almost intolerable in some places. Local hostility forced many expatriate teachers to resign and leave Libya. In one community a Libyan who was about to leave to study in England was beaten and had his car and clothes burned. A Peace Corps volunteer was transferred to that town to teach in the high school. The day he arrived he talked his way into a basketball game in progress on the school's outdoor court. He could talk the young Libyans' language, and in half an hour he was showing them how Wilt Chamberlain dunked shots. He stayed and taught. The other volunteers stayed in their communities, where they were known and had friends. In such times there is no better protection. They continued to teach.

The inspectors in the Libyan Ministry of Education, whose job it is to assess the performance of all teachers, watched the Peace Corps volunteers closely, and they liked what they saw. What they saw was what the Peace Corps had not been able to make clear in the initial abstract discussions: there could be a fundamental difference between an expatriate contract teacher hired sight unseen and a carefully selected person who learned about the country before he came, who wanted to speak the language of the people, and who—whatever his other motivations might be—wanted to be a good teacher and to be a part of the school and community.

In early 1968 the Ministry of Education officials called in Willard Whitman, the Peace Corps rep in Tripoli (we called him that even if they didn't). A decision had been made to further upgrade the importance of English in the curriculum, they said, by increasing the number of hours it would be taught and by starting it at a lower level. The latter meant teaching English in many more schools than heretofore. Libya, Whitman was told, would like to request additional Peace Corps volunteer English teachers.

"Fine," Whitman said. "How many?"

"Five hundred," the minister replied.

Whitman was stunned. When he passed the information to Washington, the reaction was the same. For a program to go from fifteen volunteers to five hundred in one jump was bold thinking even for the Peace Corps. Weeks of discussions followed. This was no longer 1963 and the Peace Corps had gone through its period of growth for growth's sake. A careful survey of schools and job potential finally produced an agreed-upon figure of about one hundred and fifty for the next increment.

The Libyans were enthusiastic. They suggested an exciting innovation of sending forty Libyan teachers—at the ministry's expense—to the training program for the new volunteers. The Libyans would teach Arabic to the trainees and at the same time improve their English through the association. This idea was carried out and, while there were problems, there were many benefits.

The large new group of volunteers arrived in Tripoli in the fall of 1968. The attitude of the Libyan government was completely changed. They were welcomed in arrival ceremonies as Peace Corps volunteers. The government, realizing the increased administrative problems, authorized a Peace Corps office and an adequate staff. The new volunteers settled quickly into their assignments. A few months later, Libya authorized an evaluation of the program by Lawrence O'Brien, the Peace Corps' able and experienced Director of Evaluation, who earlier had been rep in the West African country of Gabon. O'Brien reported that, on the whole, the program was excellent. The volunteers were well occupied with their teaching loads and making good adjustments to living in North Africa. The volunteers in the small, isolated desert towns were making friends faster and finding life more interesting and pleasant than those located in cities; but this was nothing new to the Peace Corps.

On balance, the Libya program was a good one. In teaching English the volunteers could feel that they were directly contributing to the future development of the country. Students going on to study in universities in England, Canada, and the United States would have to have excellent English; Libya still desperately needed university trained engineers, public administrators, business managers, doctors. At other levels thousands of good jobs were available with oil companies and related businesses; Libyans could learn better and take over faster on these jobs if they spoke English. With its magnificent Roman ruins at Leptis Magna and Sabratha and with its lovely Mediterranean coast, Libya had a tremendous unrealized tourist potential; again English would be a great asset.

In the summer of 1969 invitations went out for another group of one hundred and fifty volunteers to begin training; when they arrived the total number of volunteers in Libya would be over three hundred. But it was not to be.

In August of 1969 King Idris I, Libya's chief of state since independence, traveled to Istanbul for medical treatment. On September 2, a military coup was staged. The coup met with almost no resistance, and within a few hours Libya had a new government. The members of the junta were so obscure that neither the American Embassy nor the State Department could identify a single one. The leader was a twenty-seven-year-old army captain. But one thing was certain: They wanted no part of the outward-looking previous government.

With aggressive single-mindedness they moved Libya toward intense Arab nationalism. Within two weeks English was dropped from the schools. Road and building signs in English were taken down and replaced with Arabic. Restrictions on tourist travel were tightened. A number of countries were put on a boycott list for trading with Israel. Since English was not to be taught, the new government told the Peace Corps, volunteers would no longer be needed. Soon afterward, the announcement was made that other ways would be sought to decrease the number of foreigners in Libya.

Just three years after the first small group of Peace Corps volunteers moved to their assignments in Libya, the program came to an end. The training program for the large new group in the United States was abruptly broken off—as had happened so many times before—and an effort was made to find new assignments for those volunteers in Libya who had the heart to try it again in a new country.

Eight times in its first eight years the Peace Corps was asked to leave countries where it had programs in progress. Without exception the reasons for the eviction have had to do with nationalist passions, a general suspicion of Americans, or closely related political motives. Besides Indonesia and Libya, the countries which have asked the Peace Corps to pull out on-going programs are Ceylon, Guinea, Mauritania, Gabon,[1] Somalia, and Malawi.

The Ceylon program came to an end shortly after the Ceylonese government nationalized certain American private business property and failed to make provision for adequate compensation to the companies affected. The Hickenlooper Amendment, which directs that U.S. aid to a country must be suspended under such circumstances, was invoked and AID stopped operations. Peace Corps officials in Washington had earlier succeeded in

[1] In only one case has the Peace Corps left a country of its own accord. In March 1964, the Peace Corps volunteers were withdrawn from Cyprus and the program terminated. The island was in such a state of chaos that the volunteers were unable to work. Road blocks were everywhere; schools were closed or turned into refugee centers; government workers left their jobs; development programs were suspended. The decision on Cyprus was not universally approved in the Peace Corps, the feeling of some staff being that the more a country is in trouble the more volunteers should be able to render some useful service. Jack Vaughn vowed never to order a program to shut down in a country unless the lives of the volunteers were in serious jeopardy. Volunteers were withdrawn from Eastern Nigeria (Biafra) during the Nigerian civil war only after the Biafra Government advised the Peace Corps that it could no longer assure their safety. Volunteers were also withdrawn from East Pakistan during the conflict with India in 1965. In both cases, the Peace Corps continued to work in other parts of the countries.

having written into law a provision that the Hickenlooper Amendment would not apply to Peace Corps programs. Nevertheless, Ceylonese sensitivities were such that they did not want Peace Corps volunteers in the country at that time.

Mauritania, the desolate and fiercely Moslem West African country, broke diplomatic relations with the United States at the time of the 1967 Egyptian-Israeli fighting. A tiny Peace Corps program of only twelve volunteers was just settling down in the country. While Peace Corps officials made it clear that the volunteers would stay in the country, despite severance of diplomatic relations, if the Mauritanian government wished, the program was ordered out.

Despite all Peace Corps efforts, its programs in Africa have been severely affected by the political currents that swirl constantly throughout the continent. The program in Tanzania, which once numbered five hundred volunteers, declined during 1968 and 1969 through lack of requests for new groups and came to an end when the last volunteers finished their assignments in October 1969. In Nigeria, whose Peace Corps program had once been the second largest in the world with over seven hundred volunteers, there was a similar decline when the Federal Military Government in 1968 cancelled requests it had made for new groups. The numbers of volunteers pinched off to sixty-two in 1969, and the program will end through attrition in January 1971, or earlier, unless there is a last minute request for more volunteers.

Julius Nyerere, Tanzania's dynamic leader, strongly supported President Kennedy's Peace Corps idea even before his country gained its complete independence from Britain. Indeed, the very first volunteers to go into training were the Tanzania surveyors, and they arrived in time for the country's independence celebrations in December 1961. Nyerere became president of Tanzania in 1962; and the Peace Corps grew, mostly by supplying teachers for primary and secondary schools, during his first years in office. The two presidents, Nyerere and Kennedy, had much in common with their youth, vigor, eloquence, and eagerness to take their countries in fresh new directions.

Yet even from the beginning the Peace Corps was not without criticism in Tanzania. The President's own brother, Joseph Nyerere, in a general attack on the United States in the National Assembly asked, "What use is the Peace Corps if America is going to blow up the world?" And on several occasions parliament members made vague but vociferous attacks on the Peace Corps and volunteers in general, calling them troublemakers and suggesting that they were not in the country for any good purpose. In a newly independent black country the appearance of a fresh crop of white faces was almost certain to bring forth some resentment that could best be expressed by questioning the motives of the newly arrived outsiders. A wiser course for the Peace Corps might have been to keep its numbers at a much lower level in a young country that was in its first heady years of completely running its own affairs.

After the Kennedy administration, noticeable differences began to develop between the United States and Tanzania; they seldom made headlines, but they kept diplomats on edge and changed the complexion of the two country's relations. Tanzania was critical of the United States' growing role in Vietnam. The U.S. was not happy that Tanzania was accepting aid from Red China, aid that might become some of the most massive in Africa. Cold war tensions inevitably grew up, and the specter of the CIA began to be very much on Tanzanian minds. The belief seemed to be widespread that the Peace Corps was a cover for U.S. intelligence operations. I have already mentioned President Nyerere's statement that while he had never seen any evidence of CIA involvement in the Peace Corps, the problem was that members of his government believed there was.

In March 1967, Nyerere gave a press conference during which he made a surprising reference to the Peace Corps. "The Peace Corps has changed its character," he said. "Some of the idealism has gone out, and now? Now it is a problem."

I do not at all think that Mr. Nyerere was speaking about the work of Peace Corps volunteers in Tanzania. I have carefully examined all available records relating to the Tanzania program and have talked to many volunteers and staff members. I believe that the volunteers in 1967 were working hard and as well as earlier volunteers and that their job placements were probably better. Almost all volunteers have always found Tanzania a lovely country to work in and have enjoyed their association with Tanzanians; I am sure this was true of the volunteers in 1967 and that they were not unhappy or making trouble.

While it may be presumptuous to second guess President Nyerere, he never elaborated on his one cryptic comment about the Peace Corps, so one must conjecture. In speaking of the loss of idealism, I cannot help feeling that he was, perhaps unconsciously, referring to the Johnson administration and its conduct of the war in Vietnam. And when Nyerere said that the Peace Corps had become a problem, I think he meant that it had become a problem for him. Some officials in his government still very much wanted new volunteers, but others were opposed; and there were the ever-current CIA charges. I was once told by a knowledgeable Tanzanian that in fact Mr. Nyerere continued to think well of the Peace Corps volunteers in Tanzania but that the program had become a personal worry for him.

President Nyerere's Declaration of Arusha set forth his vision of a self-reliant Tanzania and a society and way of life for his countrymen that would not be based on imported imitations. This splendid statement probably spelled the death knell for the Peace Corps in Tanzania if it had not been spelled already. The irony is that the Peace Corps believes that its job is to help foster self-reliance and to assist people in finding the way of life that is best for them. With philosophical backing and leadership such as Nyerere's Peace Corps volunteers should have been able to give some measure of help in making the President's vision a reality. But once again the Peace Corps idea was no match for the combined forces of nationalism, xenophobia, international politics, and cold war pressures.

In Nigeria the Peace Corps program foundered on the shoals of that country's tragic civil war. At the time the Eastern Region proclaimed itself the independent state

of Biafra on May 30, 1967, 135 volunteers were assigned
there, mostly as teachers but also working in agriculture
and related programs. Almost at once the Federal Military
Government asked the Peace Corps to withdraw its volunteers from the East. Here was a cruel dilemma for the
Peace Corps and a diplomatic problem for the State Department. Volunteers are always officially invited to a
country by its federal or central government, and the
Peace Corps agreement is with the Ministry of Foreign
Affairs, not with state or local agencies.

If the Peace Corps failed to obey the request that it
remove the volunteers from the East, the Federal Military Government would certainly expel the Peace Corps
from the parts of the country it controlled. Furthermore,
to leave volunteers in Biafra in the face of the FMG's
instruction to withdraw them would remove any FMG
responsibility for their safety later on. But to remove the
volunteers would be an act of considerable political
significance because it would demonstrate that the Peace
Corps responded to the wishes of the FMG and not
the new Biafran government. More important, the
Eastern volunteers might be especially useful during this
time of emergency, and they were deeply committed to
their work with the Ibo people. While their work had already been badly disrupted by the crisis, most of them
did not want to leave.

We stretched out our discussions with the FMG as long
as possible, forlornly advancing our traditional rationale
that the Peace Corps hoped its role could always be to
work with people as individuals and stay removed from
whatever political crises might be stirring around them.

We were getting nowhere with our argument, however, and very soon would have had to take the Eastern volunteers out on the FMG's order. But in early July the Peace Corps representative in Enugu received word from Colonel Ojukwu that the Biafran government could no longer guarantee the safety of the volunteers. This was our signal to leave on terms that would not be offensive to either side. Whether Ojukwu was aware of our dilemma with the FMG, I don't know; but when we left Biafra, Jack Vaughn publicly expressed the hope that the Peace Corps would one day return.

As the civil war extended agonizingly through 1968 and into 1969, the Peace Corps program withered. Relations between the Nigerian and U.S. governments were continually strained, and former volunteers from Biafra now back in the United States set up a loud and persistent cry in Biafra's behalf. The FMG was unhappy with this "political interference," but of course the Peace Corps could not have done anything about it, even had it wanted to.

The Nigerians were terribly defensive. The Nigerian ambassador called the Peace Corps office one morning furious about a Peace Corps recruiting advertisement he had seen in the Washington *Post*. The ad showed a small black child, obviously hungry and sick, and the caption said, "If everyone in the world ignored things like this, maybe there'd be no world." Although not one word was said about any country or geographic location, the ambassador automatically assumed that the child was Biafran and that the Peace Corps was trying to embarrass the FMG.

Later that same day a former volunteer from Biafra called, furious because he interpreted the ad as a Peace Corps effort to get credit for helping Biafra when in fact we were not. We heard from others, expressing both reactions. The picture of the starving child evoked no pity, only political fury.

In Nigeria no new volunteers were requested, and a rising level of xenophobia was evident in the country. R. W. Apple, Jr., of the New York *Times* reported the following message was posted on the bulletin board of a major Nigerian newspaper: "Not a single man in Nigeria should have doubts as to the Peace Corps. It is a corps of spies and American imperialists." Officials of the FMG voiced no such sentiments, but they showed no inclination to keep the program alive. A final request for teaching volunteers was made in the spring of 1968, but it was cancelled shortly afterward with no real explanation. Another Peace Corps program, and one of the most important, had failed to survive the harsh political climate of Africa.

The most bizarre political use of the Peace Corps took place in Guinea in November 1966. The events leading to this use were equally bizarre. On October 28, a nineteen-man Guinea delegation, headed by Foreign Minister Louis Beauvogui, left Guinea's capital of Conakry and flew to Dakar, Senegal, to connect with a Pan American World Airways plane going to East Africa. The delegation was on its way to attend a pre-summit conference on the Organization of African Unity in Addis Ababa.

The party boarded at Dakar and the plane continued on to Accra, Ghana, for its next scheduled stop. At the

Accra airport the entire delegation was forced off the plane at gun point by soldiers of Lt. General Joseph Ankrah, leader of Ghana's ruling military government. The delegation was placed under arrest and held hostage in the hope of exchanging them for some one hundred Ghanians who Ankrah claimed were being detained against their will in Guinea.

When word of the Beauvogui delegation's detention reached Conakry, Guinea's state controlled radio unleased a barrage of abuse not only against Ghana but also the United States. Broadcasts asserted that the United States was fundamentally to blame because the "Accra puppets" were merely carrying out the instructions of the agents of imperialism. Further reports said the United States was to blame because the Pan American plane landed in Ghana; the fact that Accra was a regular stop on a long-established route seemed irrelevant. By nightfall the militia patrolled the streets of Conakry; teen-agers with rifles and submachine guns surrounded the American Embassy; a dozen militiamen with fixed bayonets on their rifles stood in front of the Peace Corps office.

The following morning the inevitable march on the American Embassy took place. Part of the mob put the embassy under siege while the rest broke into the ambassador's residence and almost demolished it. It is interesting that, as the chanting, slogan-shouting mob poured through the streets, it passed within a few feet of the Peace Corps office. No trouble occurred there, not even a rock heaved through a window.

The Peace Corps program in Guinea was three years old, but it had never been large. The present contingent consisted of sixty-two volunteers, a mixture of blue collar mechanics and English teachers. Despite the smallness of the program, it was considered one of the Peace Corps' hardest assignments for a rep because of Guinea's explosive politics and its prime position in the cold war conflict. The rep's job belonged to Henry Norman, a former practicing attorney from Syracuse; he had been with the program from the beginning and had successfully guided six volunteer groups in the country.

Norman told the volunteers in Conakry to report for work as usual on the morning of the embassy march, but by mid-day all of their Guinean supervisors had told them it would be better if they returned to their houses. Some of the volunteers had awakened that morning to find themselves actually under house arrest. Others were placed under house arrest during the day, and these house detentions generally included the volunteers serving up-country from Conakry.

Significantly, the volunteers were not subjected to any personal attacks or animosity. To the contrary, both their guards and neighbors were sympathetic and helpful. Neighbors cooked and brought food to some of the volunteers. One reported that when he gave a guard a hundred francs to buy some bread for him, the guard leaned his rifle against the house and left; when he returned he gave the volunteer the bread, picked up his rifle, and resumed his guard. In an up-country town, the regional governor personally brought his radio to a volunteer's house so that she could keep up with the news of the crisis.

By the end of the week, the trouble seemed to be abating. A special mission from the OAU had interviewed most of the Ghanians in Guinea and discovered that they were not being detained against their will in Guinea; in fact, they did not want to return to Ghana. The Ghanian government announced the release of Foreign Minister Beauvogui and his delegation. The volunteers were released from house arrest. It would have been easy to sulk, complain, or put on a display of righteous indignation. Instead, Norman told his volunteers to report back to work and to conduct themselves as they had before the crisis.

Monday afternoon Foreign Minister Beauvogui returned to Conakry. He was given a street-lined hero's welcome. The minister told of beatings and humiliation to which the delegation had been subjected in Accra. He announced that the United States was entirely to blame for the incident. Sékou Touré, Guinea's brilliant, unpredictable president, announced a mass meeting to be held the next day in Conakry's "Stadium of the Twenty-eighth of September" to consider the "lessons learned from the events in Accra" and to honor the returned delegation.

On Tuesday the stadium was overflowing and the speeches unusually abusive. President Touré himself delivered a strongly anti-American speech and concluded it with an announcement that took the Peace Corps and the embassy completely by surprise:

. . . And to begin, since today is the eighth of November, by the fifteenth of November, in one week, we ask them to send a plane or planes to remove all agents of the Peace Corps that they may return to the United States and leave Guinea.

Comrades, comrades, in your name, in your name we say to the men, to the women, who have come to Guinea in the name of the Peace Corps, far away from their families, from their country, and enduring certain deprivations which they shared with you; we say to these men and to these women, we will retain only pleasant memories of them, but we have had enough of the politics of their country. We thank them, and in dignity we send them on their way.

And we will even have a reception for the agents of the Peace Corps that they may preserve the best of memories of our people and that they may know that they can count on Guinean dignity.

For good measure, President Touré tacked on the expulsion of Pan American personnel from Guinea and the denial of landing rights in Conakry to the company's airplanes.

Since Touré had committed himself in a public address, the Peace Corps knew that he would not reverse his impetuous decision, and neither Norman nor Washington sought a reversal. The hasty and unexpected departure of the volunteers from their sites produced dozens of stories of sad and moving farewells. Two volunteers in the town of Telimele were honored with a luncheon put on by government, labor union, women's auxiliary, and political leaders. At the luncheon they were showered with gifts ranging from carved ivory tusks to decorated wooden bowls and gourd serving ladles. At a school in the village of Tolo the volunteers had a final meeting with their students; the head of the student body made a speech in which he expressed the hope that the troubles between Guinea and the United States as governments would not affect the friendship of the students of Tolo and the volunteers as individuals.

When the volunteers left Tolo the following morning, they found all of the students of the school gathered near the vehicles that would take the volunteers to Conakry. One of the volunteers described that moment:

"They stood there silently watching us pack our suitcases in the cars. Then, when the last vehicle had been loaded, as if on a given signal and in a great wave, they rushed toward us shouting good-bys, crying and shaking hands. It was the most emotional thing I've ever gone through. We all cried."

When the volunteers and staff left Conakry airport on September 15, Alpha Diallo, secretary general of the foreign ministry, headed a Guinean delegation to see them off. In his farewell statement he reiterated Sékou Touré's words that his government's action was not directed against the volunteers as individuals but was to serve as a rebuke to the United States Government. He expressed again his government's appreciation for the work of the volunteers and for their desire to serve in Guinea. In the name of the President he wished them safe journey and good luck wherever they might be.

In his reply Henry Norman said, "We have, at this time, very heavy hearts. We are leaving our friends, our colleagues. We do not completely understand, but the

Peace Corps has nothing to do with politics. We go where we are invited. We remain only during the period in which the host country wants us. . . . We will retain forever a profound affection for the people of Guinea . . . and memories of the kindness, the intelligence, the cooperation that we found here. For all of us, we are sad to leave Guinea and our friends."

With these words the "Guinea incident" became a chapter in the Peace Corps' history, but a chapter to which more than one addendum would be written. The volunteers and staff boarded a chartered Pan African Airways DC-6 and flew to their safe haven in Dakar. As they left, each volunteer received a book of Sékou Touré's essays and speeches that the President had personally asked be sent to the airport. And, in a fitting close to an episode that had more than one resemblance to a comic strip plot, the volunteers learned from the plane's intercom that their flight was under command of pilot Dick Tracy.

It would seem that the expulsion of the Peace Corps from a country should be considered a serious matter. Hundreds of lives are affected, not only the lives of volunteers but also those of students they are teaching, farmers who are experimenting with new crops under their direction, villagers they are helping to build wells or start cooperatives. Hundreds of hours volunteers have spent in studying a language and in learning about a country are wasted. Hundreds of thousands of dollars spent on training and transportation are lost. All of the time and money spent on planning a program go for naught.

Yet in all of the cases where the Peace Corps has been expelled, either from a country or a state (as in the case of Kerala in India), it is clear that none of the above considerations was seriously thought about. The Peace Corps has a written agreement with each country specifying an orderly termination over a ninety-day period should either country want to end the program. This agreement has been ignored in most cases where the Peace Corps has been asked to leave. Clearly, the countries have acted solely or predominantly out of a variety of political motives which they considered more important than the niceties of a diplomatic agreement, dislocations of human beings, or money wasted.

Both Congress and the American press have shown extreme interest in the death of Peace Corps programs. This is quite natural. But in almost every case an unfriendly congressman or editorial writer or a newsman seeking a juicier story has assumed or looked for clues that the programs were rejected because the volunteers were failing to do their jobs or provide what the countries wanted.

This has not been true. With but one or two exceptions the programs that have been thrown out or allowed to die out of a country were good programs, in a few instances among the best that the Peace Corps has managed. In almost all cases, too, the clear political basis of the country's action was obvious to anyone who wanted to see it.

The important questions that should be raised by the sobering fact that one out of every six Peace Corps programs has ended abruptly or prematurely are these: Does the Peace Corps provide too convenient a whipping boy for any political demagogue who wants to embarrass the United States? Is the Peace Corps a hopeless or even dangerous gesture of friendship in parts of the world which are increasingly afraid of and hostile to the United States? Are most underdeveloped countries stable enough to sustain over a number of years a program that will have value only if it is carried out over a relatively long time? Is the human disappointment, the frustration, and the money wasted by disrupted programs too great to justify the continuation of the Peace Corps as a whole?

It is possible to hold quite rational but widely differing points of view on these questions. My personal view is this: The struggle of the poor people of the world to throw off their poverty and achieve social justice is the great revolution of our time. That revolution is in progress in America, but it started earlier in some parts of Africa, Asia, and Latin America, and it will probably continue longer there. Until real progress is made in achieving the aims of that revolution everywhere—and I mean quite simply a way and level of life that is commensurate with human needs and human dignity—there will be no lasting peace or security anywhere.

No matter what pressures, internal or external, are exerted on the United States to withdraw from world affairs, I do not seriously believe that will happen, nor do I think it should happen. I believe that the only questions are How will we be involved in the future? And to what extent? To answer those questions we need information. If there was ever a time in our national history that we needed to know more about the rest of the world, its people and its problems, that time is now. If there was ever a time when other people needed to know more about what Americans are thinking—not our leaders but the people they are attempting to lead—it is now.

It is regrettable that the leaders of some countries have used the Peace Corps to their political advantage, but realistically we could have expected nothing else. And if the Peace Corps had not been there to catch the fire, something else American surely would or some other dramatic gesture of even more serious consequence might have been made. Professor Arthur P. Dudden of Bryn Mawr College has suggested that in a world increasingly hostile to the United States, the Peace Corps serves a useful function as a lightning rod.

Whether that is true or not, the Peace Corps can serve as a handle for a country to grasp in trying to restore or repair relations with the United States. After a break of about two years, both Ceylon and Guinea—entirely on their own initiatives—invited the Peace Corps to return to their countries. We did return in both cases, despite raised eyebrows on the part of some State Department officials and others who thought that the Peace Corps should hold out for some kind of public admission of original error, particularly on the part of Guinea. No such statement was asked for, and I am sure that to have held out for one would have meant no program resumption. The Peace Corps returned quietly (for some reason the Peace Corps' returning did not interest the press as its being ejected had) and is working in both countries today.[2]

[2] In July 1970, after the second Peace Corps program in Ceylon was about three years old, the Ceylonese government again asked the Peace Corps to leave, once more for political reasons. Whether the Peace Corps,

In cases where countries have ended Peace Corps programs through fear of the United States (Gabon) or because they were moving to political positions which they felt required the program's dismissal (Libya, Tanzania), I believe the Peace Corps' fate played a valuable role in signaling the intensity of the country's feeling. Whether such signals are understood properly in the United States and acted upon accordingly is quite another matter.

While the Peace Corps has often been seen in political terms by country leaders, this has not been true of the people with whom volunteers have lived and worked. Feelings of nationalism and xenophobia, with surprisingly few exceptions, have not been a problem for volunteers in carrying out their daily work or in overcoming the cultural and communicative problems that stand in the way of friendships. I believe that the bridges that have been built between people through the Peace Corps' having been in a country—even when the program has been broken off—may withstand the pressures of time and politics and be there for use at a future time.

It is certainly regrettable that many volunteers have been disappointed and frustrated through program disruptions, for whatever reasons. The Peace Corps does what it can to relocate volunteers in such cases though problems of language and job and country knowledge in relocation are obvious. If a volunteer chooses not to take another assignment, he is free to return to the United States without prejudice. Beyond that, I can only say that

---

if invited a third time, should accept will be a difficult decision for the agency.

there are going to be casualties in any U.S. undertaking overseas today. Persons who are drafted for military purposes realize that, and persons who volunteer for programs of peace must understand it, too.

Four out of every five Peace Corps programs have been and are being conducted with no more than minor political problems. Some of the programs will soon be ten years old and I am sure can continue for another ten years or longer if the United States Government wants to continue this small commitment to peace.

Despite its imperfections, the Peace Corps is still one of the best means that has been devised for communicating with the developing world. Some of the communication may be superficial but much of it is not. In a world where trouble always starts when men stop talking, the cutting off of such a clear channel for hearing one another would be a tragedy.

CHAPTER NINE

The Returned Volunteer in a Divided America

At the end of the Peace Corps' first decade over thirty thousand volunteers had served their full tours overseas and returned to America. Another eighty-five hundred had been overseas but had returned early for the variety of reasons already discussed. The total, while not dramatically large, still adds significantly to the number of Americans who have worked in development jobs in Africa, Asia, and Latin America. It certainly constitutes by far the largest number of young persons who have done so.

A good deal has been written about the "reentry crisis" of volunteers coming home after living and working for two years or more in an African village or an urban slum in Brazil. Unquestionably, some recently returned volunteers do have an initial disorientation at stepping back into the din of television and radio and the flash of newspaper headlines morning and night; into the rushing pace of American life, into an almost obscene abundance of food, clothes, cars; into an America much more divided, tense, angry, and violent than the one he left.

In his Peace Corps assignment, the returned volunteer probably did not see a television screen for two years; some mornings he heard a radio news broadcast and perhaps listened to some Voice of America music occasionally. If he lived in a city he probably saw a newspaper—filled mostly with local political news—every day, but if he lived in a rural area, he more likely saw one once a week. He lived among people who wore shabby or ragged clothes and who often did not have enough to eat. He became very indifferent about the food he ate in those two years; his wardrobe was a few shirts, a couple of pair of pants, a coat and tie for dress-up occasions. He fell into the leisurely pace of the life of the people of his community—the ceremonial tea drinking, the long nap at lunch time, the many holidays.

Two things upon his return he found particularly different and to varying degrees disturbing. In his Peace Corps assignment he had stood out as an object of attention, even if his job had not been a good one. If it had been good, he had probably had authority and influence far beyond anything he was likely to step into in a job in America. He was no longer "special."

The other disturbing thing was the fear of violent crime that dominated the America to which he had returned, especially in the cities. Petty theft had been a nuisance in his life overseas, but he had walked city streets at night unafraid; and if his assignment was in a village or rural area, he had known that he was safer than he could possibly have been anywhere in America.

In almost all cases, however, the disorientation of the returned volunteers has been superficial and brief. For one

thing they learn a resourcefulness and adaptability overseas that help them manage the reentry into an affluent
society. More important, living deeply and personally in
an impoverished third-world nation has given thousands
of volunteers a new and clearer perspective on their own
country and a new sense of the role they want to play in
it.

A former volunteer from India put it this way: "The
Peace Corps experience allowed me to put America at
arm's length and review it critically. I realized in India
that I have a stake in America and I'm determined to
help shape this country into what I think it should be."

Fifty percent of all former volunteers say that they
have changed their career plans as a result of their Peace
Corps service, and a large part of the shift is toward
teaching and social service work. In 1968 the Peace Corps
made a study of ten thousand former volunteers whose
career status was known at that time. By far the largest
number, over thirty-seven percent, were continuing their
education, evidence of both career changes and a realization of a need for maximum education to be effective
in today's world. Three-fourths of those returning to college were in graduate school, the rest finishing undergraduate degrees. A large number were preparing to be
teachers.

An astonishing number, over two thousand—one out of
every five in the ten thousand sample—were already
teaching, large numbers of them in urban slum and
ghetto schools. Others showed a sharp bent toward public
and social service work. Over two hundred and fifty were
working in War on Poverty programs. Another six hun-

dred were in non-profit health, labor, social service, and educational organizations. Almost four hundred were employed by state and local governments, and most of their jobs were in the area of social services. Four hundred were on the Peace Corps staff, over two hundred were working for the Agency for International Development, and another one hundred were in such international organizations as CARE, UNICEF, and working privately for foreign governments.

The city of Philadelphia, desperate for teachers for its inner-city schools, queried the Peace Corps volunteer teachers in Africa finishing their tours in the summer of 1966 about their interest in teaching in Philadelphia. Contracts were sent along with the letters of inquiry. Over 175 volunteers signed and returned the contracts and were in the classrooms when school started in Philadelphia that fall.

Robert W. Blackburn, who handled this unusual experiment in recruitment for the city, later testified before a House of Representatives committee that "we regard them (former Peace Corps volunteers) as the single best source of top-flight educators available to us anywhere."

The state of New York has established an office of Peace Corps affairs, a major purpose of which is to attract former volunteers into teaching service in the state. As an added inducement New York grants immediate probationary teacher certification to returned volunteer teachers. California also gives credit for Peace Corps teaching experience.

Without any doubt Peace Corps volunteers, almost to a man and woman, have been deeply dismayed by our war in Vietnam, and a strong motive on the part of many men in joining the Peace Corps was to delay their call to duty in that war. And former volunteers are greatly troubled by the America to which they have returned: the continuing injustices to racial minorities, the neglect of the poor, the rigidity of unresponsive bureaucracy. But with exceedingly few exceptions they have rejected the route of violence and destruction and the hippie route of withdrawal as avenues for taking up their life in America again. These men and women who have returned from the villages and the slums of the Third World have brought with them a commitment to service, and service in itself is antithetical to destroying or withdrawing.

They learned that Peace Corps service entails a commitment to work within imperfect structures—the government that invited them, the state ministry of health or education, the agricultural extension service, the Peace Corps itself (far from perfect as I have made clear)—to ameliorate problems at a people-to-people level. Dramatic change was never the Peace Corps' stock in trade.

By opting to serve in the Peace Corps, volunteers demonstrated a will to affect the world in ways which may not be dramatic or radical, but whose sum will surely improve the lot of their fellow men. They are idealists and liberals in the sense that they believe man's plight is not inexorably fixed, and also in the sense that they do not have the intellectual security—however stultifying—of dogmas and panaceas. But they are also realists and pragmatists in the sense that they believe that meaningful improvements in the human condition must be the result of hard work and dedicated, responsible action.

Another former volunteer from India, talking about his reentry into American life, said: "What I told the Indians to do, namely, to work for constructive change within their system, I have never tried in my own system and I pledged then and there that I was coming home to try for myself."

Given this basic outlook, what do Peace Corps volunteers learn in their two or more years of service overseas that can be of special value to an America in which suspicion, fear, hate, and despair are the dominant emotions with which millions of its citizens live daily?

One truth I am sure all successful volunteers learn is how difficult it is to effect even small improvements in man's condition and that evils of poverty and ignorance are not necessarily a function of the incompetence or malevolence of a handful of leaders. It is an understanding that justice is seldom achieved by overthrowing a corrupt few—though this may sometimes be necessary—but more often by working persistently to change attitudes that permeate the whole fabric of society. A peasant farmer's unquestioning belief that his daughters need no schooling is as certainly an injustice as an indifferent agriculture officer's scornful belief that the peasant farmer is incapable of learning new farming methods. Both views can be changed, but not quickly and not by petulant explosions of righteous indignation. The necessary reforms can only be enduring if those involved on both sides understand the need for them.

A second truth—of fundamental importance—that volunteers learn is that of the basic similarity of mankind: that the motive forces, aspirations, latent abilities, and behavior of peoples are really only superficially different as a result of the overlay of a particular culture. This deep-in-the-gut sense of our common humanity is, it seems to me, a tremendous asset in approaching our domestic problems, which are so largely a function of our implicit (and sometimes explicit) denial of that truth.

Another way of expressing this is that volunteers bring back a clearer view of American culture and a better understanding of people as people, not as blacks, Communists, eggheads, or yippies. A firm knowledge that labels and stereotypes are more often misleading than helpful and that intrinsically people *are* equal is an important truth to have in one's intellectual arsenal today.

It seems to me that former Peace Corps volunteers are equipped by their experiences overseas to work now in their daily lives to make these truths known and understood to their fellow Americans. This can be a most positive and important contribution to American society, and it can be carried out under all circumstances and within the context of any job—the social worker in the ghetto, the teacher in the wealthy suburban school, the architect, banker, or housewife.

Both on the job and in all social or volunteer activities —but particularly when dealing with their contemporaries and the young—the persistent reiteration of the similarity of men and the equality of men will be a noble act—as will the constant demonstration that real development or progress, though almost never fast and always difficult, is possible if we can break the attitudinal bonds with which men have shackled themselves.

In his article, "The War Against the Young" (*The*

Atlantic, October 1968), Professor Richard Poirier passionately defends the right of youth to disrupt an unessential and unresponsive establishment, but then says in a most perceptive paragraph: "The world we now live in cannot get any better merely by changing its managers or improving some of its circumstances. It exists as it does because of the way we think about one another and because of our incapacity, so far at least, to learn to think differently."

I cannot agree that the world cannot be made somewhat better with better managers and improved circumstances, but I certainly agree with Mr. Poirier's basic assertion that the world is the way it is "because of the way we think about one another."

To improve essentially our society we must change the way people think about one another. This is an arduous undertaking, but I hope I have made clear why former Peace Corps volunteers are probably better prepared for the task than any other group in America today. This, I repeat, can be their special contribution to our society.

The large-scale turning of former volunteers to teaching and to the work of developing our own depressed areas and neglected peoples makes me confident that they will play their role well.

CHAPTER TEN

A Brief Summing Up

Chester Bowles was ambassador to India for the second time during the period I was Peace Corps rep there. I came greatly to admire his knowledge and understanding of the developing world and his vision of what America's role should be in it. He took a strong personal interest in the Peace Corps and visited as many volunteers as he could when he traveled. Some time after Bowles left India and returned to his home in Connecticut to reflect and write, I received a letter from him in which he said, "With all of its imperfections I think the Peace Corps is one of the two or three really creative, positive things we have done in foreign affairs in the last generation."

I knew the Peace Corps' imperfections as well as any man, and I can still agree with Ambassador Bowles. In my judgment, the Peace Corps' work in its first decade adds up to a strong net plus, both for the countries in which volunteers served and for the United States.

From time to time, usually at congressional urging, the Peace Corps has attempted to measure the impact of some of its activities in developing countries. A long and detailed study of the work of a group of community development volunteers in Peru was undertaken by the Anthropology Department of Cornell University. The study indicated that "the Peace Corps program in the Peruvian Andes did achieve a measurable impact upon its target communities," and that villages with Peace Corps volunteers developed—in terms of schools, clinics, clubs, cooperative actions—more than three times as fast as villages without volunteers.

In Ethiopia, Gary Bergthold and David McClelland of Harvard made a study of the impact of Peace Corps teachers on their students. At the time of their study in 1968 over fourteen hundred volunteers had taught or were teaching in Ethiopia; they had taught the equivalent of a full year of secondary school for sixty-six thousand students. The Bergthold-McClelland study measured students on their level of achievement motivation, desire to improve performance, and modernity, i.e., a set of attitudes and beliefs characteristic of individuals who successfully hold modern roles in developing nations. Students who had had "high Peace Corps volunteer teacher contact" scored higher on all three of these measures than those who had not, and, states the report, "the differences were large enough that we could be certain they could not have occurred by chance."

Other effectiveness studies have documented volunteer success in educational television in Colombia, in fostering self-help projects among villagers in Colombia, in tuberculosis-control programs in Bolivia and Malawi. For the most part, however, the Peace Corps has shown little enthusiasm for quantifying the work of its volunteers or for financing any broad-based objective study of volunteer effectiveness or impact. I am sure the agency's failure to implement such research has not stemmed from a fear of negative findings. Part of the hesitation has come from the fact that developing countries are frequently suspicious of research of this type. It is also difficult to devise and expensive. The chief reason for the Peace Corps' inaction in measuring its accomplishments, however, has been a strongly held feeling by most staff and volunteers that such measuring or quantifying would lead to an emphasis on the wrong things: Instead of working with people to encourage them to do things for themselves, volunteers would be under pressure to raise so many tons of grain, build so many hundred miles of road, to put up a thousand latrines rather than convincing perhaps a hundred people to really use them.

I am sure the Peace Corps needs better measures of volunteer performance and effectiveness than it now has, but only for the purposes of knowing better how to select the right persons to become volunteers and learning the best activities in which to place them. Anyone who has worked long in developing countries and has understood the enormity of the need knows that the Peace Corps is but one tiny and unmeasurable input into the development processes of any given country. It is not without importance; but its importance lies in the quality of the association between its volunteers and the people they have come to work with; it does not lie in how much the volunteers themselves produce. As a development agency, the Peace Corps will always be relatively insignificant; but as an organization in which both its volunteers and the people with whom they live and work learn from each other and understand each other better, the Peace Corps can have real significance in the world today and for years to come.

The work a volunteer does is important, but how he does that work is profoundly more important. Mr. B. P. R. Vithal, a good Indian friend of the Peace Corps, once said to a newly arrived group of volunteers:

> . . . what we look for in a situation for which we ask for a volunteer is whether the nature of the task is such that attitudes are the most important ingredient of performance. It is in attitudes that the volunteer can make his most significant contribution. We expect he would have ingenuity, initiative, and dedication, not only because he would not have been a volunteer had he not these qualities in ample measure, but also because there is the underlying assumption that it is these qualities, and the attitudes that both create these qualities and arise from them, that have contributed to the making of modern America.
>
> It is this expectation that also places most of the limitations which a volunteer must recognize and accept. The role of a volunteer would be more in the sphere of attitudes than of knowledge or skills. Knowledge can be transmitted through teaching and skills can be imparted by training, but attitudes can be influenced only by example. Your greatest influence should therefore be exercised through example and not through any conscious teaching or preaching.

Dor Bahadur Bista, a Nepali who has done much work with the Peace Corps, has written on the same idea:

. . . In spite of what the Nepali elite might say about the "fast developing Nepal" my own observation is that elites are generally upward oriented and therefore struggling to achieve economic goals without sufficient concern for the real lives of the mass of the people. Sometimes unwilling individuals are sacrificed for prior decided economic development projects. Since the real beneficiaries of any economic achievements should be the large majority (the rural people) it is they who must achieve and maintain progressive attitudes. But this will not happen so quickly under an authoritarian system since there is little dialogue between the authorities and the common rural people. This is where I believe Peace Corps could help because Peace Corps is the only organization where its workers (volunteers) have direct relationships with the people at the lowest level without any vested interest.

Peace Corps volunteers can make the common people aware of the fact that there can be alternatives, that every individual human being has the potential and it is their right to exploit them and aspire for a progressive future oriented life.

And commenting earlier on the seriousness with which volunteers approach their work, Mr. Bista said, "After a certain amount of initial confusion and shyness, even the poorest Nepalis are capable of finding out who is a phony person and who is sincere in his efforts."

I think what both Mr. Vithal and Mr. Bista are talking about is best illustrated by a letter that Charlie Houston once received when he was in charge of the Peace Corps program in India. It concerned two volunteers in southern India who were about to finish their two-year assignment.

Dear Sir:

We the poultry farmers of this village are running poultry with the practical help of Mr. John and Mr. Henry. We have affection to see them doing practical work. Poultry is a new industry for us because before we could not know this industry. With the help of Mr. John and Mr. Henry we are running so many poultries in our area. Also it is giving a good profit in our poultry now a days and we are increasing in our standard of living.

Now we are starting a new poultry Farmers' Co-operative Society. There is much to do and buy and build. It is a lot of work to complete but if Mr. John and Mr. Henry could do work for one more year from February then it is complete and we will be running up well in our industry.

We honourably request you to order Mr. John and Mr. Henry to stay here one more year.

Thanking you.

The letter carried thirty signatures and a number of thumbprints. For the first time in their lives perhaps these farmers had learned to hope for something better—indeed, to ask for it—because they had become convinced that something better was possible and that they had the power to achieve it. The birth and growth of this attitude, this outlook are, again, what Vithal and Bista are talking about; and the Peace Corps at its best, I am convinced, has been more successful in changing the way that people (including the volunteers) think about themselves than any of our other aid-giving or development programs.

I have said much in earlier pages about the necessity of the Peace Corps volunteer having a real job and the experience or training to do it. They give him a credibility overseas that he cannot have without them. But the way he works with people, the way he makes them feel about themselves, the ideas and values he both imparts and receives through his associations—these are the important elements in Peace Corps service. When volunteers have been well selected and well placed, they can help others to a new awareness of their potential as human beings, and they have done so in thousands of cases. In the process, the volunteers have become better men and women.

Most volunteers I know feel that they gained more from their two years in the Peace Corps than they were able to give to the people they worked with. I do not think volunteers who express this view are being modest or humble. I think they are quite correct. Living and working in Africa, Asia, or Latin America today, at the level and in the way that the Peace Corps has intended, is a tremendous educational experience. Harold Taylor has written, "As deeply as I believe in the virtues of knowledge and learning, in the virtues of the informed intellect, and the present desirability of college degrees in the market place, I am convinced even more that the students of our colleges who have chosen to serve in the Peace

Corps and in VISTA have chosen a sure way to educate themselves into the contemporary world."

Many Americans seem shocked and disappointed at the notion that volunteers benefit more from Peace Corps service than do the people they work with. They are even more offended by the idea that America—because of the educational value to the volunteers—has gained more from the Peace Corps than have the countries where the volunteers worked. Such negative responses seem to me quite unrealistic. If volunteers and America benefited less from Peace Corps service, it would not mean that other countries and their people would benefit more. The fact is that officials of the countries with whom I have discussed this matter are quite pleased at the idea that the volunteers benefit greatly from service in their country. And they know that former volunteers in America knowledgeable about their country, and usually sympathetic to it, can be of continuing value to their country. One of the main accomplishments of the Peace Corps, it seems to me, has been opening the eyes of thousands of young people, making them critical—and knowledgeably critical —of the United States' presence and policies in many parts of the world.

The word one heard most often throughout 1968–70 in connection with the Peace Corps was "relevance." Was the Peace Corps still relevant? How could we make the Peace Corps relevant in 1968 or 1970? There were great debates within the Peace Corps about the wisdom of merging with VISTA to give ourselves a "domestic relevance."

The Peace Corps was of course as relevant in 1968 or

1970 as it had been in 1961—as relevant to its purposes of promoting understanding and peace. It was Americans who had changed since the Peace Corps began its work. They had discovered their own poor and they had felt the ugly reality of racism; suddenly only these problems and the desperate dilemma of Vietnam were important. Many college students felt that, with American guilt in Vietnam, serving in a Peace Corps was practicing hypocrisy. Many volunteers overseas felt they should resign and come home to work on America's social, economic, and political problems.

I have talked to scores of such volunteers and I think I know how they feel. It is hard to be away from one's country when it is in such obvious and desperate trouble, and their guilt feelings are not hard to understand. But I have tried to point out that the problems of the countries in which they are working are equally desperate—though often very different—and frequently interwoven with ours. I have tried to make the point that the guilt they feel is, in part at least, based on an innate feeling that America's problems are somehow more important than the problems of India or Peru or whatever country they are serving in. I have suggested—with what success I cannot say—that perhaps a good deal that is wrong with America and the world today is the result of such a narrow and provincial way of viewing the problems of others.

Some college students now seem to feel that the Peace Corps is square and establishment, yet it was a forerunner and a concrete expression of the assertion by youth today that there must be a better and more honest way of ordering society. In the cultural revolution underway in America there certainly seems to be a place for the Peace Corps. The work of a volunteer features self-awareness and concern for others; it gives the individual wide scope to express himself positively—all important concerns of millions of young men and women today.

So the answer is still "yes," the Peace Corps is relevant, as relevant in the decade of the seventies as it was in the sixties. The pursuit of peace through increased understanding is a terribly practical goal, and the Peace Corps remains one tangible way to work toward that goal.

But the question I have been asked most frequently of late is not about relevance but about survival. Can the Peace Corps survive in the climate of disenchantment and preoccupation with domestic problems that exists in America today? Can it exist in a world of increasing nationalism and distrust of Americans?

I naturally find it very difficult to be objective about the Peace Corps. My years in it were the most productive, creative, and satisfying of my life. The Peace Corps years gave me scores of friends and hundreds of warm memories of decent people—Americans, Nigerians, Indians—learning to work and live together. Of course I want the Peace Corps to survive, but can it?

It is impossible to imagine the Peace Corps being born in today's America, but fortunately it already exists. It has forty thousand alumni, most of whom—as I pointed out in the opening chapter—believe in the Peace Corps concept and want the agency to flourish and improve. I think theirs will be a strong voice for its continued existence.

Despite the great publicity given to campus rebellion

and nihilism, the numbers of young people today who are seeking ways to serve their fellow men and help create a better society far exceed the numbers of the past. It is clear that a significant percentage of them will want the Peace Corps as a vehicle for their service.

The Peace Corps has now functioned for ten years and —as I hope I have made clear—has learned a great deal about what a successful presence overseas entails. The zeal for large numbers and the preoccupation with image have disappeared and the emphasis is now on working closely with host country officials to place volunteers in jobs where they are wanted and needed. Political problems will certainly continue in the future, but with a smaller number of volunteers more carefully integrated into host country structures, the chances of avoiding destructive blowups are increased. Hopefully the Peace Corps will also begin to acknowledge more publicly the value of overseas service to the volunteers. This acknowledgment will, I am sure, be appreciated by the receiving countries and make the volunteers more welcome.

Leadership in the Peace Corps is going to be even more important to its success in the decade ahead than it has been in the past. If the right men and women are chosen —persons of understanding, imagination, and courage— the Peace Corps' moment in history can become a long and valuable one.

Index

ACCION, 290

Accra, 351–52, 354

Adams, Timothy, 148

Afghanistan, 113, 226–27, 237

AFL-CIO, 297

Africa, 37 ff., 50–92, 95 ff., 102–14, 180–89, 258, 284–85, 363, 366 (*see also* specific countries); community development programs in, 161; French-speaking, 174, 177, 180–83; and Kennedy's death, 140; political problems, nationalism, 312, 345–57

African Season, An, 7 n

Agency for International Development (AID, formerly International Cooperation Association), 44–47, 56, 95, 128, 198, 200, 233, 344, 366

Agents of Change, 180 n

Agra, 195

Agriculture. *See* Food crops; specific countries

AID. *See* Agency for International Development

Alexander, John, 43, 56–57, 60, 63, 169–73, 249; Wiggins and hiring of, 40

Americans Committed to World Responsibility, 14

Antioch College, 241, 247

Apple, R. W., Jr., 351

Apter, David, 243

Arabs, 335–44

Armstrong, Neil, 297

Asia, 37, 38, 50, 60, 70, 95, 112, 113–14, 133, 177, 180–81, 285, 363 (*see also* specific countries); and color prejudice, 261; and community development programs, 161; and President Kennedy's death, 140

Atlantic, The, 369–70

Azikiwe, Nnamdi, 51, 64

BA generalists, 142–73 ff., 181, 191 ff., 222, 231–39, 268–69. *See also* specific areas

Baku, 331

Balewa, Sir Abubakar Tafawa, 51

Baumann, Gino, 161

Beauvogui, Louis, 351–52, 353

Beeler, Margery Donk, 6

Bell, David, 45, 46

Bell, Paul, 277, 278

Bennett, Meridan, 180 n

Bergthold, Gary, 372